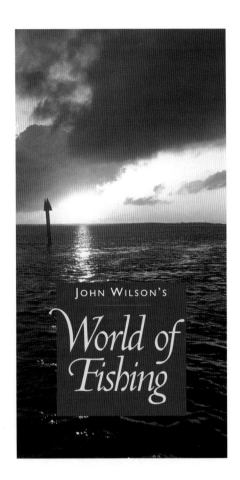

John Wilson's

World of
Fishing

John Wilson's
World of Fishing

Dedication

I dedicate this book to my wonderful wife Jo:
my soulmate and best friend.

Introduction

The following selection of articles originated in my *Daily Express* and *Sunday Express*
columns, 'Anglers Retreat' and 'Gone Fishin', reflecting my angling exploits and
subsequent adventure travels both at home and abroad throughout the best
part of a decade. Indeed, being a full-time angling writer, it is important that this volume
records my personal 'world of fishing' in which I am honestly just as happy centre-pin
trotting or upstream nymphing for dace or grayling in a southern chalk stream, as I am
scrambling across rapids in pursuit of a big mahseer in southern India, or heaving into a
brute of a white sturgeon twice my own bodyweight in front of TV cameras,
along Canada's mighty Fraser River.
I consider myself extremely fortunate to have experienced so much diversity during
my work as writer and television director/presenter, and I hope the reader will identify
with my trials and tribulations, whilst taking time to smell the roses along the way.

Good fishing,
John Wilson, Great Witchingham, 2004.

First published 2004
by Barnwell's Print Ltd. Aylsham, Norfolk NR11 6ET.
ISBN 0-9547778-0-8

Designed by Stephen Harper, Harper Design 01362 683568
Printed in Great Britain by Barnwells of Aylsham 01263 732767

Contents

'Anglers Retreat' and 'Gone Fishin' essays from John Wilson's long-running column in the *Daily Express* and *Sunday Express* 1996 – 2004.

A magnificent 35 ¼ lb common carp from Spain's River Segre.

IT'S ALWAYS TIME FOR BARBEL

By far the world's heaviest, mightiest and most powerful barbel, the mahseer, lives in the fast-flowing mountainous rivers of India. In October, before Winter frosts noticeably lower water temperatures, there is no better time to catch *barbus barbus*. And if you are to experience the exhilarating speed and power of our own indigenous barbel, for goodness' sake don't attempt to extract one from locations where the species is not prolific. Take my local River Wensum, for instance. Now although there are limited stocks introduced into a few stretches, in total they occupy a very small percentage of the river's overall fishable length. But because a handful of jumbo specimens in the 12-15 lb bracket get caught regularly and make the press with equal regularity, it's only natural, I guess, for anglers to assume the Wensum is full of barbel, when nothing could be further from the truth. It's simply that the same old recognisable whoppers are repeatedly caught and publicised.

So select a location prolific in the species, like the middle reaches of the famous River Severn for instance, where shoals of hard-battling barbel in the 4-7 lb bracket are so large that competition for your bait will be high: rivers where most gravel-bottomed, fast-flowing typical barbel swims are actually likely to contain them. Then it's a case of quiver -tip ledgering directly downstream or across the flow (to reach opposite bank runs) with your bait presented in conjunction with a heavy block end feeder rig (to lay down a carpet of attractor feed like hempseed) placed hard on the bottom. I rate the simple fixed paternoster, using a four-turn water knot as the junction between hook length and feeder link, the most effective end rig and usually opt for 6 lb test straight through, only stepping down to a lighter (3-4 lb) hook length when, despite seemingly ideal conditions, bites simply don't happen when they should.

As for baits, well, I reckon a half-inch cube of luncheon meat offered on a size 8 hook heads a long list which is limited only by your imagination. And remember, any bait that catches carp or tench will catch barbel. Cheese cubes or paste are excellent and never ever underestimate the pulling power of a big lobworm. You can try a big bunch of maggots

Fishing buddy Martin Bowler caught this 17 lbs 3oz barbel known as 'the traveller'
from the upper reaches of the Great Ouse near Bedford.

(10-15) on a size 8, or step down to just two on a 14. Match fishermen swear buy casters, and when barbel become finicky (as they can on hard-fished waters) use hooks down to size 16. And if you follow suit, make sure that the hook is up to the job, by using a forged pattern like Kamasan 3982 extra strong eyed, which I religiously use for all my barbel fishing.

Lastly don't worry if you haven't a sensitive quiver-tip rod. With nine out of 10 barbel bites the rod tip suddenly arches over with such force, due to the aggressive manner in which the species characteristically hoovers up the bait and turns across current, that it quite literally hooks itself in the process. So any 11-12 foot Avon style, or even a light carp rod, will suffice so long as you keep the tip angled up high on rests with minimal line across the surface, ensuring that current force does not pull your rig away from the swim.

There are many other ways to catch barbel of course but in the autumn as the rivers lose their growth of summer weed and speed up, perhaps with the addition of floodwater, ledgering takes some beating. And if you can catch the river fining down nicely after a spate with a tinge of colour, barbel are likely to be ravenous. So keep your eye on that rod tip if you stand up to have a pee. In fact reel your rig in rather than walk away from the rod or it might suddenly fly into the drink: a phenomenon most barbel addicts have experienced at some time or another, although I doubt they'll admit it - I won't.

WHERE TO CATCH THE BARBEL

Without question, if you are seriously seeking to catch barbel and are willing to travel, then my advice is to take out a Birmingham Anglers' Association annual club card which is available over the counter from most Midland tackle dealers. This Association ticket actually includes more barbel potential on a tributary of the Severn, the lovely River Teme, the Avon and on the River Trent. The BAA actually controls more than 20 miles of fabulous barbel fishing on the mighty Severn split up into some mouth-watering stretches between Shrewsbury and Tewkesbury. And one of the most prolific beats is a $3\frac{1}{2}$ mile wooded piece of the river starting about a mile upstream of Bewdley on the eastern bank with access to the car park at Folly Point from Northwood Lane close to Bewdley road bridge. And if you can't catch a barbel here you won't catch one anywhere; the species has in fact become the dominant fish through the Severn, although a dace, roach or chub is quite likely to happen along on your barbel rig. If you have only ever fished in stillwaters or the narrow sluggish rivers of the Fens, then the width, speed of flow and sheer majesty of the Severn will both delight and amaze you.

CONDITION THAT WORM

Now whether you plan to offer lobworms to barbel or catch perch, which are another excellent autumn option, they do need to be lively and attractive. So having collected a batch from the lawn at night with the aid of a torch (and following a period of prolonged rain is the best time), they do need to be stored properly. And even 'conditioned'. You don't know how to condition a worm? Well I'll tell you. Simply tear up some old newspaper into strips (it will only tear into strips one way and chunks the other) and soak it in cold water in the sink. You then need a good supply of clean, 2 pint bait boxes into which go a dozen or so lobworms (no more) plus a handful of sopping wet (only lightly squeeze it) newspaper strips. Now here's the tricky bit, which is talking the woman of the house into some fridge space, because you need to leave the boxes of worms in the fridge for at least a week. You will then be the proud owner (though you may be divorced!) of the meanest, liveliest, chunkiest, fighting-fit lobworms you've ever put on a hook. Believe me.

Another winter 'double' for Martin Bowler that succumbed to a paste covered boilie.

BOILIES BAG BIG WINTER BARBEL

Despite the fact that only a little over a week remains before the end of the close season for coarse fishing, March is always a month I really look forward to because so much more is now on the cards as both air and water temperatures start slowly to rise. River enthusiasts especially can expect serious action with those big barbel right now, fish for argument's sake which pull the spring balance down into double figures. And, as with carp, there are few baits more selective in putting sizeable fish on your hook than a 14-18 mm sized boilie, hair-rigged to a size 6 hook. Keep the mono or braided hook length fairly short, say 6-8 inches, with a 'flat' 2-3 oz lead anchoring the bait static on the riverbed. In confined swims where line bites might not only prove troublesome, but actually deter a barbel from approaching the bait, slip a 'back lead' on to the line so those last few feet of reel line are ironed to the bottom and unlikely to be picked up by the fish's pectoral or pelvic fins. If the situation is impossible to employ a clip-on 'back lead', then incorporate one in your ledger rig by semi-fixing a 1oz coffin lead between two swan shot on the reel line, 2-4 feet above your ledger set-up which, of course, becomes a most effective: bolt rig'.

In large river systems it is possible to employ a two-rod set-up for exploring two different swims from the same position. But on no account even think of straying away from those rods. The sudden charge-off downstream (most barbel do exactly this) can prove both violent and electrifying, so either slacken the reel's clutch or use a 'bait runner' type reel, simply 'lifting' into the fish when the rod tip lurches over. You can imagine the outcome should you forget and whack the rod back hard against a fish that has already hooked itself. Even on 10-12 lb test reel lines (the very minimum breaking strains recommended) something has got to give.

To alleviate current force against the line, angle the rod tip up as high as possible, using two rod rests. For this specialised form of barbel fishing, rods with built-in quiver tips are simply not required, an 11 or 12 foot $1^{3}/_{4}$ lb test curve carp rod being perfectly suitable for the task at hand. And should you for one moment think that such an outfit is perhaps over-gunning, wait until you become attached to a double-figure barbel heading off downstream in a heavy flow.

Lastly just a few hints and tips. Refrain from introducing the same amount of loose feed into the swim as you would during the summer months. If you have done your homework and are presenting the bait in a recognised barbel haunt, just a few hookbait samples close to the bait are sufficient. Hooking on a small PVA dissolving bag filled with hookbait samples or pellet feed whenever you recast makes good sense. And to ensure the aroma of your hookbait permeates through the water, simply make up some paste from the same mix as the hookbait and knead a good dollop around the boilie. My fishing buddy, Martin Bowler, always does this when he's after winter barbel. And as he accounts for more klonking great barbel than anyone else, it's got to be the way to go.

FRED - THE BARBEL GURU

Fred Crouch displays a modest sized barbel taken by John from the River Kennet on quiver tipped maggots. A great day out using a deadly technique.

I just love barbel fishing and that exhilarating feeling of a good fish powering off downstream, screaming line from the reel against a tightly set clutch. But there is no way I would wish only to fish for barbel (or any other single species) and nothing else, like my good friend and barbel guru, Fred Crouch.

Actually both Fred and I originally came from North London and so enjoyed our barbel apprenticeships on the River Lea at many of the same locations, from Dobbs Weir, downstream to Enfield Lock, and during the early morning in the very same park lakes and ponds where you weren't supposed to fish (though we never met in those days). While I moved away in my early 20s to live and fish abroad before finally settling in Norfolk, Fred's love of barbel during the past 40 years has allowed him to set what must surely be an unbeatable record. He has caught more than 10,000 barbel and pursued his favourite fish up and down the length of the country.

Now while there are countless carp fanatics who fish for nothing else, I personally do not know of anyone other than Fred who single-mindedly pursues another species. This makes Fred Crouch unique and the foremost authority on barbel, whose habits he has documented and studied for the benefit of all, including the National Barbel Society. Needless to say I was really looking forward to a trip made in Fred's company just a few weeks ago along a stretch of the majestic River Kennet in Berkshire, near Newbury. Accompanied by David Hallett from Slough, we three stealthily walked a particularly narrow and weedy stretch where, provided the angler keeps well back from the water's edge, barbel will forage ridiculously close into the margins over narrow gravel channels between long flowing clumps of weed; where they venture naturally when anglers are not around.

I was most surprised and not just a little impressed to see that in none of the recognised barbel swims had the marginal grasses, comprising of thistles, willow herb, red campion and the like, been beaten down or even bent over to provide a clearing for the angler. Fred is emphatic about sitting well back from the water in relaxed fashion, the ledger rod on two rests with the tip only just poking through the marginal vegetation, so the barbel have no reason to be alarmed. And of course it works a treat.

I was a little perplexed as to how anglers had landed their barbel from these same swims without the occasional stem being bent or broken, and Fred showed me how. He walked 10 yards downstream of the swim where we planned to fish, and there was the evidence - a slight gap in the tall-vegetation screen, where each barbel is eventually landed after quickly being pressurised away from the thick weed beds and downstream out of the swim, well away from feeding fish, the arched rod held high over tall grasses throughout. All this, of course, results in the very minimum of disturbance and allows the barbel to regroup and recommence feeding far quicker than they would in a swim from which a visible angler has hooked and landed and returned a fish. Makes you think doesn't it.

Fred also has a totally foolproof routine of baiting and waiting prior to fishing, in order to allow barbel time to locate the newly introduced food source and follow it up to where the hookbait will be placed. So, following a good helping of stewed hempseed and maggots deposited into the head of the 4-foot-deep clear gravel run by bait dropper, we sat back and waited an hour for the fish to move over the feed and become more confident in their feeding, before casting. There's always a lot to catch up on whenever Fred and I fish together and so the time soon passed. Then I made up a simple open-end feeder rig using a 6 lb reel line on my 11 foot Avon quiver-tip rod, with a 20 inch hook link and size 10 hook sporting just three maggots. Sandwiched between a plug of breadcrumb groundbait at each end, the feeder contained both hempseed and maggots. But Fred had a trick up his sleeve for ensuring the hook did not catch up as I plopped the feeder rig down through the weed to the gravel run. He simply pressed the hookbait into the bottom of the feeder and secured it in place with a blob of groundbait: simple yet most effective. And just 15 minutes later the rod tip arched round confidently as my first barbel of the day turned across the current, having virtually hooked itself. Fred sure knows his barbel.

A BARBEL BONANZA

You need the water running exceptionally clear over gravel to actually witness species like barbel hoovering loose feed and your hookbait up from the bottom. Fortunately that was exactly the condition of the Upper Great Ouse during a stalking session I made recently along a charming and narrow, completely overgrown stretch of the river near Bedford. The first swim I tried was one to die for. The flow came right to left beneath a wooden staging where I crouched and skirted a huge bed of bulrushes immediately downstream. Only a yard out, between long flowing beds of streamer weed, I could make out the shape of five nice barbel hugging the bottom. Three yards upstream in went a big lobworm on a size 4 hook direct to the 6 lb reel line with two large swan shots on a short paternoster link, 20 inches above the bait, to keep it down amongst the gravel. Slowly I inched it downstream to the lead fish which momentarily became obscured by the trailing streamer weed. It's a characteristic of stalking fastwater barbel in weedy runs - one minute they are there, the next they are hidden from view. The line hooked around my forefinger tightened anyway and as the quiver tip arched round alarmingly, I eased the Avon rod back into a powerful, thrusting resistance which tore off downstream at a rate of knots. Five minutes of pure enjoyment later, an 8 lb barbel slid over the landing net. A terrific start. A second cast with lobworm produced a chunky perch of about $1^{1}/_{2}$ lb but the barbel had scarpered. So I emptied 3 pints of hemp and small boilies down to the bottom using a giant bait dropper purpose-made for me by mate Mick Willis, with a view to returning later on, and continued stalking downstream.

From an entanglement of submerged willow branches shading a deep run along the opposite bank I extracted a duo of nice chub weighing around $2^{1}/_{2}$ and 4 lb a piece also on worm and then decided upon a sit and wait stint in a small overshoot weir pool after first carpeting the fast run at the tail end with hempseed and boilies. Within minutes I saw a monstrous barbel move over the gravel several yards upstream of my boilie hair-rigged on a size 10 hook, a fish easily pushing 12 to 13 lb, if not a pound or even two heavier. It was immensely thick across the back but when the quiver tip arched round an hour later I found myself attached to a bream of $7\frac{1}{2}$ lbs well and truly foul hooked in the top of its head. This explained a succession of small plinks and plonks on the quiver tip which I had mistakenly thought were line bites from barbel and not a shoal of bream, though I did eventually take a 7 lb barbel from the weir before moving back to that pre-baited gravel run where I first started the day.

The hempseed and chopped boilies had worked a treat, and it was most satisfying seeing the snout of a good barbel block out sight of my boilie hookbait a split second before the tip slammed round. Getting bigger too – this one weighed just a couple of ounces short of 10 lbs and went like stink. But my day wasn't over. Literally one last cast made to the tail of the run (to where the barbel had retreated) resulted in a slamming bite followed by a most exciting tussle up and down the swim against pressure from both current force and my 11 Avon rod. Fortunately the latter won and I got to admire and return a superbly proportioned barbel of 11 bs 3 ozs. What a day.

FOR BRIAN, A RED LETTER DAY INDEED

It always gives me great pleasure when a friend finally achieves a lifelong ambition and lands a real whopper. Such was the case when Brian Ward from Southampton popped up to fish with me on my local River Wensum. Thinking that barbel might just be on the cards, in addition to the infinitely more catchable chub with which the river is well stocked in its upper reaches, our session started at dawn near Norwich where a fast run over gravel is overhung along the opposite bank by gnarled old goat willows for more than 30 yards immediately upstream from where a sidestream joins the main flow.

As we crept up stealthily opposite the overhang where weed had collected around sunken branches, the ghost-like shapes of several sizeable barbel could be seen slowly foraging over the long gravel run. They were prime candidates for a freelined lobworm which I plopped into the head of the swim and watched carefully as it trundled downstream towards the barbel, my forefinger hooked around the 6 lb reel line, just in case my eyes watching it on the surface failed to identify a pick-up. Halfway down the run the line entering the surface twitched simultaneously as the line tightened across my finger, but I failed to connect on the strike.

On about the fifth run through, however, an identical bite saw the Avon quiver-tip rod instantly take on an alarming bend, as a barbel shook its head angrily and

zoomed beneath the overhanging willows in an effort to make sanctuary of the sunken roots. But through sidestrain and the strength-sapping action of the all-through Avon rod, the barbel was quickly steered away from the hidden snags into open water. And within two minutes a 7½ lb 'whiskers' was safely in the landing net – a great start. Now that our cover and the element of surprise had been broken, resulting in the barbel taking refuge right under the trees, I baited the head of the run with several pints of stewed hempseed mixed with a handful of sweetcorn (the intended hookbait) in an effort to bring them out to feed from the gravel run. Brian knew it was obviously going to be a lengthy wait for those barbel to regain their confidence and so took his time in making up a link ledger rig holding two large swan shots on a 3 inch link. To a 10 inch hook length the strongly forged size 10 was tied direct, presenting three kernels of sweetcorn on a hair rig made from 5 lb black dacron.

Meanwhile I crept about 100 yards further upstream casting freelined lobworms beneath overhanging bushes in search of chub. After a fat four-pounder, however, the usually 'easy to catch chub' just weren't interested in large baits. The water was crystal clear but then the River Wensum usually is throughout the summer months. And their lack of interest was rather a strange phenomenon for so early in the season. Perhaps it was due to the persistent rain preceding our trip and none too warm weather for June. Anyway – this called for drastic action and small baits. So I emptied the remainder of our stewed hempseed, several pints at least, into the head of a 2-foot-deep run alongside a huge raft of floating weed, which had collected around a submerged branch on the opposite bank, and returned to Brian, who had seen the occasional barbel venturing out over the gravel to feed on the hemp, but no bites as yet.

No wonder Brian Ward is wearing an ear to ear grin. He took this 12lbs - 2oz barbel whilst fishing with John on the River Wensum near Norwich.

The magical qualities of hempseed are quite phenomenal, as I witnessed half an hour later, when creeping back to the baited chub run. At least 30 good fish all had their heads down gorging upon hemp grains from amongst the gravel and though they scattered when I flipped in a size 8 hook holding three corn kernels with a swan shot pinched on to the line 12 inches above, they returned within minutes. By using sweetcorn on the hook I could easily identify my baits amongst the hempseed on the bottom and the first chub to suck it in was a fat 4¾-pounder which put up a super scrap at close range. Three others of a similar stamp followed within the next hour before the shoal became completely spooked, so I crept along to see how Brian was faring with the barbel, just in time to see a really large fish at the tail end of his fast run move slowly upstream towards the hair-rigged corn.

As the reflections upon the surface were spoiling Brian's view of the bottom

I gave him a running commentary of the barbel's progress as it confidently made it's way upstream sucking up corn and hempseed from amongst the gravel. As I whispered, 'It's on your bait now, ' Brian's Avon rod simultaneously buckled over into an alarming bend. But Brian was off his stool like a shot and ran several yards downstream to a position directly opposite the great fish so that maximum sidestrain could be applied in order to stop it from reaching the tangle of sub-surface willow roots along the far bank. For a while it was very much a touch-and-go, give-and-take battle but fortunately the 6 lb test and Avon rod combo did the business, and while I clicked away on the camera Brian steered the great barbel across the flow into the waiting net: a superb specimen of 12 lbs 2 ozs and by far his largest ever. What a morning!

ROGER IS SOLD ON BOLT RIG BARBEL FISHING

My good pal Roger Bayzand from Lymington in Hampshire is not only one of, if not 'the' best skipper operating along England's South Coast, he has over many, many years put a lot of big cod, ling, pollack, tope and conger my way through expertise of positioning his 32 foot catamaran *Sundance* over a particular section of wreck or rough ground. Now it was my turn to reverse the honours because, though a freshwater enthusiast for many years, Roger had never fulfiled his ambition of catching a barbel.

Sea skipper supreme and an old friend Roger Bayzand proudly presents his first ever barbel; a River Kennet beauty. Was he one happy bunny.

So I organised a day's ledgering in a super, usually barbel-packed, mill pool on Berkshire's fabulous River Kennet, just off the A4 road near Thatcham, and arranged to meet Roger outside a favourite café for breakfast at 7.00 a.m. After a three hour-plus drive from my Norfolk home, I was really looking forward to a tasty fry-up, but being Sunday the café was unfortunately closed. At the river our second disappointment materialised. Roger had inadvertently packed into the car two left-footed wellies (he has two identical pairs apparently) so he was forced to wear chest-high waders all day. Irritation was soon replaced by elation, however, when his very first cast produced a slamming bite. Literally within minutes of Roger's 14 mm hair-rigged Esterberry boilie on a size 10 hook and 2 oz running lead settling amongst the rocky bottom immediately below the main flush of white water, the rod tip arched over alarmingly.

We had been fishing for less than 5 minutes and Roger was about to realise his dream as a good barbel headed upstream ripping several yards of 8 lb line from his screaming reel, then the hook fell out. The look on his face was priceless. From that point on, however, I am pleased to say our fortunes started to change.

In addition to red, Esterberry shelf-life boilies, I had also catapulted some 12 mm trout pellets into the pool's white water, as there is a trout farm situated just off the river above the mill pool. And these soon had those barbel grubbing about for our ledgered boilies. Both single and double boilie offerings proved effective, with two boilies hair rigged to a size 8 Kamasan B982 extra strong eyed hook, best of all. Our 8 lb monofilament hook lengths were just 10 inches in length, above which, cushioned by a size 10 swivel and rubber bead, a flattened 2 oz lead kept the bait static on the riverbed. Three feet above the lead I used a large x 3 swan shot as a back lead. This ensured that barbel did not hit the line above the ledger rig and spook. An important point this. Line bites where the barbel's huge fins catch the line above the lead can easily reduce the number of bites to materialise.

The barbel were obviously concentrated into just a car-sized area of well oxygenated water immediately down from the weir sill where extra water from a land drainage pipe angled the flow towards where we sat on a gravel spit at the downstream end of the 40-yard- long pool. This necessitated long and accurate upstream casts to place our ledgered baits into a huge back eddy beneath the white water in a depth of around 10 feet. And we kept our rod tips angled up high with the aid of two rod rests for each, to stop surface pressure pulling the lines and our baits away from the target area. Within an hour Roger made amends for his earlier loss and landed his long-awaited barbel, the first I might add of eight we took during the session: the largest a superb 8 lb specimen, falling to Roger's rod. Mission accomplished or what?

Keeping the line really tight after casting with the tip bent around ensured that when each barbel hoovered up the bait and moved off, the hook point penetrated immediately. These 'bolt rig' tactics work as well with English barbel as they do with carp and produce slamming bites. There is no need to strike, simply to lift the rod from the rests and start winding. Naturally you have to watch the rod tip all the time. To turn around for just a few seconds could result in the rod catapulting into the river and out of sight. Bites are that dramatic. It is a good way of catching barbel.

THE MAGNIFICENT SEVEN

Following week upon week of drifting snow and sub-zero temperatures around the clock, with the surface of local lakes frozen solid several inches thick, and even the nearby River Wensum partly frozen across, it was really nice to set out contemplating something other than pike or chub. The thaw was welcome indeed and as daytime air temperatures had risen to 7°C coinciding with the first frost-free night for more than two weeks, I eagerly stacked my quiver-tipping gear plus a fresh white loaf and a bag of breadmash into the hatchback that evening in readiness for an early morning start. Unfortunately, and contrary to what the weatherman had promised (I wish I could be so inaccurate with my job and still expect to earn a living), when I woke at 6.30am and put the outside light on a really heavy frost had formed overnight and lay there glistening as if sticking two fingers in the air. But I went anyway and as I drove through the woods down towards the river with ice on all the puddles crunching heavily beneath the tyres it seemed as though chub were back on the cards yet again.

During mild winter weather other species such as bream, big roach (that's if the cormorants have left any), barbel, and even the odd carp, are all on the cards from the

Big 'river' bream like these do not usually occur in freezing conditions. Lucky me.

river, in addition to chub which are now by far the dominant species. So little else was on my mind whilst introducing a few golfballs of freezing cold breadmash into the head of a 6-feet-deep run overhung by a line of willows, followed by having to smash the solid point of my front rod rest through inch-thick marginal ice. The commotion alone was enough to stop anything from biting. I was in fact perched on the inside of an acute bend upon a frozen bed of rushes and soft silt which, in higher temperatures, would have resulted in two bootfuls. So I could at least thank Jack Frost for that. It was certainly a chub or nothing situation. I had a fixed paternoster ledger all ready made up on the 5 lb reel line, with a 3 lb hook link holding a size 12 hook. So on to the link went two swan shot and across and downstream towards the trailing willow branches went a piece of breadflake half the size of my thumbnail. My fingers were so cold from squeezing and throwing out the mash it was painful to press the bread around the hook shank. Only ardent chub fishermen could appreciate this and only a chub fisherman would appreciate the elation in such conditions of watching the quiver tip momentarily take on a gentle bend from current pressure against the line and then spring suddenly back.

I struck immediately and the Avon quiver-tip rod arched over into a full bend as what was obviously a really big chub begrudgingly shook its head from side to side before heading across and downriver to the end of the run taking several yards of line against the clutch. What a wonderful fight, yet despite only a moderate flow and applying as much pressure as I dared, it seemed ages before I could work this powerful ponderous fish up towards the head of the run where it was first hooked. A couple more thumps directly below the rod top plus a short run and my specimen chub miraculously turned into a slab-sided bream just before it slid into the waiting net. What a surprise – a superbly shaped bream weighing exactly 7 lbs 1 oz. Some chub, eh? And a complete fluke was my immediate reaction. But following a couple of tentative line-bite-type knocks on the tip, round it went and in came another lovely bream, even bigger than the first.

By now Wilson was, of course, well up for all this. The sun had even started to rise over the trees in the direction of Norwich, suddenly turning last summer's growth of dull brown rushes the colour of golden corn. A pair of swans drifted by, the cob looking most aggressive as they do when a human dares to claim their marginal growth. Even a cormorant flying within range almost directly overhead couldn't rattle this happy bunny as those lovely bream fed on, really against all the odds of cold, clear water and bright sunshine. Though I reckon those bream knew the really cold spell was over (despite the frosty morning) and started to feed in earnest after weeks of existing at an extremely low metabolic rate. Who knows? Perhaps the strong sunlight actually triggered their appetite.

In fact I wonder if, had I stayed on and seriously fished my socks off, a huge bag might not have materialised. But in truth I am just as satisfied these days with a photo of one or two nice specimens as I am with a netful flapping about on the bank. So after netting a magnificent seven, the best two scraping 9 lb, and losing another of a similar stamp, even with bites still happening every cast, though now noticeably more timid, I decided to pack up and pop home for a late breakfast. Good thing I did too: my wife, Jo, had virtually cleared the front patio of December's oak leaves. What a woman!.

Alan Pearce and I really put those Ardleigh bream through their paces, accounting for a super bag of fish in the 5-6 lb bracket.Thanks for baiting up Alan.

ARDLEIGH'S HARD FIGHTING BREAM, SIMPLY A DREAM

Hidden away in deepest Essex just a few miles from Colchester lies picturesque Ardleigh Reservoir managed jointly by Tendring Hundred Water Services and Anglian Water Limited. Such is the beauty of the surrounding countryside, particularly the two deeply wooded valleys, which 30 years ago were flooded to create this 100-acre-plus water storage reservoir and leisure playground, it is difficult to believe it lies within just a mile of the A12, one of East Anglia's busiest roads. But the best kept secret of all is Ardleigh Reservoir's fabulous bream fishing. There are big pike and perch here too, plus tench, roach and carp. The bream fishing, however, is absolutely fabulous as my pal Alan Pearce and I experienced at the end of June whilst filming one of my *Go Fishing* television programmes along the Wick Lane arm of Ardleigh.

As he lives much closer than I, Alan agreed to pre-bait for a couple of evenings prior to our dawn start (so necessary for attracting these massive, ever hungry bream shoals into a particular area) and upon arrival I was truly amazed to find we were the only anglers along that part of the reservoir. Talk about secluded get-away-from-it-all day-ticket fishing. Each of us fishing two 12 foot Avon-style ledger rods apiece with fixed/paternoster – cage feeder rigs, and baiting our size 10 hooks with a mixture of sweetcorn and worm, we quickly got into the bream. If anything there were too many gathered in our pre-baited area just 40 yards out beyond the marginal fringe in 8 feet of water, because every so often our bobbin bite indicators would quickly jingle up and down, denoting false bites (liners), where the deep body of the bream momentarily catches the line. We capitalised on enough real bites, however, most of which were extremely bold, and those Ardleigh bream, which averaged between 5 and 6 lb, fought incredibly strongly in the clear water. Unfortunately I managed to pull the hook from a really good tench which looked all of 7 lbs plus, just when it was about ready for the net, but soon afterwards hit into something considerably larger.

By its sheer speed and power this was obviously a big carp (which are more common in the reservoir than most anglers realise) and it led me a real song and dance on just 6 lb test reel line for a good 10 minutes before Alan finally slipped the net beneath it. A beautiful big plated scale mirror carp of around 20 lbs, which we didn't bother to weigh and returned straightaway. Simply marvellous action for the two digi beta television cameras. I must get Alan to bait the swim up again some time, because the bream were still feeding when we wrapped at 9.00 a.m. having caught a dozen or so bream apiece and with more than enough action in the can. Now why can't all my filming be this easy?

BREAK AWAY TO NET BEST OF BREAM

My brother Dave is certainly no slouch when it comes to putting double-figure bream in the net, his favourite location being the renowned Breakaway Pit at Melton, near Woodbridge in Suffolk, arguably the most prolific sheet of stillwater for specimen bream in East Anglia, if not in the whole of the British Isles. Big tench exist here in prolific numbers too, along with some jumbo-sized roach and rudd in excess of 2 lbs, plus a healthy stock of carp to 30 lb. And it's all due to a mountain of natural food in the form of brine shrimps which find their way in by the million from the nearby River Deben estuary. But the best news is this deep and most attractive 7 acre pit is open to all for the price of a day permit through the Breakaway Tackle Shop in Ipswich.

Due to brother Dave's success with the bream here over the past two seasons I decided

I was joined by brother Dave at the prolific Breakaway Fishery near Woodbridge in Suffolk.Our target was its huge bream which are regularly taken into double figures, which this fish wasn't.

to film one of my *Go Fishing* television programmes at the pit just recently. Though, of course, whenever television cameras start rolling rarely does anything ever go according to plan. Take our practice session on the day before, for instance, prior to the film crew's arrival. Bailiff Denis Gooch had kindly ensured that Dave could fish from the renowned 'Lawns' swim which ensured that a 60 yard cast placed his method feeder baits of a mainline active eight boilie on one rod and worm and maggot cocktail on the second on to a 10-foot-deep plateau. And within an hour those bream started obliging, Dave accounting for three beauties to 12 lbs 6 ozs, before I suggested that we rest the swim. After all we wanted those big slabs on camera the following day.

As sport had only really started happening at midday for Dave, I arranged our filming from midday until dusk, rather than the customary dawn start, which as it happened was a wise decision. Contrary to popular belief we do not simply keep two cameras rolling the entire time from dawn until dusk. I look for a realistic window during which time I fancy that action is most likely to happen and then go for it. So the following noon Dave and I filmed an introduction, put our baits out and sat back to await events with our fingers crossed. The first fish was a lovely 6½ lb tench and came to Dave's rod. The second, a bream of around 7 – 8 lbs, certainly one of the smallest in the lake, also came to Dave's rod, as did fish numbers three and four which were both carp of around 8 lbs. All good stuff for the cameras. By now I was, of course, receiving stick not only from my brother about my complete lack of bites, but also from the film crew. All good-natured banter naturally but where were those double-figure bream? The hours ticked by and I set a time of around 7.00 p.m. when we should have to call it a day. At 6.30 p.m. however the indicator went up to my only bite of the session and in came a superbly conditioned bream which tipped the scales at 10 lbs 1 oz. Enough said and programme sorted.

Really for anyone with their sights set upon catching a double-figure bream the Breakaway Pit has few equals in potential, believe me. Give it a try.

IT'S IRELAND FOR BREAM

If you are contemplating freshwater angling holidays abroad this summer in destinations like Ireland, Sweden or Denmark, with bream bashing in mind, with perhaps tench, rudd, roach and pike on the cards. During the winter is the time to start booking, not a couple of weeks before you fancy setting off. Actually it's through booking early in order to be there at 'prime time' between June and September that I have experienced some memorable catches from these locations, several of which have been featured in my earlier *Go Fishing* television programmes and videos. Though I just loved Sweden's Klaralven River in Karlstad, where the unique and colourful golden ide features regularly amongst massive bream hauls, and thoroughly enjoyed Denmark's River Guden which produces jumbo-sized rudd whilst breaming (that's if you can wade through the sheer density of quality roach), for overall potential you just cannot beat the Emerald Isle.

Until I was introduced to Ireland's magic by Martin Founds of Anglers World Holidays more than 10 years ago, I must admit to being somewhat reluctant to get on the ferry due to all the adverse publicity. And when I did finally start touring around to research various areas for their filming potential, I actually felt rather silly, because as everyone had indeed assured me, only in the Belfast area had the troubles ever erupted. The rest of Ireland is, of course, like going back in time, with massive river and lakeland systems simply crammed full of fish, just like English rivers were 50 years ago before water abstraction and farming practices sealed their fate. And, of course, complete with car plus all the tackle and groundbait required, you are only a few hours' drive away from the heart of Ireland once the ferry deposits you at either Dunlaoghire or Dublin, with crossing times of just 99 minutes or 3 hours 15 minutes from Holyhead depending upon which ferry line you take and how fast you want to get there.

Back in the early 1990's I helped put together some videos for the Irish Tourist Board and Polygram Video Limited, which featured several destinations along the marvellous Erne and Shannon systems, without question the top two locations if it's bream you are after. The River Shannon at 210 miles long is the longest river within the British Isles and in my opinion also by far the most prolific and majestic. Its catchment area is in fact over

For catching big bream on the float, there are few places to match fabulous Meelick Weir on the River Shannon.

9000 square miles representing one-fifth of the area of Ireland. Being 'lowland heritage' it lacks that 'valley' look of the River Severn but in fish stocks it is truly unsurpassed, varying in depth between 20 and 40 feet throughout its middle to lower reaches with densely reeded banks up to 100 yards apart. Even hot spots regularly bream-fished by visitors year in and year out are as prolific today as they ever were. Such is the quality of fishing.

Whilst centres at Carrick on Shannon, Roosky, Lanesborough Athlone (particularly in Lough Ree) and Shannonbridge are famous for providing holidaymakers with 100-lb-plus bream bags, my favourite area is the Shannon from picturesque Meelick Weir, going downstream through the town of Portumna, and on to the mouth of massive Lough Derg: a length of around 10 miles resembles a bream factory, with quality roach, rudd, tench and pike on tap should you tire of the big slabs. And once they interbreed with the bream there is going to be a wealth of jumbo-sized hybrids all along the Shannon, possibly to match even those legendary hybrid catches of the River Bann in Northern Ireland.

A TRADITIONAL START

Having left the stagings at the crack of dawn, I must have taken half an hour to row across the 30 acre lake through the mist, so dense were the lily pads, to a small clearing on the other side. Here I put the mudweights down to the bottom through five feet of water at each end of the punt with my back facing south-east so that I wouldn't be squinting into the sun when it rose. With such clear skies, a sunny day seemed imminent, and judging by the small clusters of bubbles erupting through the oily surface close alongside the pads, so too was some traditional tench fishing on the float. With the water so clear, I doubted tench would wish to roam into the centre of the clearing no larger than half a tennis court, so I introduced a few loose balls of seed-mix groundbait along the fringe directly opposite the punt, plus a scattering of sweetcorn and red maggots. I then had but a 10 yard cast to place the float up close to the lilies.

Hidden away from the world in deepest Sussex and surrounded by thick woodlands, this particular lake was not one I had fished before so my plan of baiting on the 'little yet often' principle seemed the best course of action until sport dictated how the morning would develop: always a wiser move than heaving in bucketloads of free nosh with the hope of making a huge haul, because should the tench be in a fickle mood and unwilling to clear up a big breakfast (which is exactly what happened) I could have sat there all morning without a bite. As it was bites came steadily but with such long breaks in between that action could at no time be anticipated.

With the punt moving slowly from side to side above the mudweight ropes, plus an appreciable 'draw' on the surface, my favourite float technique-'the lift'-was not on. It is simply too sensitive for boat fishing with the bait presented on the bottom in all but the most calm of conditions. So using a 14 foot float rod and 6 lb test line combination I rigged up a 5BB bodied, insert (fine-tipped) waggler with most of the bulk shot locked around the float a little deeper than the swim and a single no. 1 shot pinched on the line 6 inches from the size 10 hook holding three grains of sweetcorn. A splodge of liquid 'leader sink' (washing-up liquid works just as efficiently) around the reel's spool ensured that the line sank between float and the rod tip, positioned just a couple of inches above the surface. And this enabled me to set the hook using a sideways sweep of the long rod.

Another reason for my not using the lift was a carpet of filamentous bottom weed upon which a large single shot would catch and cause resistance to a biting tench, whereas the no. 1 shot presented little resistance, most bites being extremely positive with the float tip completely disappearing. A proportion, however, were gentle 'lifts' as a tench came off the bottom with the bait, thus noticeably allowing the float tip to rise: one reason why I chose to use a fine insert tipped bodied waggler, as opposed to a straight waggler which is nowhere near so sensitive.

Unfortunately the first fish I hooked seemed unstoppable and went charging off in the opposite direction through a veritable wall of lily stems, managing to deposit the hook in one of them. Great start, I thought. But unfortunately the fracas didn't stop others from rooting about amongst the oily seed-mix fragments and loose-fed corn that I regularly catapulted along the far edge of the clearing. So I was soon into another tench which fought incredibly hard despite my bullying tactics. Following a couple of heavy runs around the clearing, each accompanied by a glorious swimmer's roll, where hooked tench characteristically arch their bodies to porpoise on the surface before slapping their spade-like tails hard upon the water in a cloud of spray and diving down to the bottom again, my first tench of the season was soon lying in the bottom of the net – a superb female of around 5½ lbs. By now the sun had risen above the trees behind me, bathing the fish's olive green body in soft golden light, whilst I admired its powerful shape before slipping it gently, almost reverently, into the keep net.

My decision to make a traditional start with tench had not been wrong. Whilst I watched a pair of great crested grebes teaching their offspring to dive and catch young roach, and a pair of crows mobbing a kestrel each time it ventured over their territory on the edge of the woods, four more tench found their way into my keep net that morning, the best going 6 lbs 2 ozs. What a wonderful start to yet another coarse fishing season.

RAKE IT UP FOR TENCH SUCCESS

Yes, it's time to be thinking about some serious tench fishing once again now that summer weather conditions have set in, because this friendly and fascinating, hard-battling species will be feeding in earnest through to late autumn.

Why do I think tench are friendly? Well they are particularly angler friendly in that whilst feeding amongst the detritus covering the bottom of ponds, lakes or gravel pits, tench give away their presence by emitting bubbles which rise to the surface. Some of these bubbles originate from the fish's gills as they chew their food and pop up in small clusters of tiny bubbles, whilst wide patches of distinctly 'frothy bubbles' rise to the surface when tench rip nose down (as they characteristically do) through the bottom strata to disturb items of natural food, such as shrimp and bloodworms. This froth is occasionally followed, especially in really shallow water, by bits and pieces of semi-buoyant decaying plant material. Quite simply the tench has released small layers of methane gas trapped within the bottom detritus.

Naturally the angler equipped with a pair of binoculars can at the crack of dawn, when tench traditionally feed with aggression, easily pinpoint areas where they exist and, more to the point, isolate swims where they prefer to feed naturally. They will then subsequently accept hookbaits with more confidence.

Now this isn't to say that tench cannot be encouraged to feed away from natural larders. Carp anglers who practise the 'trapper' approach by consistently pre-baiting areas with boilies and then play a waiting game for the fish to turn up, often account for tench in vast numbers. In stillwaters containing far more tench than carp, the tench might actually become a nuisance to anglers with their sights set on a particularly large carp.

In heavily weeded tench fisheries, those clogged with dense beds of Canadian pond weed, or where the surface is carpeted in dwarf pond lily, wearing chest waders and getting in there with a long-handled garden rake accomplishes two things. In less than an hour's work a fishable swim can be cleared, and the bottom will be nicely stirred up, with all manner of natural food items held in suspension, just waiting for the tench to turn up.

And arrive they will, much sooner than you ever expected. I've even caught tench whilst a friend has been throwing in a weed rake. Honestly.

For deep swims purchase one of those wide, heavy rake heads from a specialist garden centre. There is an enormous choice available. But don't tell the Mrs, or you could be gardening instead of watching a float next weekend!

SUMMER TIME FOR TENCH

Once our British summer time has finally arrived, anglers with an all-round interest such as myself, often find difficulty in deciding upon which species to target. There is so much to try and cram into a relatively short timespan of a few months when all the most exciting species of coarse sea and game fishing are feeding at their most aggressive and in fighting-fit trim. I want to be enjoying catching carp off the top, uptiding for smooth-hounds and tope, quiver tipping a local weir pool for specimen bream and barbel, see my float tip lift positively amidst a fizz of tench bubbles, or watch the leader zip positively across the surface as a rainbow trout sucks in my nymph on the drop. Yes, it's all there if you can find the time; and if, like me, your sights are forever set upon whacking into specimens, because being in a minority they present the ultimate challenge rather than a bag of fish, choice of venue is of paramount importance. Take a small lake, for instance, chock-a-block full of tench most of which are never going to top three or four pounds because there is simply not enough natural food in the larder. On the other hand, consider a large deep gravel pit with only small stocks of tench and with little else in the way of either carp or bream to compete for the natural food source. Those tench will have every opportunity of reaching huge proportions.

I have in fact been concentrating upon such a water this summer, and following several of the inevitable blank sessions which go with 'needle in the haystack' tench fishing, I finally struck gold, my chosen swim being a 12-foot-deep gully close into the bank densely overhung with tall trees. By climbing the trees and viewing through polaroids, I located small groups of what looked to be trophy-sized fish. But never were there more than two or three working along the bottom of the gravel gully at any one time – so heavy baiting was out. I simply pre-baited every other day with a few handfuls of loose-fed corn and stewed hempseed and fished short, early morning sessions when feeding bubbles could be observed, laying my single grain of sweetcorn on the bottom beneath a waggler float rig. Strangely, corn produced just one bite but a

My largest tench ever caught mere feet from the bank using the 'lift method'. It weighed in at 9¼ lbs. No wonder I'm grinning like a Cheshire cat.

nice tench of around 6½ lbs, resplendent in a livery of dark olive green, charcoal fins, that little red (teddy bear) eye-and a most promising start indeed. But when I changed over to a fluffy piece of fresh white breadflake covering the size 12 hook tied direct to the 5 lb reel line – bingo! I hit the jackpot. From the moment the rod tip pulled hard over and line started screaming from the reel, I just knew this was a whopper. After fully five minutes of hugging the bottom it came up and rolled just beyond my landing net. Its rounded dorsal fin looked enormous. And that's because it was. On the scales it weighed 9 lbs 4 ozs, my largest tench ever. To turn a marvellous morning into a truly memorable one, half an hour later the float tip sank again and I netted a second tench of 7 lbs 1 oz. What a brace.

CARP ON THE FLY ROD

Ever since I can remember, the silvery roach has been Britain's most popular and commonly caught freshwater fish. During the past few years, however, and not surprisingly, carp have risen to the top of the list. Now the only trouble with carp and carp fishing is that unwittingly anglers become caught themselves in the stereotyped web of bolt rig fishing boilies at long range using a two or even three- rod set-up wherever they fish.

On large windswept lakes and gravel pit complexes this approach certainly does the business, but on small, more intimate waters, where carp can be tempted and caught at close range by stealthy fishermen, there is a whole variety of techniques to use, from freelining to float fishing lift style. You can even use your fly rod, not necessarily to fool them into sucking in a dry fly or slow-sinking imitative nymph, although I've caught my fair share of carp on each, but to present small floating baits with accuracy on an outfit that will provide unbelievable excitement. Technically this is 'fly rodding' but who cares

A 20 lb carp on a fly rod? Absolutely no problem.

so long as you catch carp? I suggest a 9½ - 10 foot reservoir-type fly rod matched with a size 7 or 8 weight-forward floating line as the ideal combination. Oh, and ensure there is at least 100 yards of backing beneath the line too. To the end of the fly line sleeve on a braided connector which comes with a preformed loop and join 10 – 12 feet of 8 – 10 lb mono as your leader using an overhand loop, just as you would connect hooks to nylon with the reel line, loop to loop.

Alternatively, and for continuing the energy of the cast through to the floating bait, simply sleeve on a 12 foot Masterline Big Butt leader (braided sleeve included) made from rapidly tapering mono, which really assists turnover even in strong winds. To avoid dragging small baits unnaturally across the surface, which results if the leader starts to sink, smear the entire leader to within a couple of inches of the hook with silicon mucilin. The hook needs to be small yet strongly forged. The pattern I use is Kamasan B982 extra strong eyed. It works wonderfully on the fly rod in sizes 14 – 10 in conjunction with small biscuit-type floating dog and cat treats and with floating carp and trout pellets.

To attach your bait, gently file a shallow groove (using a junior hacksaw blade) along one side and after adding just a touch of super-glue, hold steady along the shank of the hook for 10 seconds pressing tightly between thumb and forefinger. Now it doesn't seem as though a small mixer or pellet will stay on and withstand the rigours of casting, but, believe me, it will, and this 'groove and glue' technique offers by far the best presentation with the hook sitting directly below the bait. Have a wander around your local pet stockists and you'll find all manner of potentially effective small floaters. But remember one thing – for accurate, trouble-free casting and good turnover of the leader, keep bait size as small as possible – say ⅜ th inch square or less.

If larger baits are imperative then reduce leader length to just 6 – 9 feet, but beware of the splash made by the floater. This is why small baits are so much better to use: being lighter they create far less suspicion. Incidentally, there is absolutely nothing to stop you from presenting baits 'on the drop', just as though surface controller fishing. A bunch of maggots counter-balanced with a slither of buoyant foam glued to the hook so they can only 'just' sink can prove deadly. A bunch of casters super-glued together then glued on to a bare hook have the same effect, and I'm sure you'll think of other combinations.

Obviously, just like floater fishing using standard carp tackle, it pays to get the fish in a feeding mood first and up aggressively on the top for free offerings by regularly catapulting baits out. Then you can target individual fish, or simply wait to see if your floater gets slurped down when presented amongst a surface scattering. When your bait disappears and it comes to striking remember this – with a fly rod you do not have the perfect tool for really banging the hook home, so wait until the carp gets its head down and tightens the line as it moves off before whacking the rod upwards hard and pulling the line down with your other hand. Many fish, incidentally, know they have blundered when closing their lips, and upon feeling resistance from the line, belt off in panic anyway, virtually hooking themselves in the process.

When a fish goes charging off remember to get quickly to your feet (assuming that you have been keeping low down) and hold the rod really high up to avoid the line becoming snagged around the pads and stalks of lilies or thick clumps of soft weeds. Endeavour to play the carp directly from the reel, breaking the rim firmly but smoothly with the palm of your winding hand in order to slow it down. To the Carp, the action of your fly rod, plus sunken line being towed against water pressure, is like one giant elastic band that just keeps stretching and stretching. And you'll be amazed the size of fish that can be beaten on just a couple of ounces of carbon fibre.

Stu Makay[left] and Fred J Taylor [right] and yours truly enjoy an evening with friends beside the fabulous Red River at Lockport Bridge Dam near Winnipeg.

PARADISE FOUND ON THE RED RIVER

In complete contrast to how we British anglers put enormous value on the carp as the supreme freshwater adversary, with species like zander at the bottom of the list, North American fishermen put walleye (their zander) at the top and are not the slightest bit interested in catching carp whatever their size – strange isn't it? In fact most Americans and Canadians would really rather catch a bundle of 2 – 3 lb walleyes, which merely flap about like a bream of similar size, than have their string pulled by long, lean and unbelievably hard-fighting common carp, which throughout America average double figures and are so plentiful their sheer density in numbers takes some believing.

Take Manitoba's fabulous Red River at Lockport Bridge Dam near Winnipeg, for instance, where completely by accident I first encountered the Canadian carp phenomenon 10 years ago. I can remember then saying to guide Stu Makay, who runs the fishing at Lockport, that he was sitting on a carp goldmine and still is if my recent trip across the Pond with a group of Brits is anything to go by. Our party of eight stayed in Stu's anglers' accommodation which commands a wonderful panoramic view over the Red River immediately downstream of Lockport Bridge Dam. This is, in fact, a massive weir where a churning maelstrom of white water offers quite unbelievable boat and bank fishing for both channel catfish and common carp to over 30 lbs, plus the exciting freshwater drum, a predatory bream-like critter that is always willing to bite and particularly common in the 5-10 lb bracket. Add shiners, goldeye (catfish bait supreme), walleye, saugers, white bass, bullheads, pike and numerous other oddities and you can understand why my old mate, international angling guru Fred J. Taylor, compares the Red River system to a 'fish factory'. It's certainly the richest fishpacked river I've ever fished. Our very first serious carp session proved this at the junction of where a 100-yard-wide drainage dyke joins the Red River.

Stu ran his customised 18 foot aluminium boat hard up on to a shallow gravel bar and immediately cut the engine, disturbing a group of pelicans from their morning nap, and scattering several large handfuls of hard maize (Canadians call it corn) all around the drainage dyke side of the boat to a depth ranging between 2 and 5 feet where carp could already be seen working over a baiting from the night before. There were carp everywhere and seemingly not the slightest bit worried by our boat. Indeed it was impossible to count the tails and dorsal fins protruding from the surface film in the shallows.

Stu, of course, had seen it all before and sat back to see how his three guests would enjoy Canada's carp hospitality on the float, which proved to be the most hectic sport with double-figure carp I have ever encountered. And what a wonderful change from the overfished carp syndrome of our small island back home. No wonder more and more British anglers are travelling to Canada and Manitoba's Red River to get their string pulled. Tell a Canadian that you love carp fishing and he'll give you a quizzical look. Tell him that you actually catch the same fish twice back home and even give them names and he'll drop his drink from laughing. It is simply beyond his comprehension – not just the fact that you 'like' catching carp but that fish are so thin on the ground (compared to Canadian waters) that individual fish even get caught again-because most Canadian carp have never seen a baited hook. Which probably explains why in just four hours, float fishing from Stu's boat, and most of them from less than two rod lengths away, my two guests, Roberto Ferrario (who had come all the way from Italy) and Richard Ward from Southampton, and myself caught exactly 50 beautifully conditioned commons between 10 and 24 lbs, nine channel catfish to over 20 lbs and eight drum to around 7 lbs, all on corn and breadflake baits. On several occasions two rods were bending simultaneously and once all three were engaged with carp – not bad going for a casual 10.00 a.m. start.   And we only stopped when we did in mid-afternoon (you can only catch so many) because Stu said, ' Hey guys, let's stop at 50 eh!' Typical Stu.

Throughout the week's bonanza we sampled carp in other locations off the massive Red River system – creeks, vast swamps and wide channels – all with similar results, and beautifully proportioned common carp which even at 10 lbs simply knock the spots off a pot-bellied mirror of twice, even three times the size. Their strength and stamina has to be experienced to be believed.

Now as far as the channel catfish were concerned, well we couldn't go wrong. Sessions started by securing enough fresh goldeye deadbaits by trotting small pieces of worm at a depth of 2 to 3 feet just in front of the jetty. Each goldeye was then divided into five or six cutlets with one gently impaled on a barbless size 4/0 hook which incidentally are compulsory in Canada as is the use of one rod only at all times. Mind you, both carp and catting are so fast and furious, how anyone could look after two rods simultaneously (let alone three) is beyond my comprehension. Holding the rod and 'feeling' for bites is imperative, or the cat lets go of your bait. A foot or two of line is given the very second the ledgered bait is mouthed, followed by a firm strike if a run materialises. Pound for pound the carp fights faster, though the channel catfish will pull harder and for longer

Due to the heatwave temperatures, anchoring the boat in the swirling waters of the weir produced the most hectic pussy action during the daytime. Those who night fish really experience just how aggressive channel catfish can be. But ours was a leisurely holiday and two anglers sharing a boat often accounted for four or five cats apiece between 10 and 20 lbs in just a few hours. Best of the week was a $27^{1/2}$ – pounder, and its captor, Richard Ward, boated another of 25 lbs.

Martin Bowler helps me display a big 'double figure' colourful koi carp that I hooked whilst filming a 'Go Fishing' programme at Wintons fishery in West Sussex.

COLOURED CARP

Several weeks ago now during February when the ice covering my two-lake carp fishery for more than five weeks finally melted away, it revealed the death of what you might call an old friend, an orange-coloured mottled hi-goi that I purchased in a koi club sale held at Bressingham Garden Centre in the late 1970s when it was just 10 inches long. And now weighing the best part of 14 lb and still in splendid condition, having provided colourful sport to a number of my syndicate members over the years, it had paid the price for coming up to the surface beneath the ice and become frozen in.

The occasional death of adult fish is usually the bane of fisheries' owners and managers during the spring, when diseases that have laid dormant all winter long suddenly bloom as water temperatures rise. And, of course, again at post-spawning time when the rigours of propagation become just too much for some adult carp, spawn-bound females being most common among fatalities. But during the winter months is not the time I would expect to find many corpses, unless the surface is covered in ice for such a long period that gases created from rotting vegetation and leaves on the bottom cannot escape and so drastically reduce levels of dissolved oxygen. I can well remember the winter of 1963 for instance when, due to being covered in ice a foot thick for close on three months, my local shallow and exceptionally well-stocked carp lake in North London, where I then lived, suffered a total wipe out. And the Council had to come along with four pick-up trucks to cart the lake's entire population of gudgeon and wild carp away for burial. It was a sad day indeed for us local enthusiasts as prolific carp fisheries in those days around the London area were most uncommon.

But let me return to that lovely orange mottled hi-goi which in fact, upon purchase, spent the first few years in an ornamental pond before I decided to introduce it, and many other coloured carp, into my fishing lakes along with the stock of natural common, mirror and leather carp. Because it was for me a turning point: quite simply I had never contemplated fishing purposefully for coloured carp until I stocked my lakes with metallic carp in the early 1980s. Another name given to this hardy strain of king carp by the aquatic trade is 'ghost koi' and they are now extremely popular with garden pond enthusiasts, being considerably less expensive than true koi. I call them 'metallics' because they were so named by the first person in this country, to the best of my knowledge, to cross a pure white Japanese male ogon koi with a bog-standard German dinklespula table carp: a Mr Michael of Selby in Yorkshire.

I purchased several of his brood stock and 400 4-5 inch metallics of varying colour densities; some almost as white as their Japanese male parent, others showing little in the way of silver enamelling, just a white cast on the undersides of their pectoral and pelvic fins. Today many of these are superbly shaped carp weighing up to 20 lbs and possessing the most breathtaking colour hues ranging from metallic beige and silver to muted shades of pewter.

To some it may seem rather strange fishing purposefully for coloured carp but the truth is both koi (which in Japanese simply means 'coloured') and all natural strains of carp, plus the enormous variation of koi crosses now produced, all share the Latin name of *Cyprinus carpio*. They are all one and the same, so to differentiate for any purpose, even fishing, would be rather racist, wouldn't it? Indeed it would because they are genetically the same and are able to interbreed freely even in the wild and throw up such a galaxy of interesting variants not only in colouration but also in scaleage. It's an exciting development within freshwater fishing in the UK because more and more fisheries are now including a proportion of these hardy metallics or ghost kois for anglers to enjoy.

I am sure, like many of nature's most colourful creatures, coloured carp are aware of their colouration and the associated greater threat of predation by birds such as herons and cormorants. Metallic carp are certainly much faster at sucking in and spitting out the bait compared to the natural carp in my own lakes. Through observation over many years there is no doubt in my mind that because they spook very much more easily these crosses provide an absorbing challenge with a stunningly beautiful creature to admire at the end of the fight. Another plus is that they run and rip line from the slipping clutch at astonishing speed, and the way in which a metallic zooms up to the top and sucks down a floater, having studied it for several seconds by standing on its tail and back-flipping with its pectorals, is in stark contrast to a fat old uncoloured mirror carp wallowing through the surface film gorging down floater upon floater like in the computer game '*Pac man*'.

CARP PROVE HOT CATCH ON COLD DAY

So severe was the pre-dawn frost, I started the engine and relied upon the estate's heating system to de-ice everything while I went back indoors to fill the vacuum flask with coffee. From the reflected light of a three-quarter moon I could clearly see that both our carp lakes were completely frozen over as I drove through the woods and out on to the Fakenham road towards one of my favourite swims on the River Wensum. It was most certainly not a 'carp morning'.

I was about to fish an overgrown piece of the river which, during the 1980s, produced a galaxy of specimen roach for me to close on 3 lbs, plus the odd nice chub, but into which during recent years following the demise of the roach, a shoal of large bream had moved. Strangely these particular bream always became evident by porpoising on the surface but

This colourful winter wacker of 21 lbs came from my local River Wensum on quiver tipped breadflake, which is why I thought it was a chub. What a scrap!

only following a heavy overnight frost, which was indeed my reason for revisiting this particular swim nicknamed 'the rushes' due to a 20 foot fringe of sweet rush creeping out across the river from where I fished, almost halving its width. On the opposite bank two huge weeping willows presided over the swim creating a superb habitat with a depth of around 6 feet through the centre channel, the current flowing right to left. Having trudged across rock-hard frozen marshes as dawn broke, I managed to locate the wooden pallet which last winter I had secured with stakes amongst the floating raft of sweet rush, now completely carpeted in thick frost, and set up my quiver-tip rod with a fixed paternoster ledger holding three x 3 SSG shots and an 8 hook tied direct to the 6 lb reel line, covered with a large piece of white breadflake. The bream were not rolling as I had expected but I introduced several balls of mashed bread nevertheless and made a short cast downstream.

During the following hour the sun slowly rose while I made several more casts, each progressively further downstream, in an effort to search the entire swim, seemingly all to no avail. Not even a chub so much as rattled the quiver tip. But the kaleidoscope of burnished colours, reflections of the sun hitting marginal ice, the golden brown of last summer's tall reed mace stems, and the yellowy orange of new willow growth on the trees opposite brought cheer to my heart and reason for sitting there at such an unearthly hour before most folks had their Sunday papers delivered.

Then right out of the blue the quiver tip slowly pulled hard round and I struck into something, most certainly not a bream or a chub, or a barbel. As with many a big fish which suddenly finds itself hooked in low water temperatures, it took a few seconds for the penny to drop. Then the unseen force powered off downstream ripping line from a firm clutch setting, giving me time to reduce the stern drag by a couple of clicks to minimise torque on the 6 lb reel line. Twenty, 30, 40 yards it went before turning completely around and powering back up the swim towards me beneath the lapping branches of the willows on the opposite bank. It motored a good 30 yards above the willows but finally submitted to the continual pressure of my Avon rod, rolling on the surface in a mighty boil directly opposite. A huge carp no less which dived once again before I could fully claim control. Then the hook inexplicably pulled out – boy, did I feel gutted.

For the following hour I sat there feeling as sick as the proverbial parrot, wondering if there were any more carp in the swim and contemplating shelving the fishing in preference for walking the banks with my Nikon to capture the beauty of Jack Frost before the sun spoiled everything. But then the tip pulled round again and the clutch screamed, as yet another carp headed off downstream, which is where it stayed for most of the fight. Rarely do I need to pile so much pressure on to my Avon quiver-tip rod, but the subsequent curvature was both alarming and pleasing. The accumulative pressure of even a 6 lb line is capable of wonderful things. Hence after a 10 minute battle, I was able to draw a beautifully proportioned plated scaled mirror carp over the landing net. What did it weigh? Twenty-one pounds exactly – and I said it wasn't a carp morning!

JAMMY DEREK'S TRUE TO HIS WORD

When I met Derek Walker from Milton Keynes at the crack of dawn beside the summerhouse of my two-lake Norfolk fishery, the first thing he said was, 'I'm a jammy B John.' And of course I should have listened, but the luck or being lucky does play an important part in our sport. For some, however, it would appear more prevalent than usual, so allow me to recount our two days fishing together for an example.

After baiting several close-range swims between tall trees and dense marginal growth with loose-fed pellets whilst stealthily walking Derek around the two lakes, I suggested we used simple lift-float rigs and start at the first. I gave him a quick run-down on the fish stocks which include grass carp and wels catfish, plus various strains of king carp comprising of the odd beautifully coloured koi and ghost koi in shades of silver, beige, pewter and gold, plus some really long hard-fighting commons, mirrors, leathers and a handful of beautiful fully scaled mirrors. 'Oh, I've never caught a fully scaled mirror," says Derek as his float zooms under. Yes, you've guessed correctly, in comes a superbly proportioned double-figure fully scaled mirror in pristine condition. The disturbance necessitated a swim change and within minutes Derek's hair-rigged 12 mm pellet on a size 8 hook was inhaled by

Aren't koi carp beautiful creatures. Derek Walker caught this magnificent specimen using the 'lift' method from my own two-lake Norfolk fishery.

33

a superb and incredibly long common carp pushing 20 lbs, which gave him a hell of a scrap. It was the biggest common he'd ever caught. More photos, and we slowly progressed around the two lakes from swim to swim catching exactly the carp I had mentioned. Derek marvelled at the beauty of the golden metallic ghost koi and how they seem to fight so incredibly strongly and was delighted at landing his first ever true leather which was completely scaleless.

I was starting to lose count here and just knew I should not have mentioned that the huge patch of fizzy bubbles near his float looked like those of a catfish. 'Oh I'd love to catch a cat," says Derek and five minutes later we were admiring the 10-pounder in the bottom of his landing net. Even more astounding was his next strike. Up to the surface in a huge orange-red kaleidoscope of thrashing water came the largest true koi in the lakes, a stunning fully scaled beauty of around 14 lb, the colour of a pillar box. End of day one.

The following morning our chub and barbel sortie along the nearby River Wensum had to be shelved due to severe flooding so it was back to my lakes for the species he hadn't caught. I was only joking, yet his first catch of the day using a small biscuit floater produced an immaculate grass carp pushing double figures. And it simply carried on again with a variety of king carp ending in a shimmering white ghost koi of around 15 lbs that no one else could ever have extracted from such a dense marginal fringe of yellow water lilies. Yes Derek – you are a jammy, lucky B!

NO CARPING ON OUR LUCKY 13

In the early hours of the morning I woke to the impact of feeling decidedly warmer than the previous night. Our Spanish villa, built to keep visitors cool for most of the year, no longer felt like a fridge, and when Martin Bowler's alarm clock went off a few hours later,

I immediately predicted he'd be 'hauling' carp shortly afterwards from our 20-foot-deep pre-baited swim in Rio Ebro where it converges with the Rio Segre at Mequinenza, some 100 miles west of Barcelona. I know it's strange how a dramatic rise in air temperature makes fish start to feed on the bottom of a freezing cold river, which in no way could possibly have warmed up noticeably overnight, yet Martin did catch and catch 'big time'. Within just a few hours he accounted for no fewer than four immaculately scaled common carp (all the Spanish 'river carp' are commons) between 20 and 26 lbs on hair-rigged boilies, ledgered on a bolt rig just 40 yards our, over an area heavily pre-baited the evening before with a mixture of hempseed, maize and hookbait boilies.

Our recent four-day winter break in the sun as guests of the Bavarian Guiding Service in Mequinenza had come to fruition after all despite some uncharacteristic chilly winter weather for Catalunya. Normally fishing in shirt sleeves by midday in this part of Europe is par for the course which after all is why an ever-increasing number of Brits now spend their winters in Spain. Due to such an incredible stock of carp and wels catfish inhabiting these two fertile rivers (Mequinenza is considered as the catfish capital of Europe) anyone would indeed be pushed NOT to catch. I've never fished anywhere so jam-packed full with carp, which continually give away their presence by rolling on the surface and at least every other fish is a 20-pounder. It is quite unbelievable. From Martin's favourite swim I had in fact taken a $28^{1}/_{2}$ lbs beauty the previous morning, while our partner and fellow angling writer, Adam Penning, peaked out with a simply stunning specimen which pulled the spring balance down to within just 12 ozs of that magical 30 lb figure.

Our guide, Gary Allen, could not have been more pleased, for in less than four full day's fishing we nobbled 13 common carp over 20 lbs, and in difficult conditions. What was my best? Only a PB weighing a massive $35^{1}/_{4}$ lbs, that's all: an immaculately scaled, long and thickset common carp. By far my largest ever which despite the low water temperatures fought strongly for a good 10 minutes, making several long, heart stopping runs. But the size 6 hook held and rarely have I been so pleased to see a fish finally slide over the net. Spain – we'll most certainly be back.

ALIENS HAVE LANDED

I understand that the Ministry of Agriculture, Fisheries and Food has recently issued a news release proposing harsh new measures for protecting our native freshwater species in England and Wales, in that it should be illegal to keep or release non-native species into any water without a licence. Apparently even the strict rules currently in force governing the release of alien species into the wild are not easy to enforce and do not cover introduction of exotica into fish farms and other waters not regarded as 'wild'. therefore MAFF are proposing to

make it illegal to even keep non-native fish or release them into any waters in England and Wales without a licence. How this will affect the pet trade and in particular aquarists, who enjoy studying freshwater exotica from about the globe, I'm not too sure, but it can only be a step in the right direction and good for the survival of our native species.

In just the last decade for instance we have experienced the kind of threats which alien freshwater species of both fish and crustaceans can pose. Throughout much of southern England our indigenous crayfish has almost been wiped out by the aggressive and very much larger signal crayfish from America, originally stocked only by owners of stillwater trout fisheries as a secondary crop. Of course, and it was bound to happen, these jumbo-sized freshwater crayfish have now spread into many river systems and are fast becoming the dominant feeder down on the bottom of the riverbed. It is I think still early days and the jury will be out for a long time, but I fear the ecosystem of invertebrate life is going to be catastrophically affected by these alien mini lobsters once they become prolific everywhere.

Another crustacean to be extremely concerned about, now firmly established within the London Dockland area, but which has also been found far upriver within tributaries of the River Thames, is the Chinese 'mitten' crab which can grow to 6 inches across the carapace and which, like the signal crayfish, is not only quite capable of dominating the invertebrate life at the bottom of the river, but is also an ardent consumer of fish life in its early stages, spawn in particular, plus fish fry.

Crustacean-wise these two are, in my opinion, creatures that all freshwater anglers should be most concerned about. However, let's look at various alien fishes which may or may not be a good thing. I won't go too far into the 'zander' controversy because this rests fairly and squarely on the shoulders of the 'then' Great Ouse River Authority (I assume with MAFF permission) who took the decision of introducing a batch of zander into the Great Ouse Relief Channel at Downham Market in Norfolk way back in the early 1960s. Zander were in fact already present in a few isolated stillwater fisheries, namely the lakes at Woburn Park in Bedfordshire, from stockings made as far back as 1878. But it was the 18th March 1963 stocking of just 97 zanders averaging 8 ozs which opened the floodgates to colonisation of our river systems. Now, of course, zander are thriving everywhere and frankly, just like all over Europe, they have settled in to become part of the ecosystem.

Another alien 'plus' as far as I am concerned is the way in which the Danubian 'wels catfish' has been successfully introduced into numbers of stillwater fisheries. Again it is a fish of Europe and one which has become part of a sensible balance within many of our carp-orientated stillwater fisheries.

You see, non-anglers must understand that due to chronic water abstraction, due to the over-eutrophication of our rivers through farming chemicals, and due to the predation by cormorants upon our silver shoal species like roach and dace, the young anglers of tomorrow will start their apprenticeship not on rivers as I did, but on artificially created and artificially stocked stillwater fisheries. OK, so personally I would rather be long trotting for roach in a fast, clear-flowing, gravel-bottomed river, but if that is not possible I would rather be enjoying the fight of exotic species like catfish, carp and grass carp from an attractive manmade stillwater than simply wasting my time on a ruined river. Harsh facts maybe but true because I have watched it all happen (with photographic evidence for proof) during these past 40 years.

To my mind one of the best stock fish for modern-day stillwaters is the grass carp because it cannot reproduce in our climate. This is because its eggs need to float on the surface of a river flowing in excess of 70° F for at least two weeks whilst incubating. And within the British Isles no river is ever that warm. It's as simple as that. So if 10 grass carp are introduced no more than 10 will ever be caught. Therefore, it is a perfectly controllable stock fish, which grows to 30 lbs plus, fights hard and needs cunning to catch.

As for other freshwater exotica that MAFF have published on their hit list, such as the diminutive pumpkinseed, Danubian bleak, top mouth gudgeon etc., who needs 'em anyway?

BEAUTY PERSONIFIED

Unfortunately I don't fish my own two lakes much these days. Being so close to the house I feel I know the inhabitants perhaps rather too well. Indeed the mere fact of setting off in the early hours to mysterious waters with not the slightest inkling of what's in store, is what makes our sport so totally unpredictable and adventuresome. Every so often, however, a certain 'homegrown' challenge does present itself and just recently I couldn't resist having a go for one of several large golden orfe that have grown to specimen proportions (no doubt on all the high-protein pellets loose fed for attracting carp) and which during the summer months are forever on the move from one lake to the other via an overgrown connecting channel, slurping down emerging insects off the top.

My syndicate members occasionally catch them on small floating baits intended for carp, but of course on 8-10 lb test these beautiful creatures can hardly put up a scrap - not that orfe are actually known for their fighting capabilities anyway. The classical 'wet sack' description fits them admirably. What they lack in strength, however, they certainly make up for in cunning and extreme colouration. They are beauty personified you might say.

Now once these particular orfe have been spooked or actually pricked by carp terminal rigs, they become incredibly wary and difficult to catch and in no way will succumb to a floating controller rig where the line floats upon the surface between controller and bait, such as a cube of crust, bunch of casters, floating sweetcorn or floating trout or carp

Painted in a subtle shade of pale, orangey-pink, this, my largest ever golden orfe, sucked in a floating carp pellet and totally made my morning.

pellets etc., no matter how sensitively they are presented. And I've found the only way to fool them is to have no line whatsoever upon the surface, which necessitates crawling stealthily into a position amongst dense marginal undergrowth immediately above a route taken by the orfe and then to introduce a few free offerings. The secret being to refrain from actually lowering the floater until an orfe is just a few feet away. So long bouts of inactivity are par for the course. Suspending it within the surface film for any length of time is simply asking for an unseen carp to slurp it down, resulting in a commotion guaranteed to put the orfe off for quite some while.

To be perfectly honest I find purposefully targeting these beautiful but spooky orfe and nothing else totally addictive. They are such frustrating brazen surface foragers and will repeatedly suck in floating baits only feet from the bank whilst in full view, even in bright sunshine, but the very second a floating monofilament line appears on the surface they totally ignore your bait.

For maximum sensitivity I opted for a $2\frac{1}{2}$ lb reel line with an eyed size 12 hook tied direct and simply super-glued on a 12 mm floating carp pellet, after first cutting a narrow groove using a junior hacksaw blade. Incidentally, a 6 inch blade snapped in half provides you with a couple of these extremely useful tools, which no serious floater enthusiast should ever be without, be your quarry carp or orfe. And using a spot of super-glue to fix the bait on is so simple, yet deadly effective. Without question it offers the most natural presentation of a floating bait, short of dispensing with the hook altogether. Give it a try and you'll quickly learn to have complete confidence in the bait staying on. Indeed the bond between pellet and hook shank is so secure that removing the remnants off the hook in readiness for presenting another bait requires no small amount of scraping with your thumbnail or forceps.

Using an 11 foot Avon-style rod for poking between branches did, I'm afraid, not really allow my orfe to fight very much and following a few spirited dives it was safely in the net, all 6 lbs 6 ozs of it.

JUMBO CRUCIANS BITE ON CUE

The RMC Yateley complex, comprising of 15 lakes and a delightful stretch of the River Blackwater situated in mature woodland on the Surrey/Hampshire border, is one of the most famous fisheries in the country. And anyone can buy a season ticket. Both specimen hunters and pleasure anglers alike are catered for here as fellow angling writer, Martin Bowler, and I experienced just recently whilst filming for my Anglia Television series, *Go Fishing*, in Yateley summer pit, our target species being the deep-sided golden bronze, decidedly difficult to catch, crucian carp, which reach record proportions in this 2 acre water completely surrounded by trees. Our first task was to locate groups of crucians by looking for their characteristic clusters of feeding bubbles which can be seen on the surface at dawn when they feed most aggressively amongst the bottom detritus on natural food items such as annelid worms, shrimp and bloodworms etc., our plan then being to wean them on to our loose feed of liquidised bread and pellet crumb and breadflake hookbaits.

Crucians just love the sanctuary and reduced light levels beneath overhanging and especially partly submerged willows and we soon had them ripping up the bottom for our loose feed beside a sunken tree in a most picturesque swim just a rod's length out. Inducing a hittable bite, however, on our delicately shotted waggler rigs presented on 13 foot carbon float rods and centre-pin reels, proved far more difficult.

RMC angling manager and local big fish expert, Ian Welch, had warned Martin and me about this phenomenon and suggested we scale down to size 16 hooks presenting either punched bread or the tiniest pinch of breadflake. And he was so right.

A size 16 hook tied direct to a fine diameter 2 lb reel line, however, looks pretty light for stopping what could be a crucian carp of over 4 lb from reaching the sanctuary of sunken branches. The record crucian of 4 lbs 8 ozs did in fact come from the summer pit which is classed as a true crucian water and not likely to produce a hybrid. Hence my preference for trying Yateley. But we did manage to bag several jumbo-sized specimens, striking the tiniest of bite indications with the bait just touching bottom in 5 feet of water. My first crucian of exactly 3 lbs was in fact the largest I have ever caught in English waters and fought like stink. Soon afterwards it was Martin's turn and he took his largest ever with a buttery bronze beauty of 2½ lbs. What a wonderful session and simply marvellous action for the two cameramen who also managed to capture the antics of a young robin that sat on my rod preening itself for several minutes. It's what fishing is all about.

ARCTIC CONDITIONS BRING SCANT REWARD

While I certainly have no way of predicting weather conditions, it is a fair bet that if Mother Nature is going to throw the book at us this winter then February is the month. So with this in mind and the chance of prolonged sub-zero temperatures bringing forth frozen stillwaters and even ice over running water, what species do the most hardened freshwater fishermen choose to avoid a blank notebook? Well, for me there are only two contenders – grayling and chub. Both can be induced to feed in the lowest temperatures despite snow showers, chilling winds and even when ice threatens the river's surface.

Living as I do in Norfolk, however, with nothing on the local scene in the way of serious grayling fishing, although I do make at least a couple of trips down south every winter to the Test, Kennet and Dorset's River Frome to do battle with her ladyship, the mainstay of my cold weather prospects must lie with chub inhabiting the upper reaches of the Rivers Waveney, Yare, Bure and Wensum. In fact at around this time last winter I enjoyed several sessions close to home along the River Wensum in the most

Old pal Terry Houseago dares his quiver tip to twitch during a sub-zero chubbing session when the River Wensum actually froze 'bottom first'. Honestly!

appaling conditions and rarely blanked.

One particular day springs to mind when good friend Terry Houseago and I set off at dawn amongst heavy snow showers with quiver-tip rods and a bag of mashed bread at the ready, because simply inducing a bite would have been reward enough, such were the conditions throughout the Wensum valley on that occasion. Following a long walk across frozen meadows at Taverham, we arrived at our first choice and a favourite chub swim where a great willow tree presides over the river on the opposite bank, only to find the surface frozen across from each bank, leaving just a yard-wide gap down the middle. So about turn it was and back into the car we got, motoring to a spot a few miles further upriver at Ringland where, though initially the river seemed clear, on close inspection the entire surface contained lumps of weed locked up in ice chunks which immediately ruled out ledgering or any form of fishing for that matter. We had arrived during a rather strange phenomenon when a particular stretch had actually frozen bottom first (yes, bottom first) before breaking up and rising to clog the surface of the river.

Now I know it sounds like a contradiction in physics, but of late I've been discussing this very subject with recently retired river keeper Vic Foot, who for 55 years managed the famous Nurslings beat on the lower Test, near Southampton. Vic recalls that in the 1962/63 big freeze-up the River Test did in fact freeze bottom first with the resulting layers of ice floating up to the surface around midday complete with chunks of decaying weed growth. I believe this is called 'grue' in Scotland and it's all to do with permafrost in the ground below the riverbed. But as this phenomenon is so rare, combined with the fact that few nutcases, like Terry and myself, would actually be beside the river to ever witness it happening, small wonder it takes some swallowing.

Anyway, it was back to the car again and this time to a narrow, streamy stretch far upriver at North Elmham Mill where we reckoned the fast flow would not have iced over. And so it proved – an awful lot of walking yes, a lot of driving yes, an hour in the Bridge Public House at Lenwade yes, but eventually following an hour's warming up, our small pieces of breadflake on size 10 hooks quiver tipped close into the bank on short hook lengths did produce several tentative plucks resulting in three modest-sized chub between us. Their size simply didn't matter. We had beaten the odds by inducing chub to bite whose metabolic rate was so low they really didn't need to feed. And that's the beauty of going for species like chub and grayling in sub-zero water – both are always willing.

Finally a word about 'end rigs' for those bent on venturing out against arctic conditions, knowing that rewards will be scant. Remember to keep both ledger link and hook lengths very short, because a biting chub is only going to give the tiniest indication and not yank the rod tip round as it did last autumn. So hit any slow quarter-inch pull on the quiver tip before the bait is dropped – and take a hip flask with you.

LIVELY CHUB PROVIDE A COLD COMFORT

Angling illustrator Dave Batten and I had planned to go pike fishing on the wide tidal reaches of the lower River Waveney in Suffolk. The low spring tide on the day we'd arranged would have allowed us to trot livebaits down the deep centre channel throughout the ebb, with a real chance of contacting one of the river's monster pike. And having enjoyed some spectacular battles with specimens there to over 25 lbs in the past, by picking the best tides, it was a trip I was really looking forward to. Then the weather pattern went and changed for the worse with sub-zero temperatures setting in accompanied for two days by persistent rain, sleet and some heavy snow showers. The lower Waveney turned orange with high, filthy cold snow water, and any hope of a pike trip was immediately ruled out, clearish water with a fair visibility being imperative to stand any chance with these big, tidal river pike in the deep fast-flowing lower reaches.

'Well, there's always chub fishing on the River Wensum,' I said to Dave, who was straining at the leash for a day out away from his Apple Mac. So we ignored the fact that my local River Wensum was also getting on for two feet higher than normal, going like the clappers, heavily coloured and full of debris in the way of leaves and decaying weed, and set off anyway. Being the first really freezing cold weather of the winter, I think we both regretted making a dawn start. A strong bitterly cold northerly wind was ripping down the valley accompanied by the odd squall of hailstones. It was the kind of day when those immortal words of Fred J. Taylor, 'I'll be glad when I've had enough of this,' immediately spring to mind.

With the river flowing right to left we settled in immediately upstream of a wide right-hand bend on the outside bank, just above a large partly sunken bush where I knew the depth beneath shelved down to more than six feet and was the home of at least a dozen resident chub. With the river distinctly out of sorts, placing a static bait literally on the chub's nose was imperative and that's exactly what Dave must have done. Within a couple of minutes his quiver tip arched round as a good chub powered across the flow, having sucked up his large piece of ledgered breadflake. What fabulous fights winter chub can provide, keeping close to the riverbed throughout and straining the 6 lb test reel line to the full. This fish was no exception, but finally it succumbed to the pressure of Dave's

Dave Batten's smile says it all. Success over the adversity of appalling conditions, produced a superb chub brace when most anglers would have stayed in bed.

Avon quiver-tip rod and slid into the net, well over 4 lbs and a nice start. Sitting slightly upstream of Dave (but only two yards apart) I made a long cast and put a lobworm into the slack immediately below the bush as no further action came to his breadflake bumped directly beneath it. The first bite I missed but connected with the second, another chunky 4-lb-plus chub. But that was it from that swim. With fingers getting progressively more painful from each move we made to similar 'cert' swims in the mile or so upstream, not a single twitch did we have. Only when we tramped back to the sunken bush again as the sun started to set did our fourth bite of the day occur. Again it came to my lobworm and was from a fish pushing $4^{1}/_{2}$ lbs. Those chub wanted it on their noses and nowhere else. They were situated over comparatively small areas of the river where they needed to be continually moving position in order to avoid the stream of debris coming down. Studying surface flow patterns had indeed paid off in the 'bush' swim, and they were three chub we wouldn't have caught by staying at home.

BIG CAT HUNTERS HAPPY TO TAKE ON THE HUMBLE CHUB

As founder members of The National Catfish Conservation Group, my two good friends from down south, Simon Clarke and Keith Lambert, are used to battling with 100-lbs-plus pussies in the huge rivers of France, Italy and Spain, Simon being the Group's secretary, while Keith is editor of *Whiskers*, their colour magazine. You might then subsequently assume that neither would be particularly turned on by the option of a couple of days chub fishing along my local River Wensum. But then like all expert freshwater enthusiasts, Simon and Keith, who works for an aquatic centre and so buys and sells fish for a living, have the ability to turn their water craft skills towards any species no matter how large or small and whatever river conditions prevail.

Better still, my two house guests arrived with a more than adequate supply of the red stuff plus the largest Stilton cheese (football sized) I've ever had the pleasure of demolishing. At least our evening fishing discussions had been pre-arranged in style. In return I had mashed up in the kitchen sink five loaves of stale white bread and divided it into two plastic carrier bags in readiness for our assault on those Wensum chub, now in tip-top fighting condition due to the water fining down and the bottom cleanly scoured following weeks of prolonged flooding. So the following morning saw us three nestled in immediately below a sharp bend with the current flowing left to right at the start of a long chub-packed run, where despite a sharp frost I was convinced the occupants would play ball.

Generally speaking three anglers all quiver-tip ledgering the same swim in a not particularly wide river would reduce action to an absolute minimum. But so hard were those chub on to our lumps of fresh white breadflake covering size 8 hooks, tied direct to our 6 lb reel lines, that we had six beauties to around $4^{1}/_{2}$ lbs in the bag before bites naturally started to tail off in that swim. We then fished apart, two sharing a spot, with the third fishing another, swapping over mates as we slowly made our way downstream, so I could catch up on events with both Simon and Keith. Neither had lost their enthusiasm or talent for picking out those choice lies in each swim, denoted amongst

surface deviations by a defined 'crease' where fast currents merge with slower water close into the margins: 'exactly' the holding spot a shoal of chub would choose to occupy. And fish were at home in each and every one. Chunky, hard-battling fish, a little lean in the stomach due to week upon week of enduring dirty floodwaters, but now biting unbelievably confidently sometimes within seconds of our ledgered breadflake settling on the bottom. Following a handful or two of breadmash naturally. Day one produced a total of 19 fish averaging close on 4 lbs between the three of us. On day two we fished a much lower stretch which produced 15 fish, but the best two were pushing 5 lbs apiece.

Keith Lambert (left) and Simon Clarke show some of their River Wensum chub.

SHARING YOUR CHUB SWIM MAKES SENSE

What I like most about this time of the year with the weather turning milder and the days starting to stretch out as the coarse season for river fish finally comes to a close, is that all options are open. Just recently I have been enjoying fishing for exotic sports fish in Africa and have rather neglected what's on my own doorstep, but this I shall rectify in the days ahead, and in my home county of Norfolk by far the most obliging species throughout the upper reaches of the River Wensum is the chub. What's more, not only are chub around in good numbers, they have in recent years, commensurate with the demise of both dace and roach shoals, grown to an exceedingly large average size. There is simply a surplus of natural food in the river which was once shared between the silver shoal species. Now, with the exception of a few localised barbel and carp to compete with, chub get the lot.

Take the results of a recent session, for instance, when good friend Bruce Vaughan, who runs Wychwood Tackle in Oxfordshire, came over to Norfolk for a two day chubbing stint. As always when we fish the Wensum together Bruce and I share each swim, alternating who gets the pole 'downstream' position every other swim as we leapfrog along the river quiver tipping our ledgered baits into all likely looking runs. It is in fact a most effective way of covering every inch of each swim especially those long runs which may measure 30 yards or more, and where the chub could be situated virtually anywhere, the downstream rod making a long cast close into the bank, while the upstream one makes a short cast into the middle of the river. We then both place our baits a couple of yards further downstream on each successive cast until chub are contacted. Strangely we rarely

experience any tangles though our quiver tips are never any more than the distance we are sitting apart, which is just a couple of yards.

The best bait by far is usually fresh white breadflake covering a size 8 hook (tied direct to the 6 lb reel line) accompanied by regular helpings of mashed bread loose fed. Lobworm hookbait can produce a bonus fish or two once the shoal has become cautious of bread and in exceptionally clear water we might even scale right down to a 2 lb hook link and size 16 hook holding two maggots, a small block-end feeder then replacing the swan shots on the ledger link. But frankly, before these tactics become imperative to induce further bites, we have usually moved on to the next swim. Continuing to move when sport started to slow in each swim certainly produced the goods during our recent two-day stint. In all we accounted for more than 20 fine chub all over $4^{1}/_{4}$ lbs, with the best weighing 5 lbs 2 ozs and 5 lbs 13 ozs. A fabulous average size in anyone's book, and all putting up marvellous scraps in the fast currents, taking several minutes apiece to bring to the net. I managed to pull the hook from a considerably larger fish, I suspect also a chub, from a deep, cavernous run beneath a large overhanging willow, a swim in fact which produced a 6 lb chub for me only last summer. And so now if it was the same fish, with the extra weight for winter, I was rather annoyed at myself for playing it a little too hard in order for the hook to pull – but so it goes.

CLOSE SHAVE WITH BIG CHUB

If I hadn't shaved off fellow angling journalist Des Taylor's beard I never would have hooked into a whacking great 6 lb chub. How? Well, you see, having fished a marathon session for *Angling Link* in aid of charity at Moorlands Fishery, near Bewdley in Worcestershire, Des promised to have his beard removed if he didn't reach a certain target weight (it has to be said that Des is famous for his Grizzly Adams look-alike). Which is where I came in. Being an ex-hairdresser I was invited over from Norfolk to perform the official shaving using a cut-throat razor, of course, with a promise of some exclusive float fishing in a secluded pool the following morning.

As it happens, Des did reach the unlikely target of over 200 lb of fish but couldn't back down on his beard removal which proved a great laugh for all concerned. He raised over £3000 for charity too. Anyway the following morning, after an hour and a half's drive into Gloucestershire, we arrived at a delightful stream-fed pool bordered by tall trees along the far bank. Stocks included specimen-sized chub and roach which in the past Des had successfully caught by continually spraying casters around a carefully shotted waggler float cast to the middle of the pool in a depth of around 6 feet. These tactics worked a treat, keeping the chub feeding voraciously close to the surface, while the roach foraged on the bottom picking up casters missed by the chub. It was a demanding technique, always remembering to feed a pult full of casters out prior to casting, but exceptionally rewarding for us both sitting mere yards apart covering more or less the same area.

Exactly how many chub we caught I don't know, certainly a good 30 or so, and most were between 2 and 4 lbs apiece. Des had the lion's share because he presented his bait high up in the water all morning, while I changed from a size 14 hook tied direct to $2^{1}/_{2}$ lb test reel line, holding two casters, to an 18 on a $1^{1}/_{2}$ lb hook link presenting a single caster in order to tempt the much spookier specimen-sized roach, my target being a much prized two-pounder which I missed by mere ounces. One of the largest stillwater chub I've ever caught, which at 6 lbs 1 oz, put up a tremendous scrap on my 13 foot light float rod. I wonder if Des will take me again once his beard has grown back.

OH FOR THE DAYS OF THE SILVER SHOAL

Twenty-five years ago much of my winter fishing revolved around long trotting with centre-pin reel and 13 foot rod along my local, then incredibly roach-rich upper reaches of the River Wensum above Norwich. Believe it or not, in the 1974/75 winter alone I accounted for no less than 49 roach over that magical 2 lb mark. Such was their abundance and it's not difficult to imagine how many lesser fish of $1^{1}/_{4}$, $1^{1}/_{2}$ and $1^{3}/_{4}$ lbs were also taken whilst in pursuit of each 2 lb pound specimen. In those days bags of big roach averaging over the pound and 20 to 30 at a sitting were not uncommon catches in perfect conditions with the river running steadily, nicely coloured and just starting to fine down following a flood. Prime time indeed, with my best session ever producing no less than five roach in excess of 2lbs in one afternoon trotting maggots beneath a waggler from the Wensum between Ringland and Taverham.

Interspersed with trips to the Wensum which, save for the odd pocket of fish is now

Left: No wonder my long-time chubbing buddy Bruce Vaughan has an ear to ear grin. We accounted for a glut of specimen chub to close on 6 lbs.

Yes, I was decidedly younger here. Throughout the 1970s my local River Wensum produced a mountain of beautiful roach, like these 2 lb plus specimens.

virtually a roach graveyard in its upper reaches, were sessions on the upper Waveney, the Bure and Yare, plus some on Norfolk's lesser rivers, including the diminutive Tud, Tas and the Tiffey, which were each also capable of throwing up huge dace in addition to the occasional 2 lb roach.

I can well remember receiving a phone call in my tackle shop one winter's day from an excited young friend, one Andy Davison, who said he'd just caught two dace weighing 1 lb $2^{1}/_{2}$ ozs and 1 lb $3^{1}/_{2}$ ozs from the tiny River Tud and would I come and photograph them. I was reluctant at first because on a previous occasion when Andy had me lock the shop up early and wander the river with polaroid glasses to witness a shoal of 3 lb roach, they turned out to be chub. So I wasn't about to suffer another fool's errand.

Owning a tackle shop as I did then (for 25 years no less) and writing a column in the local paper encouraged all sorts of would-be specimen-hunting anglers to offer information about what they had caught. Some of it was genuine, but much was either pure conjecture or the angler needed to buy a more reliable set of scales. Actually I think the most frustrating occurrence was that the vast majority of anglers seemed unable to distinguish between a genuine roach of 2 lbs and a hybrid of the same weight. And Norfolk's tidal rivers especially contained massive shoals of chunky roach/bream hybrids. It has to be said, however, that I did pop along to the tiny River Tud to look at Andy's two dace, which if genuine, were extremely close to the then British record of 1 lb $4^{1}/_{2}$ ozs. And you can imagine my surprise when he lifted the keep net out because, lo and behold, nestling in the bottom, side by side, were the two largest dace I have ever set my eyes upon before or since. They were both so large, both females deeply pigeon chested as dace are at this time of the season prior to their early spawning in April, that it seemed as though someone must have made them. But they were real alright and absolutely immaculate.

Andy and I still laugh about that occasion which accurately portrays the sheer quality of silver shoal species to be found in Norfolk rivers a quarter of a century ago. And it was with these memories at the back of my mind just recently, after more years than I care to remember, that I purposefully spent a couple of days revisiting some of my old haunts along the previously mentioned small rivers. Not, I might add, expecting much at all, though I did wait for a spell of mild weather to come along - so important, together with some colour in the water, if you are seriously seeking small river roach. As it turned out it was refreshingly pleasant to actually see the top of my waggler float continually dip in most of the swims I fished on all three rivers. And while the quality and sheer size of fish once enjoyed was simply not there any more, I did catch hordes of small roach plus a handful up to a pound, all on long-trotting maggots. Obviously the cormorants haven't been able to decimate these diminutive shallow and overgrown rivers to anything like the same catastrophic level achieved on most of Norfolk's largest rivers, probably because they need, like swans, such a long flight path in and for taking off once their bellies are full. Pull!

THE DELIGHTFUL DACE

Have you caught any dace recently? And have you noticed that some are rather wiry or sandpapery to the touch with tiny white spots all over their heads and upper body? You have – well don't be concerned, it's a perfectly natural occurrence around this time of the year which continues through March until dace gather on the shallows in readiness for their eventual spawning during April. It is, in fact, only male dace, and the males of all cyprinid species incidentally, which grow these mini tubercles for the sole purpose of bumping into the swollen bellies of an egg-laden female to induce release of her translucent, pinkish eggs during the spawning act. Whereupon the male promptly fertilises them with a cloud of milt. And if you have ever wondered why it is that dace hybrids do not occur, as with other cyprinids such as roach/rudd, bream/roach or rudd/bream, it is simply because they breed very much earlier than these three species. It is in fact an annual ritual that few anglers ever get to witness because dace usually accomplish their reproduction cycle during the hours of darkness, possibly through self-preservation and against predation from birds like herons and cormorants.

Actually right now and until the coarse season for river fishing ends on 14th March is unquestionably the best time for enjoying dace fishing, due to this segregation of the sexes as an early grouping process prior to their eventual spawning. Because most of the lean and wiry tubercle-covered male dace will be occupying those really fast, turbulent and shallow runs, with the specimen-sized pigeon-chested female dace in much deeper and slower swims where the current is even paced. Exactly the kind of spots where you would expect to find large roach browsing slowly along the bottom, such as in long even-depthed glides immediately downstream from acute bends, or within the noticeably slower pace of that 'filter' lane at confluences where the waters of two rivers meet, or wherever a deepish side-stream or carrier converges with the main river. Learn to study these surface currents well and the river will reward you handsomely: who knows, perhaps with a pound-plus dace, surely every river fisherman's dream. Of course such fish are a rariety nowadays from streams and stretches of upper rivers suffering from the results of chronic water abstraction, but provided you look around some at all the old records and at rivers which have produced in the past, and provided you are, of course, willing to put in numerous exploratory sessions, you'll locate some specimen-sized dace - fish for argument's sake in excess of 12 ozs.

These smooth and rounded lady dace, however, show little aggression towards feeding and will often not bite until the light starts to go late in the afternoon, unless the river has been coloured by continual rain. They are most unlike members of the opposite sex, those ever-willing to compete males, with which you could almost fill a keep net in mild conditions. And that's another thing – for optimum prospects choose mild days to go in search of these jumbo-sized female dace. Also plan to present smallish baits like a single or double maggot or caster on size 18-16 hooks, using a 2 lb reel line and a 1 – 1½ lb hook length, and loose feed sparingly. Worms and breadbaits, even large lumps of breadflake freelined on a size 8 hook intended for chub, will get greedily gobbled up during the summer months by even moderate-sized dace. But in low water temperatures-and don't let the fact that snowdrops are out and spring is just around the corner fool you – winter dace respond best to small offerings. Moreover the bait needs to be presented really slowly, or even static on the bottom. So don't be afraid to swap the light waggler or stick float trotting set-up in preference for a stret-pegging rig, particularly if the stream or river is carrying more water than you would like. And to alleviate hand-thrown loose feed from being scattered over too wide an area, use a bait dropper to gently deposit it on the bottom at the very top of the swim.

Wear polaroids whilst walking the river looking for potential lies, preferably with bright yellow lenses, which have a high light transmission even in overcast weather and so allow you to make out the shallower parts where the big dace are obviously not. It is unlikely that you will be able to locate them visually, although I have stalked big dace on the clear-flowing carriers along Berkshire's River Kennet at around this time of the year. So remember that while fish are looking up into the light you look down against a dark bottom – don't allow your silhouette to scare a shoal before even making a cast. Walk stealthily along at least two or three feet back from the margins and tread quietly as though creeping up on a field of rabbits.

THOSE LOVELY WEIR POOL ROACH

One of my very favourite winter pursuits is fishing for weir pool roach. Indeed, simply studying the maze of current patterns and wondering what's down there on the bottom evokes for me that wonderful sense of mystery in our sport of angling. It always has. Moreover, pools are great meeting places for every species, so there's always the chance of a surprise in store: a big perch maybe, bream, barbel, even an out-of-season trout or salmon. But more than any other species, pools are likely to hold roach. Why? Because roach love a clean, sandy and well scoured bottom, never festooned with blanket weed, and as most pools are close to road bridges and mill houses in short, civilisation-which cormorants hate, there is even more chance of a healthy stock of quality roach being present. Pools are the roach habitat *par excellence*.

Winter roach have that distinct 'blueness along' the shoulders and can never be mistaken for a hybrid.

Both river and mill pools, however, can at first sight appear rather hostile and tricky to fish with all that extra winter water pouring through the hatches, creating a column of churning white foam, with great boils spewing up from the bottom as the river's heart thunders down the main flush. But don't' worry, roach hate having to expend unnecessary energy by changing direction every few seconds, and much prefer the deeper, quieter areas of steady current, choice lies being the large back eddies on each side of the pool. And if you just stand there observing the flow for 10 minutes before even taking the tackle out of the car, you'll be able to pinpoint areas (some maybe no longer than a couple of square yards) where roach are most likely to be in residence.

The 'probing' outfit consists of my 11 foot Heritage Avon quiver-tip rod, coupled to a 4 – 5 lb reel line and simple fixed paternoster ledger with a 20 inch hook link of 3 lb test. This is joined to the reel line using a four-turn water knot, leaving a 10 inch link (of reel line) to take between one and four 3xSSG shots, or a small bomb depending upon current strength. For bait I use fresh white breadflake, a thumbnail-sized piece covering a size 10 hook, and after casting a little beyond the patch of slow water and feathering the rig down to the bottom the rod is held steady at a high angle on two rests. This is to minimise the amount of line in the water liable to be dragged around by current pressure. A most important factor this.

Breadflake usually induces bites (and watch out for 'drop backs') from a larger stamp of roach, but if after several casts to ideal areas bites do not materialise, I swap the shots for a heavy block-end feeder, reduce the hook size to a 16 and gently nick on three maggots. Continual accurate casting to the same area will soon lay a trail of maggots on the bottom and in all but the coldest weather bites should materialise. During mild conditions when roach really respond to a moving bait I will search the same slack using a 13 foot rod, 2½ lb reel line and centre pin, with an Avon or balsa trotter float fixed top and bottom for maximum control.

In small pools it is sometimes possible to reach out directly above the slacker, roachy looking areas with a long pole and to slowly trot the bait along. If regularly lowering maggots down to the bottom in a bait dropper is not practical then fish over depth, 'float – ledger style', using a small block-end feeder on a short link. It can prove deadly.

Chapter Two

BRITISH FRESHWATER PREDATORS

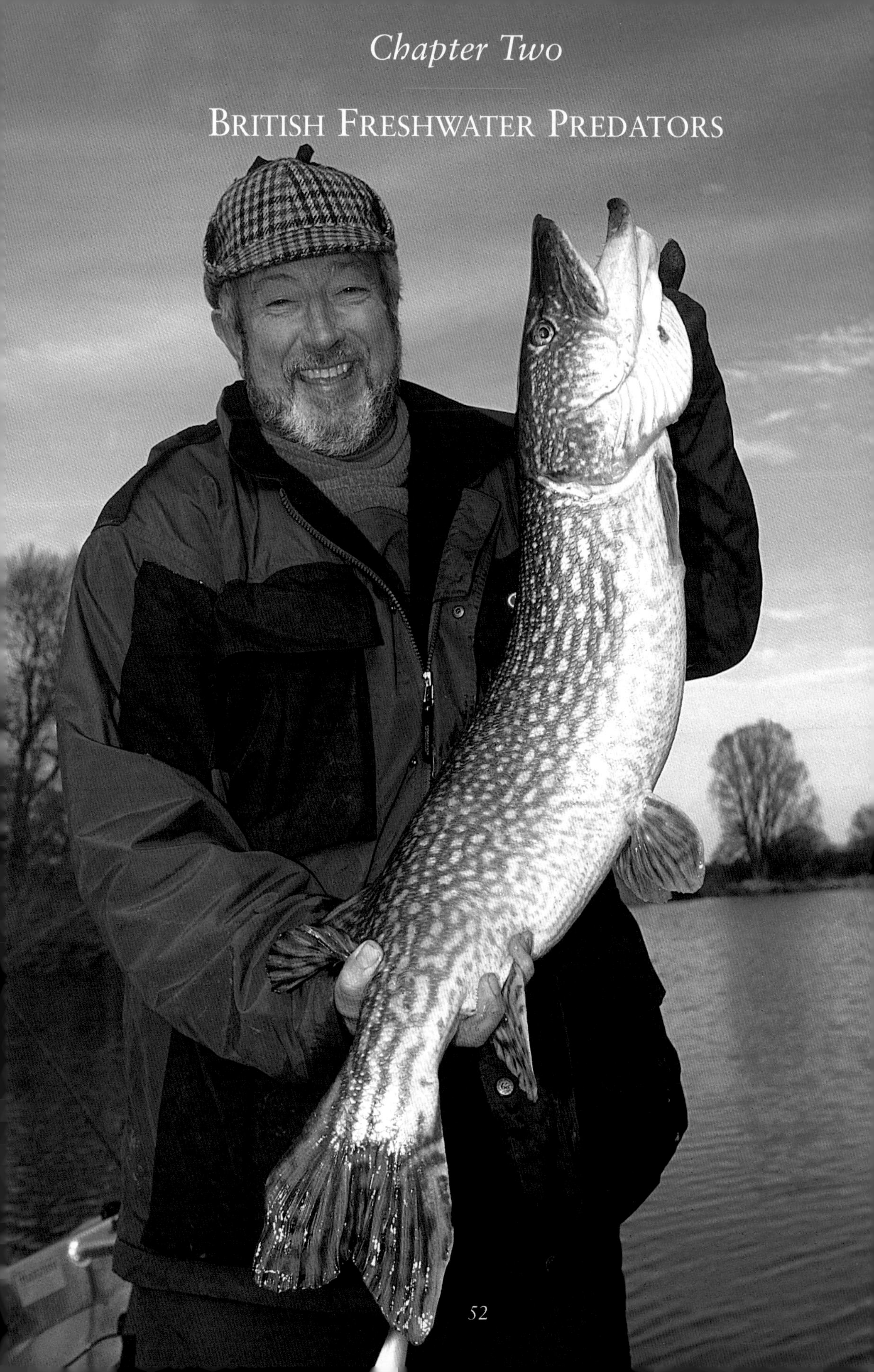

VICTORIOUS VINNIE

Days which from an early start promise to be flat and overcast with not a breath of wind are in my experience not likely to be productive for predators. But then we can all be wrong can't we? Take such a day a couple of weeks back for instance at the beginning of December when fellow journalist Pam Fisher and her husband Ben had invited me along for a piking session at their secluded Norfolk lake, when light values were exceedingly poor due to low-lying clouds and there was a distinct hint of rain in the air. Now I wouldn't have given tuppence for our chances with any decent-sized pike, which was a pity because Pam's other guests were footballer/actor, Vinnie Jones

Yes, it was Vinnie 4 – Wilson 0. But who cares?

and his pal, Phil Bradshaw, who to the best of my knowledge had never fished before. As anyone who has read Vinnie's autobiography will know, which incidentally is a most intriguing insight into Britain's most controversial footballer, the man is in fact first and foremost a true countryman whose pursuits of shooting and fly fishing come first and second. And I'd feared the lake's stock of quality pike were not going to play ball – no pun intended.

However, while we were loading all the gear into Ben's giant-sized six-man punt, I lobbed out a frozen sardine presented on a sliding float rig on Phil's behalf, about 50 yards out from the boathouse staging just into deep water and, lo and behold the float, started trundling away before everyone was ready to cast off. A little bit of instruction from yours truly about holding the rod and reel properly with two fingers locked around the reel's stem and winding down fast until all was tight before heaving the 12 foot rod back, and hey presto – Phil was enjoying the fight of a superbly spotted pike which fought like stink and subsequently weighed 11 lbs. Not a bad start for someone's first fish ever.

Once in the middle of the lake where 13 feet is the deepest we put down a mudweight at each end and fanned out a variety of static deadbaits around the boat including mackerel, smelts and sardines, and waited patiently. It was, however, Vinnie's float-fished roach that was snapped up first and by the alarming bend of his rod, by a fair-sized pike. Following a couple of powerful runs and some splashing dives beneath the punt I eventually put the net beneath a chunky fish of around 14-15 lbs. A poor day it was not going to be after all – in fact had we been perhaps trying a little harder instead of larking about, sport would have been even more productive.

Phil and I started reminiscing about our merchant navy days during the swinging sixties, while Pam interviewed Vinnie for her magazine as he worked a silver spoon close to the bottom on his second rod, methodically counting it down to the desired depth before commencing the retrieve. Unfortunately Pam's mini tape recorder switched itself off during the first hour of banter, so neither Vinnie's life history nor the two jacks of around 5 lbs apiece he accounted for on the spoon were recorded. Luckily I found two new batteries in my camera bag for Pam's machine and it was all systems go as Vinnie put everyone to shame yet again, this time with a lean fish of around 7 lbs to a freelined sardine. He obviously knew more about pike fishing than he was letting on.

By now it was lunchtime so we punted back to the boathouse for some liquid refreshment and previously cooked casserole, immediately after which Vinnie and Phil unfortunately had to shoot away to be on time for a previously arranged engagement on the outskirts of London. Thank goodness – well four nil was bad enough. But for Wilson, who until now had not experienced so much as a dropped run, it got worse – or better depending how you look at it. Ben, Pam and I decided to spend the last couple of hours at the north end of the lake anchoring at a point just inside the slope where the bottom abruptly shelves down from 5 to around 12 feet, often a productive hotspot for pike which have close access to both shallow and deep water. And this is where most of the better fish appeared to be, because for the last hour runs on both float-fished and freelined deadbaits came steadily, sardines and mackerel proving most effective for the lake's pike population which suddenly went on a feeding rampage. Most were jacks in the 3 – 6 lbs bracket but we did account for three good doubles, the best going around 17 lbs, though this particular pike could easily have gone 20 lbs had it been fatter. Its head was simply enormous. And you can guess who caught the three largest can't you? Yes, Pam. I'd been well and truly thrashed by a footballer and a member of the fairer sex on the same day, which is definitely no good for my image! How much are football boots?

A nicely marked 17 lb pike for Chris Newell

PIKE - AGAINST ALL THE ODDS

Listening to heavy rain lashing against the kitchen window panes as I filled the vacuum flask whilst waiting for friend Chris Newell to arrive, I rather wished we hadn't arranged a day's pike fishing. With the weather promising bitter-cold gale-force north-easterly winds, it certainly wasn't the day to be out in a boat on the Norfolk Broads.

We aimed, as dawn broke, for a boatyard beside the River Ant, where I had booked a fishing dinghy (the only one available) which was little larger than the average domestic bathtub with a nasty crack in the middle of the transom upon which the bracket of my electric outboard would not fit anyway. How I regretted not hitching up my own trailer and purpose-built fishing dinghy back at the house. 'Never mind' I said to Chris 'we'll pop along the road to Stalham boat yards and get a more substantial dinghy there.' But alas, none were for hire. Amazing really when you consider that Norfolk boatyards are always moaning about business on the Broads. 'Never mind' I said again to Chris, 'we'll drive to where the Norwich to Acle road bisects Great Ormesby and Filby Broads (by now we were closer to Great Yarmouth than Norwich) and see Mr Barnes'. He'll have a boat.' Which he did, but I could see the expression on Chris's face at the sight of line upon line of white horses ripping down the entire length of Great Ormesby Broad crashing against the roadside reedbeds, accompanied by torrential sleet. Variable force 6 - 8 winds somehow look more terrifying on large sheets of inland water than the sea itself especially when you're about to set out in a 14 foot dinghy which fortunately Chris offered to bale out while I unloaded the estate.

The Trinity Broads, as they are known, comprising of Little Ormesby, Great Ormesby, Rollesby and Filby Broads, cover some 800 acres to form the largest complex of angling waters in the whole of the Broads system, and because they are not connected to the network of tidal rivers only the occasional sailing dinghy and angling boats are allowed. This makes for totally undisturbed winter pike fishing and my plan to beat the weather was to make for the sheltered water of Lily Broad, a shallow 10 acre, intimate little water averaging between just 3 and 5 feet deep with a narrow entrance via the south-western end of Rollesby Broad – a 10 minute journey by electric motor from the moorings on Great Ormesby.

By 10 a.m. we were nicely settled with the mudweights down, holding the boat steady some 30 yards downwind of the broad's northerly reed-covered shoreline. This permitted a selection of static deadbaits from smelt to lamprey sections to be fanned around the boat on both freelined and float-fished rigs. And it was those positioned close to the reeds which produced pike though initially in a rather strange way. Upon casting out I accidentally hooked Chris's rod presenting an upwind bait and literally propelled it 30 yards in front of the boat. How embarrassing. Perhaps senility is setting in after all! My wife's regular little joke. Anyway, to cut a long story short, I eventually managed to hook up Chris's rod which luckily was floating and reeled it in. Then lo and behold, as he wound up all the loose line and prepared to bring his deadbait in from behind the boat, there was a living resistance on the other end which resulted in a superb pike of around 17 lbs. Despite all the odds and my clumsiness we had scored after all. And following a day of torrential rain, hailstones the size of marbles, interspersed with occasional bursts of sunlight which illuminated the reeds the colour of golden corn, we both went on to catch pike of around 10 lbs each, bringing our total to three, against all the odds. Three which we wouldn't have caught by sitting at home.

BACK-DRIFTING FOR PIKE

At the beginning of the month I enjoyed a wonderful day on the upper reaches of my local River Wensum in the company of my brother David, boat fishing for pike using a rather effective, yet unusual technique which I call 'back-drifting'. Fortunately the river was flowing steadily and quite clear with a visibility of at least 3 feet and there was next to no wind – absolutely perfect conditions for back-drifting as you will appreciate later.

As I intended us to slowly drift back downstream with the flow for at least a couple of miles, we had first to put the boat in the same distance downstream to start the day, and while I rowed upstream against the flow over all the spots we would later be fishing, Dave put a couple of balls of mashed bread into several tempting-looking chub runs beneath overhanging trees as we went along.

In addition to the pike rods and a tub of bait, we also took along our 13 foot trotting rods plus a fresh white loaf. But strangely, no matter how sensitively we trotted a piece of breadflake beneath trees overhanging the most mouth-watering swims, not a single bite did we get. Frankly I think the water was just too clear for expecting daytime action with the chub, whereas with our back-drifted small roach livebaits we enjoyed some hectic pike sport. We used just a single rod each with the bait presented sensitively beneath an inch-diameter pilot float plugged to the 10 lb reel line with a thin stem of peacock quill. One or two swan shot were pinched on the wire trace to ensure the bait kept down and the float set between 1 and 2 feet shallower than the river's middle channel. We both cast around 10-20 yards behind (upstream of) the boat so that both floats and boat drift slowly along together at current speed, with the baits covering an enormous amount of the riverbed.

In order to keep the boat side into the flow with both anglers facing upstream watching for a float to disappear, a little oar work is necessary every so often. In known hot spots such as where entrance dykes or streams converge with the main flow etc., or wide bends where the water invariably deepens on the outside, the boat can be gently manoeuvred over to that side of the river so that both baits pass over waiting pike. A peculiarity of this technique is that you soon discover pike are not spread evenly along a river's course like currants in a well-baked cake, and tend to group up probably where the greatest concentrations of their prey, in the way of a small shoal of fishes, are situated. In fact on several occasions Dave and I experienced as many as half a dozen hits all within just a 30 yard section of river.

The message here is as soon as you catch one, lower a mudweight over each end of the boat and thoroughly search the area. Sometimes we drifted for several hundred yards before one of the floats was away, often followed shortly by the other, and on two occasions we were both playing pike at the same time. When it happened it was truly electric pike fishing, but nicely relaxed in between the action whilst drifting slowly along with the flow. We actually lost count of the runs but landed no fewer than 14 fish including several doubles, the best to Dave's rod scraping 15 lbs. Obviously anything stronger than a light wind will affect the boat's drift (particularly upstream winds) and weak currents could result in more rowing than fishing – but so long as the water is clear and the baits are presented well behind the boat 'back-drifting' is a most effective and enjoyable way of catching river pike.

Brother Dave prepares to 'chin out' a fat Wensum 'double' - the rewards of 'back-drifting.

A BIG PIKE FROM NOWHERE

Worthing Fisheries, situated 15 miles west of Norwich, comprises half a mile of the River Wensum and an 11 acre flooded gravel pit holding big tench, bream, carp and pike. A pit which, though in my local domain, I had not fished for over 25 years until just recently when old friend Terry Houseago suggested we target the big pike. Boat fishing is not generally permitted on this irregular shaped, decidedly windswept deepwater pit, but as Terry runs the 'members only' syndicate we slipped my 14 foot aluminium skiff off the trailer as dawn broke, accompanied by a stiff westerly breeze and dark clouds overhead.

For the first half an hour we poodled in zig-zag fashion up and down the pit using my silent electric motor, taking account of the irregular bottom contours on the fish finder unit. Where the shallow bars were situated and where the shoals of bait fish were packed tightly together. We found good concentrations along a gully between 14 and 17 feet deep and put the mudweights down well upwind with a shallow plateau behind the boat. Our smelt deadbaits on both sliding float and freelined rigs were strategically placed on the bottom along the deep gully with one bait each cast 50 yards behind the boat up into the wind just in case. And strangely it was these baits which found pike.

Terry's was the first to go and after a spirited scrap he boated a lively seven-pounder. This we thought strange as we had not marked a single fish on the sounder over that shallow plateau before anchoring up and put it down to a fluke. Ten minutes later, however, the rod presenting my upwind bait started to nod gently followed by the ratchet on the multiplier reel clicking into action. The freelined smelt with two x 2SSG shots on the wire trace had obviously been nobbled by something heavy which ran directly upwind ripping line from the reel before surfacing in a huge, head-shaking swirl prior to crash diving. Terry and I looked at each other. 'Wizzo's done it again' he muttered, fixing up the landing net, and his words could not have been more prophetic.

Following a powerful fight, exciting to watch through the crystal-clear water, a huge-headed incredibly thickset pike hit the surface beside the boat where Terry made no mistake with the net. A beauty weighing exactly 24$\frac{1}{2}$ lbs. We then sat in the heavy rain for the rest of the day without another run!

WEIR POOL PIKE FISHING

Because the occupants of our weir pools, from the smallest gudgeon to the largest pike, are all obliged to keep moving in fast currents they consume more energy and thus, even during freezing conditions, need to feed more regularly than fish inhabiting slow-moving and still waters which can live semi-dormant for days on end. So if it's action you're after, try a spot of weir pool pike fishing. In water running low and clear best results usually come to trotted livebaits just above bottom, or working lures. A big spoon is my favourite, which with just the one treble hook at the rear, catches up on far fewer snags than diving plus. Wobbling deadbaits is another extremely effective technique which maximises on time (if you have but a few hours to spare) because you don't have to catch livebaits first. Most specialist tackle shops stock a variety of both fresh and saltwater frozen deadbaits pre-packed in

Wobbling a smelt 'sink and draw' style produces some lovely river pike.

session-sized bags. I prefer the cucumber-smelling smelt for 'wobbling' because it is light which means I can pinch up to four swan shots on the wire trace 12 inches from the bait in order to search 'sink and draw style' close to the bottom in the deepest pools, or work it without shots through shallow runs.

Whilst a pike is liable to turn up virtually anywhere except the main flush, I favour any slow back eddy close into the bank on either side of the pool and also at the very tail end where the bottom abruptly shelves up. Small areas of slack water beneath redundant hatch gates are also worth trying, as are any areas of slow, deep water. So study surface currents seriously for several minutes before deciding upon where to place the bait. When river levels are high, turning weir pools into raging torrents, you'll need to study flow patterns even more carefully. Areas of decidedly slower, deep water are sometimes created out in the middle of the pool or just to the side of the main flow. And to keep a livebait out there use a float paternoster rig, with the rod tip angled up high to keep most of the line off the surface. It's fascinating pike fishing. During severely flooded conditions when the river turns tea coloured you cannot seriously expect pike to 'chase' their food. So offer them a ledgered, completely 'static' deadbait which they will 'sniff out' with surprising ease. In aromatic preference I would select half a mackerel, a smelt or half a lamprey in that order. And remember to make several deep slits in the bait with a sharp knife, allowing their attractive juices to permeate in the water.

As when paternostering livebaits angle the rod tip up high and after opening the reel's bale arm, slip a loop of line beneath an elastic band wound tightly around the rod handle immediately opposite the spool. A biting pike can then take line without resistance from the open spool before you wind down to close the bale arm and set the hooks. Plan to fish two rods, each with a bait selectively placed close into the side of any slack or slow back eddy. Never expect hectic sport when the pool is heavily coloured. By repositioning each bait to a different spot every half an hour or so, however, a pike or two are most certainly on the cards.

RIGHT TIDE – BIG PIKE

One of the benefits of living close to the Norfolk and Suffolk Broads, with their massive network of inter-connecting tidal waterways, is being able to pike fish during the winter months without seeing another soul all day. And that's exactly the kind of seclusion my pal John (Jinx) Davey and I enjoyed just recently whilst boat fishing the lonely, reed-fringed lower reaches of the River Waveney, below Beccles - although these fast-flowing tidal reaches are not to everyone's taste and certainly not suited to the inexperienced.

In depths ranging between 12 and 18 feet and strong currents necessitating two ounces of lead to keep a ledgered deadbait on the riverbed, we find that paying attention to the tides is of paramount importance. So a current tidetable is imperative. For instance, at both high and low tide, when for a while the water becomes static prior to then flowing in the opposite direction, pike and of course their shoal fish prey must all reposition. So there is no better time of the day to expect action. Indeed it is 'the' one 'hot' period during these short winter days when big river pike go actively on the feed.

I started our account with a hard-fighting plump 14-pounder almost at the top of the flooding tide, by slowly trotting a small livebait close to the bottom through a 13 - foot - deep run beside a long line of reeds immediately below an overhanging willow. But it was our only hit from this location, so we up-anchored and moved 200 yards downriver to opposite a line of overhanging trees just before high water to be ready for the change. And right on cue, as if by magic, when slack water arrived, one of Jinx's herring deadbaits was inhaled from the riverbed. By the alarming curvature of his rod plus several heavy ponderous runs to follow, Jinx had obviously connected with a biggie which, despite full pressure from his 12 lbs reel line, succeeded in going under the boat between the mudweight ropes. But eventually, and despite some anxious moments while disentangling his line, I managed to bundle a real beauty into the landing net – a deep-bellied pike that pulled the scales down to exactly 24 lbs. The ear-to-ear grin splitting Jinx's face said it all.

A superb 24 lb River Waveney pike for my good friend Jinx Davey.

A TIDAL JEWEL IN SUSSEX

No one catches more pike from the diminutive River Adur, than local tackle dealer Joe Raczkowski.

The diminutive River Adur in Sussex may well be little more than 30 miles in length from its source to where it enters the sea at Shoreham, but for quality fish of several species, it is surprisingly prolific, especially in the lower tidal reaches. In addition to roach, bream, chub and tench there is a strong nomadic head of carp averaging double figures, good runs of specimen-sized sea trout, plus hordes of thick-lipped grey mullet which run up with the flooding tide. All of which I was totally unaware of until a recent visit to the River Adur (pronounced Ader) as guest of the Henfield and District Angling Society and local guru Joe Raczkowski, who manages the Sporting Chance tackle shop in Haywards Heath. Joe had in fact invited me down from Norfolk for a piking session along the tidal reaches which, with high and steep-sided flood banks, reminded me so very much of the network of flood relief drains throughout Cambridgeshire, Lincolnshire and West Norfolk, except that the Adur bends attractively every few hundred yards providing numerous feature swims, as opposed to running straight as a die for mile upon mile like the manmade Fenland drains. And in these coloured tidal reaches live some truly enormous pike. Joe's list of 20-pounders is both enviable and endless, topped by several beauties in excess of 30 lbs. Though to look at the River Adur, which averages around 30 yards wide and between 4 and 6 feet deep at low tide, does not give the impression of big pike potential. It is certainly a wolf in sheep's clothing and as such thankfully does not suffer from overfishing, though anyone can join the Henfield Angling Club.

I suggested to Joe that in all probability that extra food source in the form of grey mullet was perhaps one reason why the tidal river pike grow so large, but then that would be unfair to the sheer density of eels which smother the bottom. Due to the ridiculously mild mid November weather pattern our float-ledgered deadbaits and livebaits were repeatedly being attacked by eels. And despite leapfrogging the rods slowly along the river in order to maximise on the amount of ground covered, we were on a total loser. Sure we accounted for a couple of nicely conditioned doubles, plus several jacks, but the big boys (or should I say girls because all big pike are indeed females) totally eluded our efforts. In short the weather (for once) was just too nice.

I was fascinated by Joe's vast knowledge of these tidal reaches, particularly when he pointed out the shallow indentations in the mud at low tide denoting where bream shoals had been feeding. Mullet marks in the mud, bonefish marks in the mud where they feed on blue crabs – a common sight in tropical saltwater flats both I had noticed on many previous occasions, but bream never before. Joe's prophecy of pike starting to become active immediately after the turn of the tide when the water starts flooding was also right on the ball.

I'll just have to ensure that the next time I get down to Sussex our winter has finally arrived and not only concentrated the bait-fish shoals, but put the pike into an aggressive mood and put the eels finally into winter hibernation.

LANDLUBBERS ARE MISSING THE BOAT

Living in Norfolk as I do, with an unlimited amount of Broads, gravel pits, meres and estate lakes at my disposal, it's only natural that for much of my winter pike fishing I choose to go afloat. Boat fishing is, of course, the only way of effectively exploring large sheets of stillwaters, fisheries which for argument's sake are in excess of 10 acres. Fishing from the bank with a maximum casting range of say 50 – 70 yards all around the lake's perimeter is at the very best merely scratching at the surface. And there's certainly no pun intended here. Take a recent trip I made to famous Stradsett Lake, near Downham Market, for instance – a syndicate fishery open to anyone for the price of a yearly ticket. This 20 acre estate lake is one of the oldest in the country, having been built in the early 1800s a couple of years before the Battle of Waterloo. It is thus naturally extremely well established with tall evergreens on the two large islands and a foot-deep covering of rich silt on the bottom which helps to produce the specimen roach, tench and bream going into double figures for which the lake is justly famous. I was there for the pike however, and with a cold easterly wind blowing, accompanied by strong sunlight throughout the day, my decision to boat fish and present static deadbaits at long range downwind beneath sliding float rigs in the unbelievably clear water was well founded. Even then it took me most of the morning and no less than four moves to systematically work myself up the lake from the dam end before I contacted any pike.

Due to water clarity I reckoned that most of the small silver shoal species were packed tightly together in one very small area with pike all around, rather like the circle of wagons continually being attacked by Indians in standard Western movies. And so it proved. The first hit came to a smelt, fished 'sink and draw' style in around 6 feet of water virtually in the very middle of the lake: an area in no way reachable from the bank. And following a hectic tail-walking fight I eventually boated an extremely colourful and beautifully spotted pike of around 12 lbs, which as it happened was the smallest of the day. A further five runs developed, all to 'joey' mackerel presented static beneath sliding floats and fortunately I connected with them all, the heaviest pike weighing around 18 lbs.

It was certainly a day for a real whopper to put in an appearance but it never happened. However, all fought so strongly in the clear water that when I decided to pack up my right arm was seriously painful. I am after all not known for playing big fish lightly and what with six good doubles getting on for an accumulative weight of somewhere near 100 lbs, you could say I had my string well and truly pulled. The session certainly highlighted the importance of systematically grid-searching the bottom to locate pike, giving each anchorage point three-quarters of an hour or so for interest to be shown in the baits or not, before moving on downwind to cover a new area.

There is never any fear of 'deeply hooking' pike when using large spoons.

WHEN TO STRIKE A PIKE

One of the questions I am often asked about pike and pike fishing techniques is that age-old problem of when to strike. Though for me it has never been a problem because I always strike immediately, whether using live or deadbaits, presented free roaming on a wobble or static, with the realistic assumption that if it comes off it wasn't worth catching anyway. Mind you, I do not use large baits which some anglers pin their faith on, because they assume an equally large pike will grab hold as a result. In my experience all you do is miss a much larger proportion of runs from pike of all sizes. I use baits no larger than 6 – 7 inches which, let's face it, any reasonable pike will snuffle down in a jiffy provided the tackle set-up minimises resistance. Huge pike floats for instance offer so much resistance to a pike, which grabs the bait across the middle to kill it with its canine teeth before turning and swallowing; every time the pike releases the bait to swallow, the sunken float pops up and yanks the bait away. So keep resistance to a minimum and when the pike moves steadily away point the rod at it, close the reel bale arm and when the line fully tightens keep winding to account for the 25 per cent stretch in monofilament until you feel heavy resistance. Then and only then heave the rod back and keep winding so there is no chance of the line going slack. At this point the pike could easily eject the bait as it opens its jaws and shakes its head, if the rod is not bent. By now the hooks should have found purchase and you can enjoy playing one of our most exciting winter species.

Many beginners, and even knowledgeable anglers proficient at catching all other species, acquire a mental blockage when it comes to pike and, I guess through nothing other than ignorance, actually become scared of holding them. This is why whenever you notice knocks and abrasions along the flanks of a pike it is usually down to nothing other than bad handling from another angler. The truth is even a modest-size pike is equipped with large canines capable of inflicting a nasty wound, and receiving an inch-long deep slit in a finger that refuses to stop bleeding on a painfully cold day is not recommended. The answer is to wear a protective glove. The famous Normark Fish-'n'-Fillet glove, manufactured from micro chainmail, is perfect for the job. It fits either hand and being soft permits maximum flexibility. If 'right' handed wear the glove on your 'left' hand and when the pike is lying still in the bottom of the landing net insert your four fingers into its 'left' gill opening being careful not to touch the gill filaments (through which it separates dissolved oxygen from water) and press your thumb down firmly against your forefinger. You now have the perfect grip so do not relax until returning your fish.

You can unhook the pike in the bottom of the boat or on the bank (providing it is lying on a protective unhooking mat) simply by laying it on its back and curling your hand back. Hey presto, the jaws open, making hook removal a simple job using a pair of 8-10 inch long-nosed artery forceps. Alternatively if an unhooking mat is not at hand, stand up and hold the pike up. Again its jaws will open obligingly for hook removal. The use of semi-barbless trebles allows you to perform the task in seconds, and you already have the fish gripped tightly in readiness for a trophy photo.

CORMORANTS AND DO-GOODERS ARE THREATENING THE ENVIRONMENT

My good friend Dick Brigham is not only an accomplished taxidermist, he is also, which is why we seldom fish together, a field sports writer and nature photographer. Dick goes after the birds (of the feathered variety) while I fish. It's as simple as that really, although just recently we have shared a couple of interesting boat fishing trips together after pike. The first, just before Christmas on Norfolk's Ormesby group of Broads, I shall not elaborate upon because neither of us had so much as a mauled deadbait from dawn until dusk, though as usual we did become engrossed in deep conversation about our changing angling environment, and how such influences as do-gooders and cormorants are ruining a status quo that has survived since time immemorial.

On our second trip just recently to a 15 acre deepwater lake also in our home county of Norfolk, we fared rather better and still managed to put the world right by the time we pulled up the mudweights at dusk to call it a day, having accounted for several thick set double-figure pike. The first, a 12-pounder, came to one of Dick's float-fished herrings and fought incredibly strongly. This was due I surmised to rather better water clarity than we had expected. Pike really do motor when they can see where they are going. Frankly I would have wished for much less than the lake's 8 – 9 feet of clear visibility, particularly as we were pinning our faith entirely upon static deadbaits. Such conditions were infinitely more suited to livebaits, wobbled deadbaits, or working artificial lures, but as always the pike know better. Strangely the latter two techniques failed to instigate so much as a single follow and as we had only deadbaits on board we persevered with smelts and herrings presented static on the bottom. We managed just a single pike from each new area covered by raising the mudweights every hour or so and allowing the boat to drift 50 yards down the lake before lowering them again. Systematically covering the bottom in this way is most effective for locating pike that are not in an aggressive mood. Sooner or later, more through the law of averages than anything, one of the baits came to settle close to a pike and bingo! It can't resist those permeating juices of the fresh deadbait any longer.

The second pike, almost a carbon copy of the first, came to one of my smelts and

Dick Brigham with 12 pounder that fell to herring

interrupted our favourite subject and dialogue concerning what is currently happening throughout many of our inland waterways, gravel pits and lakeland systems. Blame can be pinned ultimately, I am afraid, on a totally gutless Environment Agency and toothless Ministry of Agriculture, Fisheries and Food who should both be pushing for cormorants to be put on the vermin list so they can effectively be culled, before there isn't a single silver shoal fish left. What many people do not understand, including the government and such do-gooders as those who introduce otters into the wild and into rivers almost devoid of silver shoal fishes, is that cormorants are responsible for a catastrophic pyramid of events. You see, once the shoals of roach, rudd and young bream for instance have been eaten by the 'black death', thus ruining a lake's healthy pyramid of fish stocks, there is little for our indigenous inland predatory waterbirds to eat. Worse still, not only do kingfishers, grebes and herons find the cupboard bare, but pike do too. So when clutches of young moorhens, cootes and ducks leave the nest in the spring, with next to no shoal fish left to eat, pike have no option but to consume far more young water birds than they would in a balanced cormorant-free environment: a chain of events incidentally which both the BTO (British Trust for Ornithology) and RSPB sadly react to by keeping their heads buried in the sand. And if all this isn't bad enough, along comes some bright spark who wouldn't know the difference between a roach and a kipper, and releases otters into a river almost totally devoid of silver shoal species – their staple diet. So where does the otter go? Straight from the river into the nearest well-stocked gravel pit carp fishery, lovingly landscaped, stocked and managed by anglers through no small amount of cost and hard work, to chew its way through valuable carp to 20 lbs and more. Yes, the black death has an awful lot to answer for.

One of my floats twitched and slowly glided across the surface following the pike which 13 foot down on the lake bed had picked up another of our static deadbaits. This pike, a beauty of around 15 lbs, was particularly thickset across the shoulders with a deep belly and testament to how predators at the top of the food chain should look, when there is a healthy pyramid of silver shoal species to prey upon.

Police officer Jason Davies arrested this superbly shaped 25 lb plus specimen.

A PIKE BETWEEN FRIENDS

In the company of two old friends, Jason Davies and the late Len Head, I enjoyed a most memorable day with the big pike of a Norfolk gravel pit, all of which fell to mackerel and sardine deadbaits. Of course it is no secret that ledgering static deadbaits during these cold winter months is arguably the deadliest technique for tempting not only pike of a high average size but also monsters exceeding that magical 20 lbs barrier. And static deadbaits are currently at their most effective not only because the weeds have died away, which aids presentation, but because during low water temperatures pike spend much of their time lying in and scavenging from that bottom depth band. The method works in clear water, coloured water, running water and in all stillwaters whether deep or shallow. But don't make the mistake of simply slipping a bomb on to the reel line above a short, standard-sized wire trace, or you could suffer a lack of runs due to that age-old problem of 'line bites'.

It seems rather strange to me that most anglers never seem to associate line bites with pike yet take enormous trouble in overcoming the problem from tench, bream and carp in particular. Being the longest of all these species, however, pike are prime candidates so please don't miss out by spooking a potential catch even before it has sucked in your deadbait. The remedy is to use a long 22/24 inch wire trace with a mono uptrace (as reel line) of the same length above. This ensures that sufficient rig actually lies along the bottom and so won't be picked up by the pike's body or large fins. The running ledger above the uptrace swivel, comprises of swivel and 1- 1½ oz bomb joined by just 4 inches of stiff 20 lbs mono which will alleviate tangles.

In shallow waters where the angle of line between bomb and rod tip is minimal, line bites pose few problems. But in deep meres. reservoirs and particularly in deep gravel pits like the one Len, Jason and I were fishing, which shelves down to over 20 feet, a steep angle of line is, of course, unavoidable. Actually from our dawn start I have never known such hectic action with predominantly huge fish, brought about no doubt by a sudden mild spell accompanying a stiff south-westerly breeze. Presenting whole 'Joey' mackerel on both rods my first run from a deep gully situated between two islands around 60 yards out produced a plump-looking pike of around 12 lbs following a wait of mere minutes of clipping on the drop-arm indicator. This was followed by another belter on the same rod within minutes of placing a mackerel back into more or less the same spot. And the very second upon winding down and heaving the rod back I instinctively knew it was a big mama. Jason walked up to my swim to see what all the commotion was about, as simultaneously the indicator on my second rod flew off. So as I already had my hands more than full with the unseen whopper steadily taking line across the pit against a firmly set clutch, Jason did the honours and whacked my second rod back and into what was obviously another biggie. What a pickle! But what fights we enjoyed.

Jason's pike tired first and tipped the scales down to almost 22 lbs, while I followed shortly afterwards by putting the net under a really deep fat fish that subsequently weighed exactly 24 lbs. Jason and I were laughing about the situation and decided to accept the 22-pounder as a 'pike shared between friends', seeing as it had come on my second rod, when an excited yell from Len just 50 yards along the bank really toasted the occasion. For he too had (during the commotion) also hooked and landed a whopper: a pike of just over 20 lbs – and again a static deadbait proved to be the winning offering.

During the next couple of hours sport continued at an electric pace with Len adding a 14-pounder to the tally while I took five doubles of between 11 and 18 lbs plus a couple of jacks, before Jason well and truly stuffed us both by landing a superb specimen of $25^{3/4}$ lbs from a deep gully running parallel with the opposite bank. What a day!

THE TECHNIQUES OF PIKE FISHING AFLOAT

It wasn't until I spent several hours the other day sorting through thousands of pike fishing colour transparencies on the lightbox in the hope of finding something suitable for a fellow angling journalist's forthcoming book, that I realised only a very small percentage of my own pike trips are actually done from *terra firma* these days. OK – so I am spoilt living in rural Norfolk with dozens of wonderful escape outlets on my doorstep in the form of huge windswept and reed-lined broads of up to 300 acres apiece, though in truth whenever I seek pike in this country or abroad, if I can get out afloat to catch them, as opposed to shore fishing, then so much the better. Indeed, and we are obviously talking big waters here, like the broads, lochs, loughs (the Irish word for big lake), and the waters of the Lake District, plus any of our huge manmade reservoirs etc., there is so very much more scope when exploring far away areas by boat, than minimising potential within the comfortable confines of the margins under a brolly.

So first things first, when setting out afloat you need to be kitted up with good quality waterproofs in the shape of a three-quarter-length coat and over-trousers, or an all-in-one waterproof suit with a fleecy, one-piece body-warmer underneath. Better still in my view is a bib and brace which incorporates over-trousers, covered by a three-quarter-length jacket with a built-in hood. Then if our variable winter weather suddenly starts to improve halfway through the day with a drastic rise in air temperature you don't have to sit there sweating uncomfortably, you simply remove your top coat. As an enormous amount of body heat is lost via the head I recommend a warm hat, preferably one with a peak, thus eradicating the need to be constantly squinting against reflective glare. I always take a pair of polaroid sunglasses along when boat fishing, not necessarily to see through clear water, although they are handy for watching the reactions of pike following the bait or lure, but more for visual comfort. To enjoy birdwatching, I always take along a pair of binoculars

I just love working lures for pike amongst the mysterious depths of big reservoirs like Grafham Water.

mine are 10 x 42 magnification.

As cold feet can be an acute, even painful problem, I suggest a good pair of thermally insulated waterproof boots, often referred to as 'moon boots' because to allow for the extra thick bottom insert plus foam and synthetic-lined inners these boots end up looking two or three sizes larger. But really who cares? Gloves are a handy option if only to put on after hooking on baits and unhooking pike, which leaves your hands sopping wet and freezing cold. Obviously a dry piece of old towelling is worth taking along too. Neoprene gloves with or without the tips of the fingers removed (for extra sensitivity) are a most worthwhile investment for boat fishing and as back-up for extra warmth during long hours of inactivity and for rowing in cold winds. I also own a pair of thermal fleece-lined mittens. Well – why get cold if you don't really have to? I prefer to leave the macho image to the likes of Clint Eastwood.

I also have a similar attitude towards eating out in a boat and go with two large thermos flasks. One contains black coffee and the other boiling hot water only for adding to instant meals such as 'Pot Noodles', which seem to taste so much nicer when you are out in the freezing cold, particularly if you add a spoonful of curry powder before stirring and remember to take along some crunchy freshly baked bread rolls for dunking. They are far more warming than cheese sandwiches anyway. In recent years hot bacon rolls have become my favourite winter warmer – so a frying pan and small gas cooker go along.

In case of torrential or even consistently heavy rain it is wise to pack a couple of plastic bin liners in your tackle bag so that things like your camera and any spare clothing can be kept perfectly dry. And just in case darkness looms over the water before you can get the motor started or work out which boat dyke (from dozens that all look the same) your craft was tied up in, a small toolkit and powerful torch are indispensable additions. For unhooking pike so they are returned in as pristine a condition as they come out I take along a 3 x 6 foot roll of half-inch-thick dense camping foam to go over the boat's duckboards. Not only does it protect the fishes flanks against loss of mucus and disturbed scales should it flap about, a soft protective flooring also cushions your own movements. And this is most important, especially when trying to catch spooky pike inhabiting shallow, and clearwater fisheries.

A common denominator with most hire craft unfortunately, particularly fishing dinghies, is that the mudweights supplied are rarely heavy enough or the ropes long enough. There is nothing more frustrating than being blown away from a hot spot which is really producing once a reasonably steady wind gets up, due to one or both mudweights proving inadequate. To remedy this I have for many many years now always taken along my own pair of mudweights shackled to 30-foot-long half-inch-diameter soft nylon ropes. Thin ropes really bite into your hands in cold weather. My mudweights are actually homemade by filling 2 and 3 gallon (I have two sets of varying weights) plastic tubs with cement. Prior to filling two quarter-inch-diameter holes are made in the centre of the bottom of each plastic bucket so that an exaggerated 'U' of quarter inch steel rod can be threaded through to form a lug around which the end of the rope is fixed. The bucket is then up-ended upon soft earth or sand so the steel lug drops down into its correct position and filled with a good cement mix. Once the concrete is set you have fabulous designed mudweights covered in plastic (the bucket) which helps protect the side of your boat when hoisted overboard. But for goodness' sake don't forget to swish the weight around before lifting over the gunnel or you'll deposit a foul-smelling mixture of sticky bottom silt all over the boat.

HANDLING PIKE SAFETY

Now that temperatures have dropped and we are once again into the swing of winter fishing, let's look at a subject which many freshwater anglers never seem to be really happy about 'handling pike'. Due to their armoury of teeth, sheer physical strength and large size pike certainly look intimidating and as a consequence may not always be handled quite as lovingly as they should during hook removal. In fact, as we no longer clout pike over the head to eat or give to the cat, they should be returned to the water in the very best possible condition in order that when they fight another day someone else has the pleasure of enjoying their majesty. After all, pike are one of the heaviest and certainly the longest predators (next to big eels and pussies) British freshwater anglers are ever likely to encounter. But first things first.

Obviously a capacious landing net is imperative for engulfing and subsequently lifting a good pike from the water and depositing it on *terra firma* or into a boat and my advice would be to obtain the largest you can afford. There are no prizes for pike that won't fit into your net. A triangular, deep-meshed net of at least 36 inches or better still 42 inches does the job admirably. I prefer those with lightweight glass fibre or carbon fibre tapered arms held tight like a bow across the front by nylon cord and which fit into a T-block that screws into the landing net handle.

Now unless the bankside is comfortably carpeted in sphagnum moss or long grass upon which to gently lay the net once your pike is safely inside, invest in a foam-filled unhooking mat to protect its scales and body mucus once it is lowered down for unhooking. Regular boat anglers like myself find that a roll of dense (camping) foam or even an oblong of carpet underlay is just the job for protecting the pike from flapping about on bare boards and hurting itself. Now for successful unhooking you require just two items – an 8-10 inch pair of long-nosed artery forceps (it doesn't matter whether they are straight or curved) and a protective glove for your left hand, assuming you are right handed. A heavy-gauge latex cotton-lined industrial glove will suffice provided it is tight fitting, but in my opinion there is nothing on the market to beat Normark's 'Fish-n-Fillet' glove. This extremely supple glove (which incidentally fits either hand) is actually made

Unhooking even large pike is easy using long nosed artery forceps and a micro-chainmail glove .

from microfine chainmail across which a sharp knife can be drawn without fear of an accident. So for the simple routine of unhooking pike it is perfect. Start by turning the pike on to its back (kneeling astride really large fish helps to keep them still) and insert the fingers of your left (gloved) hand into its left gill opening making sure that the sensitive and extremely delicate gill rakers (through which it extrudes dissolved oxygen) are not disturbed. And when fully inside clamp down upon your forefinger with your thumb (still on the outside) in a firm vice-like grip. Now this does not hurt the pike and is the safest way of handling it. To facilitate hook removal, gently curl your hand towards you and, 'hey presto', the pike has no option but to open its lower jaw. Its upper jaw cannot move of course, being a continuation of its skull, and once you have appreciated that it is the lower jaw which in fact hinges open, unhooking suddenly becomes a formality, not something to dread.

The hooks should then be eased out carefully with the long-nosed artery forceps through the front, or first dislodged via the opposite gill slit if they are situated well back in the throat. Learn to treat the pike with firm respect (never release your grip until the hooks are completely withdrawn) and even deeply hooked fish can be dealt with in seconds provided semi-barbless hooks are used. Incidentally, while the pike is still lying on the net, should you wish to weigh your catch don't fuss about with separate weigh slings or bags etc., simply slip the arms from the T-block and roll the net up to accommodate the hook of the scales, then deduct the weight of the wet net afterwards. Lastly, before returning your pike, right now is most certainly the best time for taking a trophy photograph while it's still knackered. So don't be tempted to retain it in a tube or sack for photographing later (unless absolutely necessary) because once it livens up again after a short rest, trying to hold it still for the camera can prove extremely difficult – so get used to this set routine.

A WENSUM WHOPPER AT LAST

The nice thing about living within walking distance of a river as I do is that you get to know not only its physical characteristics but also its many moods, a prime example being the meandering upper reaches of my local River Wensum here; depending upon height and clarity, it's often possible to predict where certain species will at least be situated. I know, for instance, that when the river is running low and clear chub will pack together along the deepest most even-paced glides, while pike take up residence in the quieter choice lies either behind sunken willows where the water is slack or on the outside of wide bends in slow back eddies.

One such wide and deep bend sprang to mind just recently where on several occasions in the past I had accounted for some good chub hauls, the best consisting of no fewer than 21 chub in a short afternoon session, all averaging between $3^1/_2$ and $4^1/_2$ lbs and I recalled that several were badly scarred from pike attacks. The bend certainly deserved some serious pike attention but it was something I had simply never got around to. With Michael Fish assuring the continuance of a glorious 'high' however, which was responsible for unbelievably mild conditions (14th February being the warmest ever on record at 66° F) and the Wensum running low and incredibly clear, how could I resist adding a pike rod plus a few small roach to my chubbing outfit for a long awaited dawn assault at the deep bend?

During the first hour or so until the sun started to filter through the water I concentrated on quiver tipping breadflake for chub close into the bank immediately below the bend, and accounted for a fat fish nudging the $4^{1}/_{2}$ lb mark which was full of fight in the fast current; but nothing followed. I couldn't buy another bite from chub I knew to be there, which was I suppose just as well for I was itching to try for pike on the outside of the wide bend where an enormous 6-foot-deep slow back eddy simply screamed out to be fished. I mounted a 6 inch roach on a duo of size 8 trebles, set 5 feet below a 1-inch-diameter pilot float, plugged to the 10 lb line with a stem of peacock quill, and standing well back from the margins so the sun didn't throw my shadow over the water, gently plopped it into midstream where the current pattern slowly drew it downstream and around temptingly into the back eddy. Wham! Almost instantly the float disappeared accompanied by a long flash down below as the early morning sunlight illuminated the flank of what was obviously a double-figure pike. It weighed 14 lbs to be exact, once I had deducted the weight of the wet landing net, and led me a merry song and dance all over the wide bend, making run after run and full use of the strong centre flow to its advantage. Beautifully spotted with a neat head, as only river pike are, it was popped into a sack and secured close into the marginal sedges rather than returned immediately - possibly to ruin the chances of additional sport. A sensible move as it proved for the float plopped under again more or less in the same spot.

I struck hard and kept cranking fast as the pike came towards me indicating that perhaps it was only a modest-sized fish. It stayed deep, however, and when virtually beneath the rod tip suddenly woke up, making a tremendously powerful surge diagonally across the 30-yard-wide bend, crashing through shallows on the opposite side like a bat out of hell and continuing on upstream against a firmly set clutch. Was this my Wensum 20-pounder at last, I thought? I had come so very close on several occasions during a love affair with the river spanning over three decades. I had caught goodness knows how many specimen pike from 20 to over 30 lbs from the Broads, the Fens, gravel pits, estate lakes, reservoirs and just about everywhere else locally, but never my beloved River Wensum.

By now the unseen force was fully 50 yards from where it had first grabbed the roach and still motoring, so I grabbed the net and ran upstream making line as I went. It was one of the most exciting fights I have experienced with any pike from any location, and that includes the tail-walking wonders of Canada's far north. This fish just wasn't going to give up easily, treating me to breathtaking run after run, including several glorious, nerve-racking rolls and lunges in midstream as I gradually increased forearm pressure along the rod butt in an effort to bully my prize into the net. I wanted to see it safely on the bank more than badly. Now, how 41 inches of pike went into my 24-inch-diameter chubbing net don't ask me, but it did, head first and with surprising ease - all $22^{1}/_{2}$ lbs of it – boy, did I drive back to the house a happy bunny.

GRAB SOME ZANDER ACTION

One of the key points learnt from fishing in Spain's Rivers Ebro and Segre during the past three years is how quickly zander are able to home in on artificial rubber lures or mounted bleak deadbaits, worked close to the bottom, despite thickly coloured conditions. At home, at least in my neck of the woods in the county of Norfolk, zander are most commonly found in the River Great Ouse and along the inter-connecting system of Fenland drains, such as the Relief Channel, the Cut-Off Channel, the Middle Level Drain etc., and in heavily coloured spate situations I still invariably tend to pin my faith on an anchored, freshly killed small deadbait. Yet one look at the zander's huge light-reflecting eyes suggests that here is a predator purposefully designed for feeding at night and for attacking its prey of small silver shoal fishes like bleak, dace, roach and rudd, in extremely low light values, such as you find in coloured clay pits and whenever the drains for Fenland rivers are heavy in spate and running like strong tea.

I truly believe we British predator anglers, myself included, suffer from a mental blockage with zander due to our pre-conditioning with how the pike's feeding habits change when it cannot actually 'see' its prey. Which I guess is why we tend to opt more for the 'smell' factor, that is using aromatic deadbaits whenever the water becomes thickly coloured, as opposed to persevering with artificials and relying more on the zander's acute sense of sight and vibration.

Over in Spain the Drachkovitch deadbait mount is much used. This presents either a freshly killed bleak or a soft rubber lure with an excellent hook-up rate. In the UK small big-lipped deep diving plus sporting ballbearing rattles work most effectively in addition to Drachko-style mounts and soft, synthetic rubber shad and minnow-tail lures. I particularly favour the 'wild eye' jigging shad heads, split tails, vibro-tail jigs, rattle grubs, rattle hot craws, etc., etc. My overall favourite, however, is the 'vitala ribbed soft plastic synthetic fish' which is available in 10 electrifying colours. I have taken countless nice zander on this vibratory sensation and have even put it to good use when after the legendary Nile perch of Lake Nasser in Egypt.

Now the weather will shortly be warming up, it's well worth persevering with these artificials. For optimum results remember to use a non-stretch braided reel line coupled to a stiffish lure rod. Soft-tip rods dampen and suppress the kind of action which needs to be created for these particular lures to score.

THE DRACHKOVITCH RIG

Guide Gary Allen hoists up a splendid 'Rio Ebro' zander hooked on a Drachkovitch-mounted synthetic lure by Simon Clarke.

The huge wels catfish of Spain's Rivers Ebro and Segre are legendary but what marvellous sport with specimen-sized zander up to 20 lbs there is also to be had in the Rio Ebro, for a distance of 30 miles both up and downstream of its confluence with the Segre at Mequinenza, just a two hour westerly drive from Barcelona. Zander are not indigenous to the system, having been introduced along with a rich food source in the way of the silvery bleak, by German anglers. And apart from presenting a live bleak beneath a float rig, by far the most effective technique to catch quality zander is to work a freshly killed 5-6 inch bleak up and down 'sink and draw' style close to the rocky bottom mounted on a Drachkovitch rig. Rubber shads incidentally can also be used.

Now if you are old enough to have used or can visualise one of the 'Archer flights' of yesteryear you will comprehend how the Drachkovitch rig works. Invented by Frenchman, Albert Drachkovitch, this versatile deadbait mount, available in several sizes to suit various target species from trout to big pike, comprises of a lightweight V - shaped spring wire stem inserted down the deadbait's throat, to which at the top clip is attached a ball weight of between 4 and 12 grams. This is to ensure the mounted deadbait nose dives attractively after being twitched upwards by the rod tip. Also attached to the clip is around 6 inches of stiff copper wire, which is threaded through the bleak's shoulder and then wound around the body to ensure it stays in one piece for as long as possible. Lastly two single trebles joined to wire (one short and one long) are pushed into the bait's flank and tail root (on opposing sides) to ensure a hook-up from whatever angle the zander grabs hold. And it works so very, very well.

Several zander may be caught on the same bait before it starts to disintegrate and due to the fine wire round-bend trebles, the prongs of which will bend if pulling hard for a break or snag, rig loss is kept to a minimum. A small fixed spool reel loaded with 20 – 30lbs test braid, used in conjunction with a sensitive-tipped 9 foot spinning rod, is the ideal combo for working this rig. The braided line permits close control of the bait after closing the bale arm and commencing the 'sink and draw' routine, once it has touched bottom where zander are grouped up in packs. Very often at this precise moment, either on the lift or as the bait flutters attractively downwards, a zander will hit.

Generally the cast is made downstream and across so that each time you raise the bait it works across the flow. Our guide at Mequinenza, Gary Allen, actually lumped into a beautiful 12 lb zander on the very first cast, whilst demonstrating the technique and I cannot wait to try it along my favourite zander-packed stretches of the Great Ouse system and in local lakes. Incidentally, DIY enthusiasts who find Drachkovitch rigs difficult to obtain from UK tackle shops should easily be able to construct them.

WARMER DAYS PERFECT FOR ZANDER HUNT

The unusually mild weather at the beginning of January which produced temperatures as high as 13 and 14° C promoted two things: it encouraged two pairs of greylag geese to start looking for nesting sites in the larger of my two lakes (the earliest I can ever remember); and I was talked into joining brother, Dave for a midwinter trip in search of zander - a species we usually only bother spending any time on during the autumn and early winter. Our chosen destination was the lower reaches of the Great Ouse, near Ely, which following a week of continual rain was nicely up with a strong flow, but more importantly thickly coloured to a shade of strong tea.

Now I've mentioned before that during typical winter weather with prolonged bouts

Brother Dave caught this plump zander from the Great Ouse ledgering a 4-inch dead roach.

of sub-zero overnight temperatures zander seem to do a disappearing trick and become almost impossible to catch. But any spell of mild weather soon brings them out of the doldrums and on the hunt for their staple diet of small silver shoal fishes. Coloured water, however, is imperative for any chance of consistent action during daylight hours. One glance at the zander's large glassy eyes suggests that they are not only nocturnal feeders but also exceptionally well equipped for catching small shoal fish during low light conditions. Hence the zander hunter's preference for coloured water. And so Dave and I were more confident of the prevailing conditions when we met at a favourite swim on the Ouse where depth shelves down to around 14 feet on the outside of a wide bend. Huge overhanging willows fringed by tall reedbeds at the upstream end of the bend provided the perfect habitat for zander which are in fact the most sensitive of all our predatory species: sensitive that is to any kind of resistance created by the angler's terminal tackle (something all would-be zander enthusiasts should bear in mind).

We geared up two Avon-style rods apiece with 8 lb test reel lines and running ledger rigs comprising of a 1 oz bomb on a link above the top swivel with a cushioning bead between. Traces were soft, 15 lb test wire to which a pair of size 10 semi-barbless trebles had been attached, scaled-down pike traces none-the-less, to accommodate our 3-5 inch freshly killed roach deadbaits.

Now whilst the occasional zander may belt off and attempt to pull the rod in, as most pike would do having sucked up a static deadbait, most will not. They are so unbelievably intolerant as I was to experience on the day, having decided to use drop-arm indicators in order to combat the strong flow of the river. In fact I missed out on the first two bites which failed to pull the line free from the indicator clip. The rod tip nodded once, the line lifted and the bait was subsequently dropped like a hot brick. Meanwhile brother Dave, who was using clip-on ledger bobbins and putting up with the continual pull of the river which occasionally gave false bites, was enjoying a real field day, albeit from some of the most gentle zander bites he had ever experienced, the majority consisting of little more than 6 – 10 inch lifts or drops of the bobbins. And unless a strike was made immediately the small roach was ejected within seconds.

Dave enjoyed fairly consistent action throughout the morning accounting for a couple of 2 lb schoolies, a brace of seven pounders and then a plump fish which led him a real song and dance around the marginal sedges and which at first sight looked as though it might even go into double figures. On the scales, however, it weighed 9 lbs plus. My brother's continued crowing about my complete lack of fish prompted me to switch indicators from drop arms over to clip-on bobbins and thus made all the difference, allowing me to hit a couple of tentative lifts, both of which resulted in zander of between 7 and 8 lbs. The bites were actually less positive than I would have expected if ledgering worms for perch or bream, but that's zander fishing. And upon striking those predators had the small deadbait well and truly inside their mouths. It was indeed a lesson in just how sensitive these enigmatic fish can be when the mood takes them. As is our normal practice when presenting freshly killed deadbaits to zander, Dave and I pierced each bait several times with a sharp knife to allow their scent to permeate more easily in the coloured water: an old trick but one that does seem to produce more runs than unpierced deadbaits. Though we finished the long dawn until dusk session having grassed 10 nice zanders and dropped a further three, we still felt that had the sun not shone continually, thus greatly increasing light values down there on the bottom of the river, we might even have encountered one of the larger, double-figure specimens for which this part of the River Ouse is renowned. Can't wait until the weather turns mild again!

My good friend and fellow angling journalist Dave Lewis travelled all the way from Wales, to bag this magnificent brace of 'zeds' from the Great Ouse at Ely.

DAVE GETS HIS ZANDER

As I had to be over at Ely in Cambridgeshire at 8.00 a.m. sharp for a pheasant shoot on the Thursday morning, I decided to leave much earlier than the hour's drive necessitated in order to have a good look at the nearby River Ouse - and for good reason. Fellow angling journalist

Dave Lewis and his wife Allison were coming over to Norfolk from Wales for a social weekend, giving Dave and I the chance of sneaking an early-morning session after zander as he had never caught one, if conditions were favourable. Fortunately the Ouse itself was still heavily coloured after all the rain during November and ideal for zander, but fair honking through. So I drove around to several favourite spots hoping to find an area of deepish slack water close into the bank where we stood a good chance of catching using small, ledgered deadbaits. That's the beauty of the Ouse network of inter-connecting rivers and drains: there is such a wonderful choice of locations, and I soon found an ideal spot where huge willows deflected the strong flow across the river, leaving a nice slack on the near bank. A swim incidentally which had always produced zander for me on previous visits, so I was confident of Dave scoring.

Come early Saturday morning, however, despite our setting up in the dark to ensure we had at least an hour's fishing during darkness before dawn broke, usually prime zander feeding time, our ledgered freshly killed small roach deadbaits remained untouched. We were fishing two rods apiece and as always for me when targeting zander specifically bite indication was through lightweight bobbins clipped on the line between reel and butt ring set on a 12 inch drop. I find zander extremely sensitive to resistance and not the marauding predators many anglers still conceive them to be, one reason I prefer bobbins to drop-arm-style indicators from which a biting zander will not always pull the line.

Dawn broke with a chilly south-easterly wind and clear skies, promising strong sunlight: completely the reverse of what I consider ideal zander conditions and I was feeling less optimistic by the minute. At 20 minutes to 8.00 I said to Dave 'Let's give it until 8.30 and if there's still no action we'll move on to the Old West River' (a 20 minute drive away to another favourite spot). But at a little after 8.00 I saw the tip of one of his two rods knocking followed by the bobbin jerking upwards. Within seconds the world suddenly seemed a better place and following a spirited fight in that dogged, head-shaking way that only zander scrap, Dave Lewis was staring down the mesh of the landing net admiring his very first zander.

During the following hour, at a time when I certainly would not have expected zander to be feeding aggressively, the bobbins just wouldn't keep still, though we often had to wait for a strikeable bite to develop. Several nice fish then came our way, the largest almost pushing double figures, before the feeding spell ended as abruptly as it had started. By then, however, for my good friend, Dave Lewis it was a case of 'mission accomplished'.

PERCH ON THE BOBBIN

During recent years sizeable perch have really made a phenomenal comeback from the disease which ravaged the species throughout the 1960s and 70s and at present there is no better time for coming to grips with stripies of 2 lbs plus. Moreover, when continually high river levels rule out any serious running water action save for the odd floodwater haven, and you fancy a change from the routine of pike fishing in stillwaters, why not enjoy a spot of bobbin ledgering for perch?

In stillwaters big and small, from vast reservoir and gravel pit complexes to farm ponds of just half an acre, the sensible approach is to look for feature lies by plummeting around to locate the deeper holes, troughs and gullies where perch overwinter close to their staple diet of small shoal fish which automatically pack together in deeper areas once their cover of weed dies back and low winter temperatures set in. Perch are also attracted to marginal

Richard Bowler's smile really does say it all. This handsome, monstrous perch of 4 lbs 5 ozs was caught ledgering a deep bend on the upper reaches of the Great Ouse.

features with deep water beneath like big overhanging tress, particularly willows, whose lower limbs dangle beneath the surface providing both diffused light and cover from a maze of lesser branches which sprout a thick membrane of sub-surface roots. In completely featureless waters it may be necessary to fish with both baits ledgered far out into deep areas, while in others, especially those smaller, more intimate fisheries, you can hedge your bets by fishing one bait close up to a willow along your own or opposite bank, with the second bait placed into a deep hole out in open water. It's always a suck it and see situation and the best combination for perch ledgering is an 11 – 12 foot Avon-actioned rod coupled to a fixed-spool reel holding 6 lb test. My terminal rig comprises of a 20-24 inch hooklink of $4\frac{1}{2}$ lbs test with a size 6-4 eyed hook at the business end and at the other a small swivel to which the reel line is tied. Running above the swivel is a large Drennan ring with a 5mm cushioning bead between. The 5 inch link is made from 30 lb Masterline black mono for its stiffness which alleviates tangles, with (depending upon distance) a $\frac{3}{4}$ - $1\frac{1}{2}$ oz bomb on the end.

Now for the bait: there really is nothing to beat big lobworms and in case you are wondering how I can lay my hands on a good supply of lobs in the dead of winter even when the ground is rock hard, well I store them amongst strips of dampened newspaper in a large wooden box. Simply make hay while the sun shines by collecting worms after dark off the lawn during bouts of mild wet weather. Then you'll never be without.

It is imperative to angle the rod downwards on two rests with the butt ring resting against the front head (an electric bite alarm is optional here) and pointing directly at the bait to minimise resistance. Now while all kinds of super-duper swing-arm, and quiver-arm indicators are currently available, nothing beats the simplicity of a clip-on ledger bobbin with a 2 foot retaining cord attached to the front rest. After casting the line is wound up and the bobbin clipped on the line between reel and bait ring with a 14-16 inch drop. Now small perch are renowned for giving short, sharp jerky twitches and jingles of the bobbin. If you have ever observed them through clear water attacking a big worm, you'll see them quickly suck it up, usually by one end (this accounts for those inexplicable missed runs), run with it, blow it out, suck it up again and so on. Whereas quality perch, fish of 1 and 2 lbs upwards, invariably engulf your worm and move positively away, causing the bobbin to steadily rise all the way up to the butt ring in a totally authoritative manner. Trouble is, while small perch have trouble engulfing a whole large lob, those of say 6 oz upwards do not, so you may need to wade through various shoals and size groups and change swims a few times in order to make contact with the bigger perch.

You'll also notice that suddenly on both rods, even with baits presented 30 – 60 yards apart, movements on the bobbins are simultaneous. It's as though someone has suddenly flicked on the feeding switch and a feeding phenomenon we humans cannot possibly comprehend. But you can also make your own action happen by winding the bobbin up tight every few minutes and pulling it down a foot or so, thus moving the worm along the bottom. Perch have the habit of just lying there staring at their next meal if it looks as though it can't get away, rather like a cat does with a mouse trapped beneath its paw. But when the bait does a runner – bang, they nail it instantly. Try it and see. In fact continually moving the bait towards you is by far the best way of locating fish within a large area, if bites do not materialise.

To complement shortish casts (up to 25 yards) in small waters catapult broken worms out and regularly spray the area with maggots to keep small bait fish active, while in big waters loose feed in the way of broken worms can be sandwiched between plugs of breadcrumb groundbait at each end of a large open-end feeder which replaces the ledger bomb.

BIG PERCH MAGIC ON THE OUSE

I think it was my old mate and angling guru, Fred J. Taylor, who once said, and I quote, 'To be successful on the Upper Ouse you have to fish as though you've just missed a bite and be expectantly ready for another.' Well, Fred really did hit the nail on the button with that one and it's advice that will stand you in good stead for catching those significantly wilier specimen fish inhabiting not only the Upper Ouse but diminutive rivers all over the British Isles. Trouble is in cold, overcast weather with rain spitting into your face it's not always easy to charge yourself up as though you've just missed a chance and are already for the rod tip to twang round again when it hasn't moved for two hours. Is it? And I was reminded of Fred J.'s immortal words just recently when as coincidence would have it I was myself sat beside the upper reaches of the Great Ouse in pursuit of what have become my passion these past two winters: big perch.

The wind was howling across the meadows interspersed with rain and for a couple of hours I even succumbed to erecting the umbrella for a bit of warmth - not something I like doing incidentally simply because its sudden presence upon the skyline, overshadowing a narrow piece of river, could easily scare the perch I was seeking. And the water had become reasonably clear after recent flooding with a visibility of at least 2 feet. Summer water conditions almost, accompanied by decidedly wintery weather – not a good mixture at the best of times. I had in fact first fished the Upper Ouse one winter over 40 years ago (I lived in North London then) as a junior member of the Enfield Town Angling Society. The late Dick Walker had invited the club along to a wonderfully overgrown fishery at Stony Stratford, a stretch he rented with the Taylor brothers, which in those days was famous for producing some huge chub. I can remember exactly what I caught: a bag of quality dace and good roach, all long trotting maggots, but through inexperience I lost a couple of sizeable chub which had no trouble at all wrapping my light hook length and size 6 around a bed of decaying bulrush stems. But it proved a great learning curve and when Dick himself walked round to chat with each and every one of the club's members individually, including me, it wouldn't have mattered if I'd blanked.

A few years later Dick allowed a friend and me to visit his stretch and try for the specimen chub during the summer months using black slugs and crayfish for bait. It was real hit and hold fishing in the narrow

I couldn't believe my good fortune when this huge perch surfaced. It weighed 4 lbs 7 ozs and like most big stripies I've caught from the Ouse, gobbled up a large lobworm.

overgrown reaches of the Ouse, stalking on all fours Indian style, a lone chub in a clearing amongst dense bulrushes and then trying to horse it out through the greenery before it could get its head down. I simply loved it and have taken great pains in stalking and creeping up upon specimen fish inhabiting small clearwaters ever since.

These and so many other past memories of days spent along narrow winding upper reaches of our lowland rivers drifted through my mind as I sat there waiting for my first genuine perch bite of the day. Since a dawn start with nothing but the continual plucking on the line from signal crayfish trying to devour my big lobworm on a size 4 hook, I had in fact moved swims several times spending half an hour or maybe an hour in each, with just a jack pike of about a pound to show for my careful stalking. But no perch. And as it was getting on for late afternoon I decided to stick it out in a favourite haunt where sunken bushes play host to small groups of big stripies along the opposite bank of an acute deep bend in the river. Despite the wind rocking my two rods in their rests, I lifted up the quiver-tip rod fishing worm at the end of the swim to shake off yet another crayfish when - wham, the tip buckled over and I was fast into what seemed like a big perch. It certainly stayed deep while I worked it upstream, but then suddenly those old rubber lips hit the surface and I had to settle for a chub, but a nice thick-set fish of exactly 4$\frac{1}{2}$ lbs. An hour later, not long before I packed up, call it a premonition or whatever, somehow I sensed the near rod fitted with a bobbin indicator would produce and sure enough shortly afterwards it jerked steadily upwards in that unmistakable bite of the perch. Even on 6 lb test and my soft-actioned Heritage Avon rod it managed to rip off line against the clutch, making several deep diving runs before I could get it under control and up on the surface ready for the net. The best fight I've ever had from a perch - probably due to the fact that it was my best ever perch no less and it pulled the scales down to 4 lbs 7 ozs.

A PERCH SESSION TO REMEMBER

Following a memorable February day along the diminutive reaches of the Upper Great Ouse above Milton Keynes, in the company of my nephew Richard Bowler, when I landed a magnificent 3$\frac{3}{4}$ lb perch, plus a two pounder, both whilst trotting worms around a slow eddy in a deep bend of the then extremely clear river, I was disappointed on arrival to find the Ouse bank high and coffee coloured two weeks later. Three days of incessant rain had turned every ditch and sidestream into raging torrents but at least for February the weather was surprisingly mild despite a continual downpour which started when Martin (Richard's brother) and I arrived at the fishery at 7.30 a.m. and was still coming down when we finished at 5.00 p.m. Never before in fact can I remember actually sheltering beneath the brolly for the entire day though. Strangely, however, it did not deter the big perch from biting, although our initial decision of concentrating upon the same deep bend where I scored two weeks before proved a total failure due, I am certain,, to a farm drainage dyke immediately above the bend spewing its filthy water into the river.

A complete lack of bites, save for the attention of bait-robbing signal crayfish which in this part of the Great Ouse virtually pave the bottom, and are continually active (except when perch are on the prowl), meant that the perch had been sickened by the filthy orange water which no doubt included a proportion of silage. So around midday I walked to the top of the meadow well above the farm dyke and catapulted a couple of dozen broken lobworms into an acute, deepish bend where a huge mat of brown rotting bulrushes lining the inside bank would have provided a superb hideout habitat earlier on in the season throughout the summer and autumn months, with a view to my moving in just above the bend for the remaining few hours of the day. It was the best bit of forward planning I've ever done. On arrival back at the deep bend Martin was about to lift out a crayfish firmly attached to his lobworm. That did it for me. Ten minutes later I was nicely settled in at the upstream bend with my 13 foot float rod presenting a stret-pegged worm close beside the bed of decaying bulrushes in a depth of 7 feet. Once the float had settled at a half-cocked position denoting that the bait was static on the riverbed, I cast out a second rod presenting a x3 swan shot ledger into the middle of the bend, pointing it directly at the

huge lobworm, and clipped on a bobbin indicator between butt ring and reel. When I looked up again to find the float it had disappeared and my instinctive strike resulted in a lovely throbbing headshaking resistance down deep, so characteristic of a big perch. With just a $2^1/_2$ lbs rest reel line on the centre pin I was afraid to bully it, and so enjoyed a spirited fight until it was up on the surface and ready for the net – all 2 lbs 2ozs of it. A fine start.

No sooner had I popped it into a pre-soaked sack at my feet, when the ledger bobbin jerked twice and slowly climbed to the butt ring in that classical, confident way big perch inhale a lobworm. And what a big perch it felt too. Taking line against the clutch it powered upstream for a few yards before turning back downriver, across the swim, boring deep all the time, and it stayed close to the bottom while I pumped it cautiously upstream to where I sat beneath a gnarled old oak tree, watching the rod tip didn't catch in the branches above. It seemed an age but finally my perch came up through the coloured water into view and thrashed the surface, displaying its massively deep flanks and fat belly. Perhaps with more pressure than I should have used I quickly bullied it straight into the waiting net and heaved it ashore. On the scales it weighed exactly 3 lbs 10 ozs. My second largest perch ever. What a day and it was far from over.

After introducing some more broken lobworms into the middle of the bend I eased another worm on to the size 4 hook and plopped it out to exactly where the big perch had come from. Within less than a minute the bobbin shot up and I struck into yet another biggy which after just four or five seconds unfortunately slipped the hook. I automatically feared that this would unsettle the shoal which it certainly did for a good hour or so. Then almost simultaneously bites came on both rods as the shoal again moved over the carpet of broken worm pieces.

The float was first away and I struck into what felt like another whopper which bored away downstream taking several yards of line before I managed to turn it level with the end of the rush bed. Unfortunately it veered inwards towards the near bank and became stuck fast in the bed of decaying bulrushes, and when I pulled steadily the hook came free. Was I gutted, though I had little time for self-pity because from the corner of my eye I witnessed the ledger bobbin jerking slowly upwards to the butt ring. This time the hook set firmly as the fish belted off downstream against a firmly set clutch, obviously another whopping great stripey by its head-shaking antics and dogged resistance. My Avon quiver-tip rod and 6 lb reel line were stretched to the full with this fish which led me a merry song and dance by screaming off upriver past where I sat, just missing a sunken branch, before I could get it back again under control and beneath the rod tip ready for netting. It was by far the largest perch I had ever seen in over 50 years of angling: a monstrously humpbacked specimen sporting wide dark-brown stripes, beautiful crimson fins, an incredibly fat belly (full of crayfish no doubt) and a huge mouth. And it pulled my dial scales down to 4 lbs 1 oz exactly. Boy, was I over the moon.

By now Martin had moved into the sedges bordering the next bend downstream but his ledgered lobs could attract only small perch. I experienced yet another lull for over an hour before the float suddenly shot away again resulting in my last perch of the day, another superbly fat specimen of 2 lbs 3 ozs and it was stuffed full of broken worms, coughing up the remains of at least 20 into my hand after removing the hook. Four perch weighing together 12 lbs.

Difficult to believe I'll ever better such a catch. At least those were my thoughts as Martin and I trudged wearily yet happily back to my Jeep across muddy meadows, with the rain still falling heavily.

BACK LEDGERING FOR STRIPIES

Now unless I am purposefully upstream ledgering when river fishing for species like chub, roach, bream, and perch in particular, casts are of course made directly downstream or downstream and across in the accepted manner. The first cast is usually made short and then each successive cast just that little bit further until a shoal of fish is located. Standard stuff no less. Trouble is I am sure this in part is the reason for fish spooking; the ledger rig coincidentally often lands directly on top of the shoal. And, of course, the further you cast greater is the disturbance of your ledger hitting the surface. In deep holes this may not prove a problem but in swims of just 2 or 3 feet deep the fish could panic off as a result.

For the past two winters, however, I have been employing a different technique, almost a reversal of standard tactics in fact, which I simply call 'back-ledgering' and it has helped me account for good numbers of specimen perch plus the occasional chub from the often shallow, winding upper reaches of the Great Ouse in Bedfordshire. Incidentally, throughout the winter whilst in search of perch I rely totally on lobworms for bait and these I break in two and either throw or catapult downstream into the chosen swim throughout the day, two or three worms at a time and on a regular basis. This really gets perch working through the swim and on the look-out for more. So don't set off for a day's perching without at least a hundred lobworms.

Favourite swims are wherever large willows or alders overhang and even lap the surface creating dark caverns beneath. Perch, of course, love these hideouts from which they can ambush their prey, but they are quite willing to forage further upstream once they get the smell of broken lobworms permeating through the swim. Now rather than cast short and then work progressively further downstream, I make a long cast to the very end of the swim. The rig incidentally is a simple fixed paternoster ledger with a 6 lb reel line and size 4 on the 20 inch hook length. Two size 3xSSG shot on the link can be easily flipped 30 yards downstream so it's best not to sit too close to where you expect the perch to be situated. In fact keeping them at distance so they have little reason to spook is really what back-ledgering is all about. So from the start plan to fish at a fair range – at least 20 yards plus. Now if nothing seems interested in the worm after say five minutes (no longer) at the very end of the swim, lift the rod tip up, wind the reel a couple of times and put the rod down again. This delicately moves the worm two feet up the swim and a little bit closer to you. And this you repeat every so often working the bait up the swim until bites happen, while you regularly introduce broken worms as loose feed. It goes without saying at this point that the rod should be positioned on two rests with the tip angled upwards to alleviate undue current pressure upon the line. With this systematic method of searching the swim each time you ease the rig up off the bottom and allow the shots to resettle, the worm will 'flutter' enticingly up and then down, so be on your guard for those 'instant' bites which usually occur within a second or two of repositioning the worm. And as with all perch bites, don't be in too much of a hurry – allow the fish to get the entire worm into its mouth before lifting the Avon quiver-tip rod back into a firm but smooth strike.

In really slow currents you can even point the tip at the ledger rig, angle the rod downwards supported on two rests and clip on a ledger bobbin between reel and butt ring. This is an incredibly sensitive method of bite detection creating the very minimum of resistance. Overall, however, I rate a finely tapered quiver tip the most versatile indicator, taking into account a whole variety of different swims you may need to explore along a river's course, from deep slow bends to fast runs.

To alleviate resistance to a biting perch I often lift the rod gently from the rests when the quiver tip gives a preliminary twitch and angle it downstream towards the fish which subsequently feels even less resistance. A positive pull round of the tip then usually materialises within seconds. It's a lovely way of specialising in catching large perch without spooking them. Not all swims, however, will contain jumbo-sized stripies. Sometimes from the start of settling into a new swim the tip just won't stop jingling from the attentions of small perch. So whenever this happens my advice is to move immediately. It's harsh but it's positive.

JOHN (JINX) LANDS A WHOPPER STRIPEY

A piking trip along the tidal River Waveney at Beccles with mate John (Jinx) Davey was to have been my last outing before the river season ended, but the ridiculously mild weather which followed suggested those jumbo-sized perch inhabiting the overgrown winding reaches of the Upper Great Ouse above Bedford might just be feeding. And as John had never before caught a big perch we set off in the early hours to be at the river for a dawn start for one last fling, armed with over 200 lively lobworms apiece. Strangely,

and despite the river running nicely at normal level with that lovely winter green colour, until early afternoon our ledgered lobworms attracted only a few small pike and one chub of around 4$\frac{1}{2}$ lbs. We tried all the favourite locations frequented by big stripies, such as deep holes on the bends, caverns beneath overhanging part sunken willows and deep runs alongside thick beds of decaying sedges and reed, with not the slightest interest from perch of any size; it was as though not a single perch existed in the river.

Fellow perch enthusiasts Martin and Richard Bowler were also at the river and experiencing exactly the same. Then quite suddenly at around 3.00 p.m., as though someone up there had flicked a switch, we all started to get bites from perch in swims several hundred yards apart. Neither the river nor the weather pattern had seemingly changed. We were still presenting the same paternoster ledger rigs using 6 lb reel lines and size 4 hooks holding a big lively lob on each. But now with but a few hours of daylight left those big perch were on the move all along the river.

Fishing way downstream of John and me, Richard Bowler accounted in quick succession for several nice perch of between 1$\frac{1}{2}$ and 2$\frac{1}{2}$ lbs apiece from a deep slack close into a bed of sedges. Then it was my turn as the quiver tip lunged round in that typical aggressive way perch inhale a big worm. A nice fish of around 2$\frac{1}{2}$ lbs resulted but those which followed got progressively smaller. John Davey, however, who sat halfway between Richard and me on the inside of a wide bend where a thick bed of dense rushes screened the margins, was about to strike gold. His first bite produced a perch of around 1$\frac{1}{2}$ lbs. The next fish was a pike of around 1$\frac{1}{2}$ lbs which in turn was grabbed across the middle by a pike of at least 12 lbs. And immediately following the subsequent fracas John's ledgered lobworm was grabbed by the perch of a lifetime. As it slid over the net following a powerful scrap of several minutes I could have sworn it was well over that magical 4 lbs mark, but John was delighted to settle for the scales reading 3 lbs 14$\frac{1}{2}$ ozs, almost doubling the size of his previous best.

As always it was most satisfying sharing in a friend's success and a wonderful end to the river season.

Chapter Three

TROUT, SALMON AND GRAYLING

TOUGH ON THE TWEED

Mention the 'junction pool' to any serious British salmon fly fisherman and he'll immediately know you are referring to where the diminutive and picturesque River Teivot converges with Scotland's majestic River Tweed at Kelso, a location steeped in history, rich in wildlife and, when on form with the Tweed flushed from rain, arguably the most prolific salmon beat in the whole of the British Isles, save for the bridge pool on Ireland's River Moy. But what the Tweed lacks in overall numbers it certainly makes up for in quality. Even today 20 - and even 30 pounders are there for the taking on fly should suitable water levels coincide with your arrival. Something for yours truly which has yet to happen, I might add, but I do keep trying.

Take my recent trip, for example, when my wife Jo and I accompanied by Max, our ridgeback/bull mastif cross, checked into the Ednam House Hotel in Kelso which overlooks the junction itself.

A nice River Tweed grilse for Giles Wilson, caught in difficult conditions.

What a superb setting, and in Alistair what an understanding host who allows a 13 stone dog to share one of his best rooms and the rest of the hotel with its owners. But then everything about the hotel is geared towards the well being of its guests who are there for one thing only – salmon. The crack, meeting up with old friends, the packed lunches, bar talk, dinner talk, salmon laying out in the reception hall for all to see, later to be frozen and sent on or mounted etc., etc. Here the king of the river certainly rules OK! When you can catch him that is.

Once again my arrival had met with the weather undecided. Previous trips had disastrously coincided with too much rain sending the Tweed over the banks and so low you could actually walk across in trainers. Honestly! Due to high summer levels at least now at the end of September there were plenty of fish in the river. Unfortunately most were stale and rather dark but amongst them was a reasonable percentage of fresh run silver fish. All it needed was a day's heavy rain for the river to rise those valuable few inches to get everything moving and thus snapping at our flies. But alas, after three difficult days the Tweed had in fact dropped an inch and was as clear as my local River Wensum. Nevertheless our party of six stuck to their guns and relentlessly put flies through the choice lies at the Bridge Pool, at Hempsford and at the junction itself. My partner, Giles Wilson from Northampton, no relation incidentally, broke the spell with two nice grilse early one misty morning from Hempsford, but from then on couldn't buy a pull on any pattern. We went from big brass tube flies, down to lightweight aluminium patterns, to waddingtons and finally on to small low-water flies. We even tried floating lines. But the ghilllies said slow sinkers or an intermediate and I rather think they know best.

Whilst you wouldn't want to play a big salmon on a 10 lb leader and size 10 or 12 double, if you can't even hook one then the chance of landing it is even more remote. So I tried everything towards inducing a pull. Apart from those few precious casts in the morning after the pools had been rested for the night, when a fish just might have been on the cards, we decided to fish from late afternoon all the way into darkness in the hope of some action, and scrap the afternoon session. A wise move as it turned out. In fact my luck changed halfway down the junction pool with the light all but gone when a grilse of around 6 lbs snapped up a double size 12 stoat's tail. It put up a scrappy fight through the fast run in the half light and instantly made the world a better place. This was followed almost immediately by a chunky grayling of 2 lbs plus. Then I missed a juddery pull, no doubt from another grayling. Then it was too dark to see – end of story for me.

Three days of hard fishing for one 6 lb salmon. Was it worth it? Of course it was, and would you believe on the very morning we drove back to Norfolk midweek, the Tweed had risen by an inch or so overnight. I rather fancy everyone got into fish towards the end of the week, and if they did they will have certainly earned them.

KING OF THE RIVER

On any pre-selected day I reckon that the salmon is just about the hardest fish to try and catch to order in British freshwater. Yet with just a day and a bit of actual filming time at my disposal this was my target just recently in order to complete for Meridian Television a section in one of my *Go Fishing* programmes. To help share the problem and the pressure I contacted friend Graham Purbrick, who manages the famous Testwood Salmon Fishery on the lower Test, south of Romsey in Hampshire. This consists of over three miles of double-bank fishing plus sidestreams and weir pools including the large tidal pool from which carp and even the occasional bass are taken in addition to salmon and sea trout. Having caught salmon here in the past on trotted shrimp and with a running bomb rig Graham suggested we try the ultimate challenge of attempting to beat a salmon using 8 foot lightweight brook rod outfits consisting of size 6 floating lines, a leader tapered to just a 5 lb tippet and a small goldhead nymph on the business end. The technique, which for want of a better word I call 'dibbling', has been perfected by Graham on the River Test and will instigate interest from the most unco-operative salmon in all those near bank swims immediately behind stagings, beside boardings and wherever large stones have been placed to attract salmon. The secret is to let the heavily weighted nymph reach bottom quickly following a short roll cast made square on and then to lift it steadily upwards to the surface, where every so often a salmon will follow due to a mixture of curiosity and territorial aggression and nail it just before or actually on the surface. Hairy stuff indeed, to say the least.

As with traditional downstream and across fly fishing you move half a pace down the run on each successive 'dibble' until it's been covered and then move on to the next likely lie. It's a great way not only of covering numerous runs in the course of a day but also of dealing with all those short and awkward or overgrown lies which are next to impossible to work using a traditional double-handed rod. Moreover it permits two friends to methodically search a particular beat leap-frogging one another from lie to lie, often quite close together, enjoying all the usual banter that arises from fly fishing.

Graham struck gold first with a lovely fresh run sea trout of about 4 lbs from immediately below the bridge pool on only his second cast. Took the nymph on the drop too. We then covered a good couple of dozen lies apiece including the tidal pool, all to no avail, whilst making our way upriver to where Graham had placed a succession of large stones close into the steep-sided banking as prime lies. The salmon obviously liked them because at the end of the first run up popped a nice fish of around 10 lbs for my nymph, and I allowed it to get its head down, just like I do when floater fishing for carp, before pulling into it firmly. Except I struck into thin air – it must have missed the nymph completely. I couldn't raise the same fish again but from a little further downstream a solid thump halfway up the lift resulted in a perch of fully $1\frac{1}{2}$ lbs – not what I'd expected at all.

Graham then produced a brownie of around $2\frac{1}{2}$ lbs from a small weir pool and that was day one finished, without a single salmon. On day two, however, only an hour before the camera crew were due to wrap, we tried the tidal pool again just on the turn of the tide and, 'bingo', Graham struck gold with a fine cock salmon of around 8 lbs which supplied both cameras with the acrobatic footage we so badly needed. Phew!

*Jovial Keith Sharp helps me display a set of caribou antlers whilst filming my
'Go Fishing' TV series in Canada's barren North West Territories.*

BISECTED BY THE 63rd PARALLEL

It was great to receive a newsletter just recently from an old friend and fishing guide, Keith
Sharp, up there in the frozen wastes of Canada's North West Territories, which believe or
not actually contain almost 10 per cent of the world's freshwater and where 'ice out'
doesn't happen until as late as June, maybe even July some years. Then following three
short months in which everything breeds whilst man hunts and fishes it freezes in again
come September. A harsh life indeed even for the indigenous Innuit Indians, but one that
jovial 23 stone Keith (he's probably even heavier now) who runs the superb fly-in fishing
camp at Ferguson River and Lake Lodge, which lies due west of Rankin Inlet at Hudson
Bay bisected by the 63rd parallel, wouldn't swap for anything. A fact I soon realised
several years back when filming one of my *Go Fishing* programmes for Anglia and
Channel Four Television in Canada's arctic north in the company of Martin Founds of
Anglers' World Holidays and Keith Sharp who, as an ex-Brummie, swapped his
predictable life in the UK close on 30 years ago to share the frozen tundra above the
treeline with caribou, arctic fox, grizzlies, musk oxen and Alma, his Innuit Eskimo wife
and nine children. And I'll never ever forget as long as I live our harrowing experience of
pulling a boat across a quickly melting ice floe several miles wide. They do say that filming
programmes abroad for television is a doddle – if only they knew.

Actually it all happened quite innocently really. Keith knew we required another boat
for our second cameraman and innocuously suggested that Harvey, the pilot, fly the three
of us out from the main lodge at Ferguson Lake in the Cessna float plane to a small island
20 miles away where he had left an aluminium hulled boat plus a few provisions. During
dinner, which included the most immense steaks (caribou) I had ever seen, Keith mumbled
something about an ice floe but it all sounded so exciting I wasn't listening. That is until
an hour later when, with darkness only two hours away, Harvey's Cessna headed back to
the lodge while we fitted the outboard engine on to Keith's boat and set off towards his
outpost camp at Yathked where the mighty Kazan River joins the Ferguson immediately
above Kazan Falls, a maelstrom of crashing white water and granite boulders holding
grayling averaging over 2 lbs and some of the world's largest lake trout which grow to 60
lbs and more.

As Harvey was due to fly the film crew out early the following morning to meet us, our
wellbeing would not be considered until then, which was just as well because within an

hour of setting off in the direction of Yathked in our way was an enormous ice floe across which clear water could only just be seen on the other side. And while I was thinking do we go around or across it, Keith gunned the boat up on to the foot-thick ice floe and cut the engine. Whereupon we got out and proceeded to lug the surprisingly easy to pull 18 foot hull (despite its weight of over 600 lbs) in the direction of clear water, Keith at the front and Martin and I on each side. No problem at all, that is until quite suddenly the formidable and hitherto reassuring 23 stone figure of Keith Sharp disappeared through the ice in a resounding crash that would have done a bull elephant proud. The boat lunged forward into the jagged hole made by Keith and so Martin and I jumped in and quickly grabbed the floundering buccaneer by his collar when he bobbed up, who with help of scrambling trunk-like legs on to a piece of thick ice, rolled over into the boat at the first attempt, completely drenched with a least a bathtub of freezing cold water.

It was now all but dark with a most breathtaking sunset ahead of purple, orange and yellows illuminating clear water still a long way off, and though technically summer the cold soon started to affect our exhausted condition. We had, however, no option whatsoever but to plod on and endure a mixture of rowing and pulling the boat across the ice, often making long detours walking along on the solid bright white areas. Wherever the ice was thin it was noticeably darker and when it could be felt cracking beneath our feet we transferred most of our weight onto the gunnels of the boat. When more and more gaps in the ice appeared Keith showed us how to use the boat as a bridge by pushing it across from one chunk of ice to another and then pulling it up on to firm ice once we had walked across to resume pulling. In areas large enough we pushed the boat in and used both paddles and engine for a few yards until walkable ice was located again, Keith then using the engine (all our strength had gone) to run the boat up and we continued on our way.

At around 2.00 in the morning I noticed the most strange phenomenon. Having always previously associated mosquitoes with stagnant water and the tropics here we were in the freezing cold and being unmercifully bitten by more mosquitoes than I had ever seen in my life before - or since incidentally. However, like all nightmares ours came eventually to an end when almost frozen to the bone and totally exhausted from walking, pulling and shoving, stinking of frozen sweat and after several hours of wondering whether we would actually be able to make it, we broke through the last of the ice floe into clear water with a mixture of cheering, hooting, whistles and laughter, appreciated unfortunately by no-one other than ourselves. We were, Keith told me later, over 300 miles from the nearest form of civilisation at Baker Lake and that being another small fishing lodge similar to the Ferguson set-up.

One of the many 20 lb plus lake trout we caught on big spoons and fly from the junction of the Kazan and Ferguson Rivers.

Within half an hour we made Keith's remote Yathked outpost camp and sorted out some bedding after a strong brew and warm up over a tiny spirit stove, and got our heads down until morning. What did we eventually catch? Well the fishing certainly lived up to Keith's promises with everyone in the crew actually catching lakers of 20 lbs plus, even from the shore on both spinner and fly.

SUCCESS AT AVON SPRINGS

Back at the beginning of June, I spent a really super day down at the prolific Avon Springs Trout Fishery near Salisbury shooting some footage for a fly fishing video on behalf of *Trout Fisherman* magazine. So with an immense amount of work to get through while the sunny weather held, I met up with the magazine's editors, Chris Dawn and Andrew James, plus contributor Charles Jardine, at 8.00 am for an early start. Which as it turned out was just as well, for although we were bang in the middle of what should have been the height of the mayfly season, those dainty little three-tailed aquatic flies knew better and were refusing to come off in hatches of sufficient size to make the trout start feeding with gay abandon. There is a name given to this particular time of the year and it is called 'duffers' fortnight', which suggests that anyone, regardless of their casting prowess, should be able to catch on the dry mayfly with absolute ease. Such is the gluttony of trout when the yearly mayfly cycle commences – which when you are trying to capture the gentle art on video, is something useful to have up your sleeve. In fact, only a week before, Chris and Andrew had made a recce trip to the fishery which comprises of two clearwater lakes plus a mile of the delightful upper Hampshire Avon (the very stretch incidentally once keepered by the legendary Frank Sawyer) and marvelled at how the brownies in the river were responding to their imitations. But as everyone knows, no two days fishing are ever the same, and so we decided to leave the dry fly fishing for after lunch – so hoping that the afternoon would provide some heavy hatches. And in the meantime, in order to put something bankable and quickly in the can so to speak, Charles Jardine and I made our way up to the top lake which is a sprawling, thoughtfully excavated stillwater interspersed with willow-clad islands and long reed-lined promontories. Owner Barry suggested that behind the top island in the deep water of where a spring percolates through the chalk bed was probably our best spot for some hectic footage, and he was not wrong. Even before I could finish delivering an introduction to camera, Jammy Jardine was into a good rainbow on one of his special long-tailed damsel nymph tyings, and for a good hour several nice rainbows came our way, the best to Charles at a shade over 8 lbs. On one hilarious occasion we actually each hooked into trout at the same time. It seemed that fishing fine with just a 4 lb tippet and long 16 foot leaders was really paying off during the early morning, but when the sun finally filtered through, turning the water to glass, those rainbows simply weren't interested in our artificials. A changeover to the lower lake produced a pretty 4 lb rainbow for Andrew James, once a gentle wind got up and rippled the surface, but it was hard work. So we decided to capture some aquatic insect life for Charles to identify and show in close up, relating each creature to the imitative patterns he would later tie. Unfortunately I wasn't to know the camera would fall from its mount on the high set of tripod legs while I squatted below to hold the bucket steady for cameraman Paul Bennett to focus on what was inside. Bang – all suddenly went black as 30 lbs of Sony Betacam hit me fair and square on top of my head, ramming my lower half from just above to just beneath the surface. The wet backside I could live with and even the egg-sized lump on my skull, but as I fell clutching the bucket to my chest our catch of creepy crawlies either went back into the water or into my waistcoat pocket. It's the first time I've ever had a pocket full of live shrimps. An hour later the guys had netted out another batch and we shot the nature insert without further mishaps.

With just three hours of the afternoon remaining it was Chris Dawn's challenge to produce something on an imitation mayfly from the river and he chose an acute bend where several superb brown trout could be seen sucking down the occasional mayflies as they hatched. Although some interest was shown, not until Chris swapped the dry pattern for a slowly sinking mayfly nymph did the action start. They were in fact far more interested in the emerging insects and Chris promptly accounted for an exquisitely spotted brownie of around 1½ lbs which took just a couple of inches beneath the surface. Then all hell broke loose when what I judged to be the largest brownie on the bend snapped up the nymph, making Chris run downstream along the bank in an effort to keep up. It came crashing out completely clear of the water on several occasions and led Chris a real song and dance on his lightweight brook rod outfit for a good 10 minutes, which for the camera was unbelievable footage. Its weight – 8 lbs plus – and one of the most beautifully spotted brown trout I have ever seen. Incidentally, Avon Springs is available on a day ticket to anyone.

TARRANT TAMES THE TROUT

With the check-in time at Gatwick for 6.30 a.m. on the Wednesday morning (a Zambian tiger fish adventure ahead), driving down and back again on Tuesday the day before from Norfolk to Hampshire and the famous Dever Springs Trout Fishery seemed all too much. But I went anyway. And was I glad I did, arriving in good time to meet owner Con Wilson, who proudly showed us over the new fishery lodge (to cater for corporate events) which overlooks the largest of Dever's two clearwatered, well stocked trout lakes. Trout fanatic Chris Tarrant was due to arrive later for the official opening and sit-down lunch after finishing his programme on Capital Radio, which gave us four hours of splendid, if somewhat difficult, fishing before things got under way. My last visit here to Dever Springs, which incidentally is just off the A303 Andover road in Hampshire, was back in the middle of February. And I can remember wondering at that time why more fly fisherman do not enjoy sport during the winter months. Tradition has it, of course, that they prefer to avoid frozen hands from stripping in a fly line during the cold months, and the trout's spawning cycle causes hen fish to be swollen with eggs and cock fish to go black and rather manky from fighting each other. So everyone leaves well alone until the spring. But at Dever Springs, a trout fishery stocked only with triploids which are neither male nor female and stay silver all year, packing on weight as opposed to eggs and milt, sport can be enjoyed all year through. You can have both brown trout and rainbow trout

A lovely brace of double figure 'rainbow' and 'blue rainbow' trout for angling fanatic Chris Tarrant and me.

triploids. The egg is simply given pressure-shock treatment after fertilisation, resulting in a sexless trout which fights like stink and looks always to be in tiptop condition regardless of the season.

Now, however, the water temperature was way up accompanied by an exceptionally hot and sunny morning, making Dever's trout extremely finicky. I offered an immaculately tied size 10 olive damselfly nymph to more than a dozen sizeable rainbows without so much as the turn of a head. Contrary to popular belief the trout of small, regularly stocked, clear stillwater day-ticket fisheries do not simply crawl up the rod. The observant fly fisher, however, does have the opportunity to watch his quarry's reaction to various imitations. With some hefty double-figure fish present I couldn't step down too light, but swapped the 6 lbs leader for a fluoro carbon point of just 4 lb test and the inch-long damselfly nymph for a hot orange size 12 beaded buzzer only half the size. The secret was then to plop in the lightly leaded imitation well ahead of a patrolling trout and when it had descended to the same depth, twitch it gently.

Fortunately for me the first likely customer was a big 'blue' rainbow (an interesting colour variant) which made a beeline for the tiny buzzer and sucked it in greedily. I lifted the rod tip smartly and wham – off shot the trout like a bat out of hell ripping line from the reel in several screeching surges. Lovely stuff and a good 10 minutes elapsed before I was able to net the beauty. What a fascinating spectacle to witness through Dever's incredibly clear water and my largest blue ever at 11¾ lbs; arguably the closest of all rainbow trout variants to the North American 'steelhead'. After a couple of standard rainbows both pushing the 6 lbs mark I wandered over to try the larger lake where, would you believe I, went and successfully stalked another 'blue', also over 10 lbs. Two double-figure blue rainbows in one day is something I doubt I'll ever repeat. Whilst playing the second beauty, Tarrant arrived on the opposite side of the lake so I allowed my fish to crash about heavily just to wind him up. But he only went and hooked a double-figure rainbow on his third cast, having borrowed a rod from friend Brian Furzer for a quick session prior to the opening of the lodge. I don't know how he does it.

CHALKSTREAMING FOR EVERYONE

A beautifully spotted River Test brownie for Andy Davison, taken at 'mayfly time'.

I get the impression from talking to some anglers that in terms of cost and accessibility the delight of chalkstream fly fishing is way beyond their reach. And while it's true to say that the most prolifically stocked and well-keepered stretches of river on the Test and the Itchen could set you back between £1,000 and £2,000 for a seasonal rod (still less than a heavy smoker spends annually) there are in fact numerous day-ticket fisheries offering a mixture of both lake and chalkstream trouting. Avington Trout Fisheries near Itchen Abbas in Hampshire for instance is a prime example and includes an extremely pretty stretch of the diminutive River Itchen. Also in Hampshire famous big fish water Dever Springs at Barton Stacey also has grayling and trout in the adjacent and clear-flowing River Dever. Before you leave Hampshire, the renowned Orvis Tackle Shop in Stockbridge high street can arrange day-ticket fly fishing on several well-keepered local beats of the Test between Bossington and Timsbury and on a marvellous piece of the Itchen at Kingsworthy. During the mayfly season is the best time by far to visit these unique chalkstreams.

In Berkshire the famous upper reaches of the River Kennet and its narrow carriers also provide superlative sport with trout and grayling for the price of a day-ticket. Try the prolific Barton Court fishery a few miles upstream of Newbury. Fancy one more? OK, how about Avon Springs fishery near Salisbury in Wiltshire which boasts a wonderful stretch of the Upper Acon, famous for grayling and brown trout, in addition to two clearwater lakes, the river being adjacent to the very beat where legendary Frank Sawyer was once river keeper.

So you see, chalkstream trouting is certainly not restricted to toffs only. Today fly fishing everywhere from reservoirs to the most enchanting chalkstream is now within reach of us all. And to fully enjoy what these little rivers have to offer, a $7 - 7\frac{1}{2}$ foot brook rod, coupled to a size 3 or 4 floating line is I think imperative. With a longer rod and heavier lines you'll only want to cast further and that is not what chalkstream trouting is all about. Far better to keep well back from the marginal growth and visually stalk fish at close range by using short, accurate casts presenting a dry fly or upstream nymph. Remember too that purposefully casting low and sideways not only scares fish far less and reduces entanglement with overhead trees, it allows you to present the artificial to trout occupying those choice but awkward lies beneath overhanging branches.

As always with chalkstream trout, particularly brownies, if the artificial is not inhaled on the first or second drift through, it is much less likely to be taken with each successive cast. So endeavour to place the dry fly or nymph accurately on your first shot slightly further upstream than would seem necessary (to take into account the deceptive speed of flow in these clear-flowing rivers) and slightly to the side (your side) of the target fish. Get it right and when presenting a weighted nymph you will be rewarded by observing the trout's jaws momentarily open to inhale the artificial as it purposefully moves across the current to do so.

CHALKSTREAM MAGIC

I always relish the opportunity of stalking quality-sized trout. This hefty rainbow fought like stink in the diminutive River Anton at Rookesbury Mill.

What I like most about famous Rookesbury Mill Trout Fishery, situated beside the A303 road on the outskirts of Andover in one of the prettiest parts of Hampshire, is that in addition to two clearwater lakes, visitors may also try their hand at stalking both brown and rainbow trout in a charming overgrown chalkstream, namely the tiny River Anton which meanders between the lakes.

It's wonderfully exciting day-ticket trouting as friend Andy Davison and I found out when accepting Nick Carbury's kind invitation to an open day a few weeks back, along with other keen fly fishers such as Chris Tarrant, Peter Cockwill and Chris Sandford. Nick's hospitality is second to none and both Andy and I accounted for several hard-fighting rainbows in the 4 – 6 lbs class before a splendid lunch was served.

The trout didn't exactly come easily, however, because it was a chilly, overcast morning when very little was working or showing within the upper water layers. I cannot ever remember a year when I have needed to wear a thick jumper beneath my fly waistcoat on so many occasions. As for technique, well my decision of presenting weighted nymphs on one of the new Cortland 444SL ghost-tip fly lines, which incorporates a 15 foot crystal-clear monofilament sinking tip at the business end, really did the business. Quite simply those trout wanted the artificial presented horizontally and slowly, 3 – 5 feet down, and in no way would they chase upwards. The strange on/off spring weather this year has an awful lot to answer for.

After lunch I decided to stalk the crafty brownies in the River Anton and on upstream nymphs took two beauties, the best weighing around $3^{1}/_{2}$ lbs plus a rainbow pushing double figures. And what a superb scrap such monsters put up in the narrow stream. On an 8 foot brook rod, size 5 line and a 3 lb tippet, it is indeed difficult to think of a situation where light tackle is more rigorously put to the test.

The following morning Andy and I visited the legendary River Test near Stockbridge, where we in fact stayed overnight. Fortunately the weather changed for the better and by 10.00 a.m. the sun was fast burning through the low cloud cover. Perfect conditions for stalking River Test brown trout in the traditional way with the dry fly. It is ironic really in that during the cold and frosty winter months when I travel down from Norfolk to Hampshire specifically to fish the very same stretch of river for her ladyship the grayling, on long-trotting tactics using maggots or red worms, the trout are a positive nuisance. When spring arrives, however, and you try to fool them on an artificial fly, these very same trout seem to have grown eyes in the back of their heads and are incredibly suspicious of just about every pattern presented to them.

The terrestrial-born long-legged hawthorn fly was hatching from the adjacent fields in reasonable numbers during the morning and my first two brownies, including a wonderfully spotted $2^{3}/_{4}$ pounder came to hawthorns. A changeover first to an iron blue followed by a pale watery produced nothing despite a few olives coming off, but when I put up a small grey wulf which beautifully represents the mayfly, another two brownies plus a small grayling came along, despite any show of naturals. Chalkstream trouting is certainly an education. I only wished I lived closer so I could enjoy fishing the dry fly more often.

A TROUTING HAVEN IN THE TAS VALLEY

Having written books and articles about where to fish in Norfolk and Suffolk for over 30 years now, I thought I knew of every wet nook and cranny that holds fish within the county. After a recent trip to Grove Water day-ticket fishery, however, which lies just upstream from Duffields Mill in the Tas Valley on the A140 road less than 10 miles south of Norwich, it appears not. This veritable jewel, totally hidden away in the Rainthorpe Estate owned by Mark Bedini, comprises of around half a mile of the delightful, ever-twisting River Tas and a $2^{1}/_{2}$ acre manmade boomerang-shaped clearwater lake. The river itself is narrow, shallow and still wonderfully overgrown although much of its rebirth as

Grove Water fishery manager Tony Smith stalks wild brownies along the charming little River Tas. We first fly fished together over 30 years ago.

a brown trout fly fishery is due to the clearance of pathways, riffle making and weed planting carried out by the fishery's manager, Tony Smith, who just happened to be an old friend of mine. Tony had in fact been on to me for ages to come and view and I only wish I'd taken up his offer earlier for I quickly became lost in a totally unspoilt wildlife haven.

With brook rod in hand I followed Tony through a deeply wooded valley, spotting brownies plus the odd shoal of roach and dace in the clear water of the tiny River Tas. Amongst an interesting variation of holding pools, glides, riffles and gravel runs between weed beds there exists a natural head of wild brown trout to which small stock fish are periodically added. Superb catch and release stalking for the river trouter who wants a challenge instead of filling his creel. In the lake, which is regularly stocked with rainbows to 5 lbs plus, visitors may take a four fish limit for the price of a £20 day ticket (which includes the river) and then continue fishing catch and release. Tony insists upon unhooking with forceps in the water so trout are neither handled nor netted, a policy I personally should like to see more fisheries adopt. Depths vary between 3 and 10 feet in basically a long and narrow lake with islands and promontories providing numerous movement areas. The banks are lined with beds of bulrush, sedge, yellow iris and reed, and I particularly liked the odd bed of water lily both white and yellow which provide canopy habitats during the heat of the day. There are excellent hatches of mayfly, sedges, damsels, dragonflies and in the evening buzzers in plenty. In fact I started fishing black buzzers, went on to emergers and found the best taking pattern by far (on the day) to be a small Montana fished slowly and erratically a couple of feet down. In a two hour spell Tony and I accounted for a dozen or so really hard-battling rainbows to around 3 lbs, and I thoroughly enjoyed a real surprise in the form of two immaculately scaled roach of about 3/4 lb apiece. These, believe it or not, are apparently present up to the 2 lbs mark. It really was fabulous sport on my little 8 foot brook rod, size 4 floating line, and long 3 lbs leader, black flies definitely being order of the day. Only five anglers per day are allowed at Grove Water Fishery, taking into account both river and lake.

GETTING CLOSE TO THE ACTION

Living as I do in the county of Norfolk, which boasts not a single reservoir, means that to enjoy those long exhausting, exciting battles with rainbow trout, I must motor due west into Cambridgeshire and Northamptonshire where Anglian Water is exceptionally well represented in trout fisheries by Graffham, Rutland, Pitsford and Ravensthorpe reservoirs. Just recently I decided to sample what was on offer by visiting Ravensthorpe, which is not only the oldest drinking water reservoir in Britain, it is also the oldest reservoir trout fishery dating back to 1891. My host was Nathan Clayton, head warden of both nearby Pitsford and Ravensthorpe reservoirs, whose knowledge of these fascinating stillwaters is second to none – so I was in good hands.

Drifting by boat with the wind across the reservoir, from the western to the eastern shoreline, was Nathan's recommendation - and he was spot on. With massive hatches of damselflies showing during our visit, both the emerging and nymph patterns were accepted readily on our floating line set-ups. And we enjoyed a field day. Incidentally, anyone can book a day's bank or boat fishing at Ravensthorpe, which promotes 'catch and release' trouting. For a £17 day permit you can keep two fish to eat, whilst gently releasing all others caught using a barbless hook which is mandatory, or you can take out a sporting catch and release everything ticket for £14 plus £10 for the boat. It all depends I guess whether you want to return with a trout supper or not, or really have your string continually pulled.

Most of the rainbows taken by Nathan and me averaged between 2 and 3½ lbs and fought like stink, though one lucky angler took to the scales a brace of double-figure rainbows, the heaviest a new fishery record of over 16 lbs, so a monster is always on the cards.

By now I was contemplating yet another option on offer at Ravensthorpe – float-tubing. Feeling rather like a 'redundant duck' kitted out in chest waders, flippers and a 'Steve Parton float tube' I slowly reversed into the water from a concrete ramp (it's impossible to walk straight ahead wearing flippers) to test this, the latest angling craze to hit our trout reservoirs. Basically the fly fisherman sits within an inflated rubber ring (hence the float tube label) and is fully manoeuvrable via thrusts from his flippers, and can literally go anywhere up or down the reservoir – it's fabulous. I had just an hour to enjoy this unique experience in the late afternoon, accounting for no fewer than three plump rainbows plus a couple of missed pulls, all to a fritz damselfly nymph. Frankly I just loved being out there and can't wait for another excuse to go 'tubing'. I think it is being actually in the water close to the quarry that makes float tubing so appealing.

Sharing a boat on Ravensthorpe Reservoir with head warden Nathan Clayton didn't do my chances of hooking into rainbow trout any harm at all. We had a field day.

THE LAND GOD GAVE TO KANE

A canoe full of gill-netted lake trout are admired by young Innu Indians, beside the trappers tent in which I slept at Labrador's Kamistastin Lake.

Following a long haul from Heathrow to Halifax, plus internal prop jet flights from Halifax to Deer Lake and from Deer Lake to Goose Bay, my journey into the province of Newfoundland and Labrador was almost at an end – but not quite. I was met at Goose Bay by Englishman Jon Cumming of Friends of the Innu UK, and following a quick tour of the Innu Indian settlement, we met Canadian photographer Ted Ostrowski, and loaded all our gear into a De Havilland Beaver float plane – our final destination being Mastastin Lake. Called 'Kamastastin' by the Innu Indians who for over 8000 years have laid claim to this land, the lake is situated due west of David Inlet and south of the 56th parallel. Measuring some 14 miles by 8 it is a massive sheet of cold, unbelievably clear water, but more importantly it is home to huge lake trout and most exquisitely coloured arctic char. The climate of the area is in fact sub-arctic, where the ice and snow which covers everything all winter doesn't melt until June and then starts freezing over again come the end of September. Until being encouraged into living within government-run settlements the Innu led a completely nomadic life for thousands of years, hunting porcupines, bear, goose and caribou in addition to catching and smoking fish. Labrador does, in fact, boast the largest concentration of caribou in the world, estimated at in excess of half a million animals, but few Innu hunt them now. Suckered into an easy, predictable but boring life in the settlements, the nomadic self-supporting ways of these gentle Indians is fast eroding, with the result that alcoholism and suicide are very real problems. As in so many situations the world over, from the Australian Aboriginals to American Indians, their unique culture has been repressed by the greed of the white man. The Innu, however, are fighting back and hoping to set up country wilderness camps for hunting and fishing to attract tourists, which is more or less where I come in, having been invited by the Innu to help research fishing potential of the Kamistastin lake and river system.

During the two hour flight from Goose Bay to Kamastastin where our guides, John Pierre Ashini and ex-pat Tony Jenkinson, had gone ahead to set up camp, my eyes were continually drawn to the wilderness through the clouds several thousand feet below. And I immediately contemplated the immortal words used by the famous explorer Jaques Cartier who described Labrador as 'the land God gave to Cain'. It certainly did look cold, harsh and forbidding.

The roads ended only a few miles north of Goose Bay leaving a true wilderness land mass best described as being similar to a mixture of the Falkland Islands and British Columbia, where I fished several years back. And though in midsummer, areas of snow could still be seen. Water in the form of lake and river systems was everywhere, interspersed with tundra, bog, forests of black spruce, birch and red willow, and I wanted to put the plane down everywhere so I could sample it all. Thousands of square miles of virginal game fishing. There was, however, time enough for we were soon skipping over waves at the eastern end of Kamastastin Lake where three white tents and a pile of cut logs were the only sign of civilisation I had seen during our 250 mile flight – talk about being isolated.

We were warmly greeted by John and Tony and their families who much preferred the isolation of Kamastastin to the inherent problems of government settlement life and shown to our trapper-style tent where a traditional carpet of spruce tips had been arranged to cover the ground. With a basic iron stove for both warmth (at night) and cooking, it took us no time at all to fall into the Innu way of life, and our very first meal consisted of smoked arctic char.

During the following week we grid-searched the marginal contours along the lake's shoreline with my portable fish finder/sonar unit and found that in places the lake floor actually ran off the 120 foot depth limit, less than the equivalent distance out from overhanging cliff faces. But although quite awesome to contemplate, the lake's depth did fluctuate enormously and by far the best hot spots for char and lake trout were where rivers entered in relative shallows of between 5 and 20 feet. Here we caught on both wet fly and spoons superbly coloured char to 8 lbs and lakers to over 15 lbs. But in truth during a week on Lake Kamastastin you can only scratch the surface, my favourite location being at the lake's outlet where it becomes the Kamastastin river which cut through a steep-sided pine-stacked gorge. Here the arctic char provided unbelievable fights on a wet fly or on lures in the countless pools, the most efficient lure by far being an 18 gram toby. But I do warn anyone planning such a trip during August that in addition to mosquitoes, you have the fierce biting black fly to contend with. Frankly it's not everyone's cup of tea but I loved it. Sadly there is no happy postscript to this report, because due to the discovery of an incredibly rich nickel deposit at Voseys Bay there is a Canadian government plan to dam Lake Kamastastin across its outlet to provide power in the form of hydro-electricity.

Now far be it from me to stop progress but which is more important – the Innu Indians re-establishing their culture in the land they have nomadically roamed for thousands of years, or the get-rich-quick attitude of Uncle Sam? I'll leave you to decide. Either way, if you are interested in combining great fishing with a real chance to get away from it all and don't mind roughing it, then Labrador is your kind of province.

GET YER BOOBIES OUT

So called because there is a pair of buoyant polystyrene balls tied in at the head end, the colourful range of fly patterns affectionately known as 'boobies' work wonderfully well early on in the season when the water is cold. It's all to do with water temperatures really and in which depth band or layer the trout are working. In large stillwaters like reservoirs and vast windswept lakes for instance, which take some while to warm up once winter's over, right now the trout are more than likely still to be holding station deep down close to the bottom. The same could apply to gravel pit complexes where depths exceed 15 feet. And it is a worthless exercise retrieving a lightly weighted, imitative nymph just a couple of feet beneath the surface in water 20 feet deep, when most of the trout are still actively feeding within just a few feet from the bottom, and subsequently loath to chase upwards

Big 'reservoir' rainbows hooked deep down on 'boobies' put up an incredible scrap.

into the higher top water layers.

This is why the 'booby' really produces during the early season when other patterns do not, simply because it works in reverse to all other flies which rise when being retrieved. The booby works downwards towards the bottom when you pull, because the heavy sinking line is actually below it lying along the bottom, causing your booby to quickly float upwards when you pause due to its pair of buoyancy balls. But remember, whether boat or bank fishing, if presenting boobies it is essential to allow the line to reach bottom before attempting to work the fly, so use a W.F Hi D fast sinker which gets straight down and, more importantly, stays there ironed to the bottom throughout the retrieve. Standard and most other sinking lines will not have the same effect – believe me. You'll soon know if the line has landed and is working along the lake bed, because it tends to collect the odd particle of silt and weed. If in doubt, however, cast out and put your rod down for 30 seconds. One minute should suffice in depths of 25 feet plus – sit on your hands if need be. Then commence the retrieve, but don't walk away from your rod. On numerous occasions I've experienced big fish nobble the booby 'on the drop' and even whilst it's been hanging there suspended completely motionless above the line prior to starting the retrieve.

A party piece often practised by my old mate, the late Trevor Housby, was to cast a booby out, rest his rod against the marginal sedges or reeds and simply sit back waiting for the reel to start screaming. Hardly fly fishing true but it worked with deadly effectiveness everywhere we fished together.

I find the most effective retrieve for really cold conditions is to inch the booby back in short, steady pulls between just 2 and 5 inches, with a long pause between each. Just enough movement for the marabou tail feathers to emit a tantalising pulse or two. So make each cast last a long time. I think this works best because obviously the trout is not going to give chase as such if the fly has moved but a few inches. Indeed it doesn't need to. One gulp and the artificial is history. It is the tantalising sudden downwards and upwards movement of the suspended booby which catches the instant attention of cruising trout in clear water, particularly rainbows. And the secret of this technique is that during the retrieve, which might take several minutes to complete from casting to recasting, at least one or two fish may be cruising along through the same depth band within sight of this strange and succulent looking food item.

To ensure your booby is presented within mere feet of the bottom down in depths of 30 feet and more, reduce leader length to between 3 and 5 feet. When trout start to move into higher water layers as they might do on a bright, sunny day, then increase leader length and experiment with various coloured boobies accordingly until action occurs. My favourites are black or orange. As most of the line follows the contours of the lake bed and drapes down from the surface in a huge bow up to the rod, there is absolutely no chance of whacking into short bangs and pulls as you would whilst surface fishing with a floating or an intermediate line. Fortunately, however, most trout swallow the booby as though it's the last imitation in the lake, resulting in really strong takes, the heavily sunken leaded line helping to set the hook as the trout moves off.

BROWNIE BATTLE TO REMEMBER

At a time when much of my local, once roach rich, River Wensum between Norwich and Fakenham is suffering badly from chronic water abstraction, over-eutrophication through farming chemicals, silting and cormorant predation, it is indeed nice to know that at least one man is doing something to improve this, the loveliest of Norfolk's rivers. That man is friend Basil Todd, owner of Wensum Valley Hotel, Golf and Country Club in Taverham, six miles west of Norwich City, where visiting anglers and golfers can now stay (two day

Having sucked in a mayfly nymph along a fast, gravel run, this 6 lb Wensum 'brownie' took me all over the river. Lovely stuff.

minimum period) and enjoy a most breathtaking view of rolling hills down the valley between carefully manicured greens, with the River Wensum meandering through lush water meadows at the bottom. Incidentally, those who stay here also have access to several well stocked lakes and ponds controlled by the hotel.

Naturally I went along for the superb fishing that ex-farmer Basil has now created over the past eight years by thoughtful man management. With the help of a JCB several large riffles have been made by heaping mounds of the gravel bed, for years hidden beneath silt, to within a few inches of the surface. At these locations the river has also been widened to ensure the water flows fast and bubbly, full of oxygen, to attract quality brown trout which are periodically stocked. This re-creation of habitats has a most important secondary benefit in that coarse species use these same riffles as spawning sites, and as I walked along huge shoals of fry were evident throughout the entire $1^{1/2}$ mile beat – a most heartening sight. In addition, a huge network of clogged-up drainage dykes just off the river have been opened up, deepened and landscaped and stocked with roach which should, in the future, help to supplement the river's dwindling roach population, judging by the amount of fry I saw. What with the planting of willows on the bends to both consolidate the banks during winter flooding and provide shelter for groups of large chub with which this part of the Wensum is prolific, the future looks bright indeed.

But how did my fly rod and I fare? Well, starting at the downstream end and slowly working my way upriver peering into every likely-looking run through polaroid glasses, it was my intention to single out trout using the upstream nymph – a size 10 mayfly nymph. There were in fact one or two mayflies coming off, but nowhere near enough to start the trout rising. Due to some work being carried out a few miles upriver water clarity was less than 2 feet and in some of the deeper runs I was fishing totally blind, watching the end of the fly line as the current brought my leaded nymph back down the run. The first take produced a 6 inch out-of-season chub and from a deep bend immediately upstream came another which I immediately slipped back gently. But what a chub - it was well over 5 lbs. I shall have to visit the fishery again once the season starts on 16th June because I saw numerous specimen chub which are known to run well in excess of 6lbs. Basil tells me he has also seen large barbel taking up residence in some of the deep, swift gravel bottom runs immediately upstream of the riffles. So all his hard work in creating both a trout and coarse fishery has obviously paid off. As indeed it did for me whilst making my way back downriver, having pulled the nymph from the lips of a brownie I judged to be the better part of 6 lbs halfway along the beat. Boy, was I sick.

So after giving it a rest for an hour I crept into position again several yards below where it was last holding station just out of the fast water immediately below a wide riffle. It had returned, and following a couple of refusals it suddenly snatched the mayfly nymph. Then all hell broke loose as it went careering across the wide shallow bar, sending specimen chub from between the weed beds which I hadn't seen, in all directions. The fight of a big river brownie - and Basil tells me they have been caught and returned here to over 8 lbs is usually quite spectacular. This fish was no exception, one minute crashing through the shallows and the next screaming line from the reel making 20 yard dashes downriver. It was a battle to remember with a superbly spotted cock brownie that I quickly returned without weighing. My original estimate of 6 lbs plus was if anything conservative.

GUDGEON AND TROUT

I experienced a wonderfully nostalgic weekend just recently with an old friend, vintage fishing tackle enthusiast Chris Sandford, down in deepest Sussex on his local stretch of the River Rother, catching brown trout and, believe it or not, gudgeon - yes, gudgeon. Exactly how long ago it was when I purposefully set out to catch this lovely little fish I shudder to think, because it's getting on for 50 years back. Kids in those days used porcupine quill floats and maggots were called 'gentles'. But don't ask me why. I used to catch gudgeon from the River Lea in North London where I then lived. The gravelly shallows were full of them and they were always bold biters.

So it was a real case of de ja vu last week, reliving my boyhood memories by catching

Having allowed me to fish from his lawn, antique tackle guru Chris Sandford even helps with the netting - and a superb 'brownie' to boot.

gudgeon on trotted maggots and watching the float bob and twitch before diving under. And those River Rother gudgeon were the largest I've ever caught anywhere. Some were as long as my hand honestly. I'm sure Chris fed them up. In addition to dace, roach, chub, barbel, perch and of course gudgeon, the Rother in the Petworth area also contains both brown and rainbow trout and much of it is available to all, simply by joining the local Petworth Angling Club. Chris has caught sea trout to over 9 lbs from this delightfully overgrown little river and was rather keen to see how I fared in one of his favourite weir pools presenting the upstream nymph.

After rather reluctantly packing the float rod and maggots away I put up an 8 foot brook rod, size 4 floating line and long leader tapering to just a 3 lb tippet. The chosen nymph was a dragon, goldhead beaded black buzzer, which had just enough weight to sink below the white water at the top of the weir sill before being carried by the flow through the main run to where I was positioned at the tail end of the pool. Now I love this sort of fishing which calls for short accurate casts and the loose line to be quickly gathered while eyes are glued to the leader where it joins the fly line on the surface.

On the second throw the leader tightened quickly when the nymph was halfway down the run and I pulled into an acrobatic and exceptionally hard-battling wild brownie of about 1½ lbs which just kept on going in the bubbly water until almost totally exhausted. After a short rest for a cuppa I then accounted for a rainbow of similar size and finished with an even larger, beautifully spotted brownie of over 2 lbs, all lovingly returned. By the smile on my host's face I had passed the Rother test, both in gudgeon and trout.

It was great fun to be fishing with Chris Sandford again, who is actually Britain's leading authority on vintage fishing tackle. At this year's Game Fair, through his tackle road show, Chris will be offering free valuations and advice on items brought to him by the public in return for fundraising donations in aid of SPARKS (Sport Aiding Medical Research for Kids). This worthy organisation is supported by sporting celebrities with events throughout the year and has since 1991 raised in excess of £7 million and funded over 100 medical research projects with associated equipment.

BROWN AND RAINBOW ACTION AFLOAT

Weigh-in time at famous Hanningfield Reservoir; a happy competitor displays one of the numerous big 'double figure' rainbows taken during the competition.

If you like getting away from it all and the thrill of boat fishing or the challenge of distance fly casting from the shore in big windswept stillwaters, then I'm certain you won't be disappointed with Hanningfield Reservoir, near Chelmsford in Essex, where a 6 fish day ticket limit (boats are extra) costs just £15. Because this picturesque SSSI fly-only-fishery, controlled by Essex and Suffolk Water Authority, not only covers a massive 900 acres, it has equally large trout to match. On the wall of the comfortable lodge is a photo of Hanningfield's record rainbow, a monster of 24 lbs, and no doubt there are very much larger specimens there for the taking.

Fish in the 16 – 20 lbs category are caught consistently throughout the season which opens in March and goes through until December. In fact I can think of no better venue within the British Isles for anglers hoping to catch their first double-figure trout. The number of quality trout here is simply enormous. What's more, they are small-headed, immensely deep-bodied, full-finned beauties with flanks of burnished silver that have actually grown on in the depths of the reservoir, from their original stocked size of around just 2 lbs, and do they fight!

My boat partner, Andy Davidson, was certainly impressed during a recent trip we made to Hanningfield, despite the potentially difficult conditions brought about by an entire week of successive sharp early-morning frosts, not exactly the kind of weather we expect for mid April. But we went anyway, partly because someone had landed a monster of 18 lbs 6 ozs only the day before and partly because as depths in the reservoir average in excess of 15 feet, and with large areas of between 20 and 45 feet, any sudden drop in air temperature rarely affects sport to the same degree as it does smaller shallow fisheries.

Hoping to get our string well and truly pulled, we decided to concentrate at the deeper water around the cages where anchored buoys are placed for the convenience of boat fishermen, which alleviates the pain of freezing cold fingers from hauling up the anchor chain each time you want to move position.

On past occasions I had fared well using a Hi D line presenting a buoyant 'booby' fly way down close to the bottom on a short 5 foot 8 lbs test cast. It is a slow, too methodical way of fly fishing for some but in deep cold water where the larger trout are more liable to be patrolling fairly close to the bottom I rate the effectiveness of 'booby' fishing very highly indeed. It is imperative, however, to be patient and wait for your entire Hi D (density) fast sinking line to lie on the bottom before commencing a ridiculously slow and erratic retrieve. That way you'll know the super-buoyant bobby is floating leader length directly above the bottom and jerking and twitching attractively downwards to each tiny pull of the retrieve. When you stop pulling the booby floats upwards again.

Now a take can literally happen at any time and unless the rainbow really swallows the fly and hooks itself against the weight of the line when it zooms off, as many do, you need to pull hard with your retrieving line and keep the rod bent in order for the hook not to fall out. I think it largely depends upon the aggression of the trout on the day. I've had many a big fish almost pull the rod out of my hand and days when it becomes infuriatingly difficult to keep fish on. And this was one of those days. In fact from our first dozen or so hits we landed but two rainbows. The hook pulled from what I thought was something really big, following a long run of several yards, but then takes became more solid and in quick succession I enjoyed quite exhilarating fights from two silver-bodied rainbows weighing 6 and 8 lbs respectively. Then it was Andy's turn, as he struck into three superb brown trout one after another, all between 3½ and 4½ lbs - what fabulous sport.

FLY OR SPINNER

It was indeed a pleasure to net this jumbo-sized rainbow for my old pal Susheel Gyanchand of Bangalore. On so many occasions has he arranged fabulous mahseer fishing for me in South India.

When fly fishing in clear water for trout that are being obstinate and not the slightest bit interested in delicately presented imitative patterns, I am sure that there are occasions when we each wish we could bend the rules and try a spinner or other artificial lure, maybe a worm even, and to hell with the purist approach. Well, just recently for the 160 anglers who took part in the Fred Neville Charity fishing competition at popular

Hanningfield Reservoir in Essex just off the A130 road, this wish was granted. Competitors at this lighthearted event, which incidentally raised £3750 to be split between the Littlehaven Children's Hospice Appeal and the Royal Marsden Breakthrough Breast Cancer Appeal, were permitted to both fly fish and troll or spin using artificial lures. In short only bait was banned, and the subsequent results were staggering to say the least, and not at all what you would expect.

Now I've got to be honest here and admit to taking what I thought was the easy option. Well, what with rain falling steadily for most for the day, coupled to the fact that I was playing host to my two buddies from Bangalore in southern India, the decision was made to leave the fly rods at home and put our faith in plugs, spoons and spinners. Whenever Susheel and Sachi take me mahseer fishing or wild boar shooting in India they lay everything on, and so I was keeping my fingers crossed they would enjoy the hard-fighting, specimen-sized trout of Hanningfield Reservoir, despite the miserable weather. I took along an assortment of gear from 8 foot fixed spool reel combos to single-handed Six Shooter baby multiplying reel outfits, plus three huge boxes of spinners and sinking, diving plugs. And from 9.00 a.m. to the finish at 4.00 p.m. we must have tried them all, with by far the most success coming to a 6 gram red and white 'Rattlin' rapala. The jittering, side-to-side action of this particular sinking diver which also emits rattles (hence its name) from a ballbearing-filled chamber, was unquestionably what those Hanningfield rainbows wanted on the day. But we had to work hard, continually varying depth until success came. Sometimes a take would come within a second or two of commencing the retrieve, having counted our lures down to depths in excess of 20 feet. On other occasions the trout were aggressively chasing fry near the surface and consequently would hit only within the upper water layers.

From around 20 or so hits we shared a final catch of 13 trout landed, the best just touching 7 lbs; though I cussed when the hooks pulled free from a real slab close to the boat, which looked well into double figures. With over 60 boats out, the most intriguing aspect of this quite unusual event was watching how anglers fared in the boats close to ours, because on the day those who stuck to their principles and fly fished, were the most successful by far. And presenting a buoyant booby on a short cast and Hi D sinking line, so it worked just above bottom, really sorted out the whoppers. Not our plugs and spinners. In fact the top fish of the day, which accepted a white booby, was a superbly conditioned rainbow of 20lbs $\frac{1}{2}$ oz and provided its captor, Mickey Dodkins from Rochford, Essex, with only the second 20-lbs-plus wild 'grown' on rainbow ever taken in the UK. What's more it was the first trout he had ever caught. I'm tempted to say 'beginners luck' here, but then Mickey's boat partner, John Hammonds, had earlier this year set a new British record at Hanningfield with a monster rainbow of 24 lbs $\frac{1}{2}$ oz. So someone knew what they were about.

On this most enjoyable day which ended after the weigh-in with a superb buffet compliments of the management, many competitors achieved personal bests and there were no fewer than 16 specimens over 10 lbs amongst the 1000 or so trout caught. Top trophy for the best bag went to Len Childs from Kent, with a total weight of 49 lbs 1 oz including a superb fish of 13 lbs 1 oz, and the best brace went to Peter Love of Essex and Suffolk Water with rainbows of 12 lbs and 12 lbs 7 ozs respectively. All I can say to the hard-working management team at Hanningfield, apart from 'Well done', is 'Will Wilson receive an invite next year?' because frankly I can't wait for this annual event to come round again. Incidentally Hanningfield is a day-ticket fishery which opens from 1st April to 11th December.

ANDY GETS A WHOPPER

Having stalked monster trout stocked into even small crystal-clear stillwater fisheries through polaroid glasses, to then hook and land a particular specimen by sight casting demands an enormous amount of stealth and cunning. Big rainbows especially appear an easy target when they adopt a particular route, and it would seem that any imitation dropped within their path of vision is going to be instantly inhaled. But not so, and the stalking fly fisherman must quickly learn from the trout's reaction to his artificial and adapt tactics accordingly to stand any chance of success.

Take a recent trip I made down to the renowned chalkstream-fed two lake day-ticket fishery at Dever Springs for instance, in the company of my old buddy Andy Davison. Our host, Con Wilson (no relation), owner of Dever Springs, had also invited along trout guru Bob Church and TV personality Chris Tarrant amongst a dozen or so enthusiasts – so the banter at least was guaranteed, and continued throughout the day broken only by a sit - down lunch at the local hostelry. That's what I like most about trouting, it's so civilised. Though someone eavesdropping on our conversations would perhaps give me an argument, but it's all great fun nevertheless.

We were, of course, all after the same goal, whopping great deep-bodied superbly spotted rainbow trout, ranging from around 5 lbs upwards to over 20 lbs. And it is, of course, even more frustrating not to catch when you can plainly see the very fish that would make your year. Twenty-pounds-plus rainbows look simply awesome through water as clear as gin, and after several hours of anticipation and frustration stalking a particular whopper, individual specimens are easily recognised. But it doesn't make them any easier to catch.

Most guests accounted for sizeable rainbows within the 6 – 10 lbs bracket including myself, the most effective patterns being damselfly nymphs and black buzzers. But I had absolutely no joy with a fish I nicknamed 'Jaws' which must have refused my imitations on a good dozen or so occasions.

Andy Davison, however, concentrating on the larger of the two lakes, adopted a cunning ruse to account for his largest rainbow ever. Presenting a heavily weighted 'Czech nymph' which was refused on a couple of occasions, Andy allowed the nymph to lie on the bottom whilst waiting for the trout to swim by again. And when it did he twitched the nymph upwards in front of the huge rainbow. Bingo! It was immediately engulfed and following an amazing battle went 18 lbs 4 ozs on the scales. Biggest specimen of the day.

CATCH AND RELEASE

An immaculately spotted, still-water brown trout for Norfolk fly fisherman Grant Kennedy.

There has always been indecision and no small amount of controversy amongst stillwater trout fishery owners about the rights and wrongs, indeed the ethics of catch and release. Is it right to crunch the barb of the hook down and release our trout or should all stocked fish be despatched for the table? Well, generally speaking, the explicit rules governing most fisheries do enforce the latter in order to maintain a healthy, continually changing stock of catchable trout. But then I am sure we have all been guilty at some time or another of bending down and slipping the hook carefully from a trout whilst it's still in the water, particularly in overstocked fisheries where there is a chance of returning home quickly having reached a four or five fish limit in as many casts. So what would a totally catch and release fishery be like? Well by complete coincidence just recently I was able to sample the fly fishing on two such waters within the space of a week or so, and very interesting they each proved to be.

The first is controlled by my good friend and top tackle manufacturer Mick Willis of Leighton Buzzard in Bedfordshire, and is little more than an acre, having been excavated at the foot of a small valley fed by crystal-clear spring water. Depths shelve to 15 feet and its oblong shape is nicely bordered by marginal sedges, reeds and overhanging willows. I was invited along by Mick and his wife Carol, who periodically stock a few fresh trout in the way of sizeable rainbows to make up for the occasional one taken for the table. A management policy that certainly seems to work because though spooky at times, using both black buzzers and weighted nymphs whenever the trout went deep to sulk, we three enjoyed a great morning's sport until lunchtime with rainbows to over 7 lbs – all released.

Obviously such a small water could not be maintained commercially and fished daily on a catch and release basis. After all, anglers want to catch fish and when the majority of the stock are spooked, hooked, lost or released (day after day) they simply clam up and refuse all offerings. But as Mick runs the lake on a small syndicate basis it is never overfished and thus maintains an enjoyable challenge. Equally enjoyable was the long-tailed bird sitting upon a fence across the other side of the lake which for the 20 minutes it moved from post to post I mistakenly thought was a young sparrowhawk. Then quite suddenly, in fact within a few seconds of Mick asking me what I thought it was, the bird said, 'Cuckoo, cuckoo,' and we both admitted it was the first we had ever knowingly 'seen'.

The second catch and release water I fished, situated in West Norfolk and managed by friend Grant Kennedy, is also little more than an acre which has been most thoughtfully excavated with a central island that is fishable from a narrow bridge. Thick reedbeds afford dense cover along sections of the bank and depths shelve to 14 feet in places. The water is cold, clear, pure and runs in from a powerful spring with almost the force of a fast-flowing stream exiting via the sluice end. But here's the best bit, all of the rainbows and most of the brown trout it contains are doubles. I was like a kid being let loose in a toyshop, except that I soon realised such a small stock of educated monsters, all of which had probably been caught if not hooked and lost and released before, were not going to be a pushover. In fact they inspected each and every tiny nymph I put before them with more caution than the craftiest carp.

I found the challenge most absorbing, especially watching their reactions to my artificials through the gin-like water with polaroid glasses. I wouldn't have believed rainbows could have been so obtuse and selective, but all had been stocked at just a couple of pounds close on five years before and having grown on to such large proportions within such a confined and food-rich fishery, were incredibly streetwise. They were also superbly proportioned with huge, spade-like tails and perfectly shaped fins.

With little hatching in the way of fly life other than a few terrestrial hawthorns, most of which were unfortunately being blown away from the lake, Grant stuck to working heavily weighted bugs down deep while I concentrated upon the surface layers and a slowly sinking pheasant-tail nymph, stalking individual fish which followed most distinct patrol routes. So rather than continually chase them around I kept well back and let them come to me. Not that they showed the slightest interest in my offerings. For three hours nothing – then within the space of 10 minutes Grant took a smashing brownie of close on 8 lbs and I banged into a superbly conditioned rainbow of $10^{1/4}$ lbs which sucked in my nymph on the drop. And that was it. The lake clammed up again. So in no way could catch and release on such a small lake be considered a viable proposition in commercial terms. Not that I'm worried – I just hope Grant invites me back again soon.

Jeanette Church not only ties superb flies, she also knows how to fish them effectively, as this brace of big 'double figure' rainbows from a southern stillwater proves.

GO ON, TAKE HER TROUTING

As a kid living in bomb-ravaged North London during the 1940s and 50s, I grew up believing that fly fishing for trout was the prerogative of the tweed-hatted brigade only. In fact not until I purchased my first fly fishing outfit at the tender age of 14 from Don's of Edmonton, did I realise that anyone can enjoy catching trout on artificial flies. Perhaps I suffered from inverted snobbery, a personality complex – or who knows what? But what I do know now is that those early formative years, whilst fly fishing along the upper reaches of Isaac Walton's River Lea where ironically there were few trout, taught me so very much about water craft: to wear polarised glasses and to creep and crawl stealthily, to catch roach, chub and the shy biting dace. In fact it taught me everything except how to catch trout though there is of course little difference. But at such a tender age how was I to know that particular part of the old River Lea contained next to no trout? I simply and naively assumed that if I presented an artificial fly a trout would result.

It was nevertheless a great apprenticeship and one which over 40 years on has stood me in good stead for catching numbers of the salmon and trout family wherever I fish all over the world. Because the simple truth is all species can be caught on artificial flies. And if anything, trout, due to their aggressive nature, are by far the easiest. Which brings me to the fact that nowadays many women are joining their husbands for a day out on the reservoir, river or lake to catch spotties. They find it both interesting and challenging with a meal or two thrown in by the end of the day. So guys, here indeed is a very real chance of luring the woman in your life to at least share your sport.

Candlelit dinners with a smoked trout entrée, pan-fried trout with almonds, poached fillet of rainbow covered with a mustard sauce, all could be yours. All you have to put up with every so often is the Mrs actually catching more or bigger trout than you do, but surely it's a small price to pay to keep your loved one happy, isn't it?

A prime example of such marital bliss must surely be my old pal and tackle manufacturer, Bob Church and his lovely wife Jeanette, from Northampton, both England international fly fishers no less. Both naturally catch lots of trout, lots of big trout, and I'm sure Bob won't mind me suggesting that Jeanette actually ties better-looking flies than he does.

So now that spring is most definitely in the air and with a good quality, versatile outfit of rod, reel and line, plus a selection of flies liable to set you back under £100 (certainly less than a cocktail dress) what excuse have you for not taking your lady trouting? Exactly!

DAMSELFLY NYMPHS RULE - OK

East Coast skipper Stewart Smalley, from Aldeburgh, and I spend more time together bass fishing from his 20 foot boat out of Orford than anything else. So I was pleasantly surprised just recently when he accepted my invitation down to Hampshire to fly fish for trout at the renowned John O'Gaunts fishery at Kings Somborne, two miles south of Stockbridge in the fertile Test Valley. I featured this particular, extremely well managed, trout fishery recently in Series 16 of my Anglia and Meridian Television series, *Go Fishing*. A shoot in which I tried for the first time a revolutionary new Cortland 'strike indicator' weight-forward floating line dubbed the 'Zebra' line, because it comprises of alternate 18 inch segments of black and white. With such distinct sections of line 'skating along the surface' as the trout sucks the nymph in, even the tiniest of pulls are visibly registered. And I was eager to try the line again at John O'Gaunts to ascertain whether its effectiveness was justified (I couldn't stop catching) or that I simply hit the trout in a silly mood.

On arrival at the fishery a good ripple covered the larger of the two lakes which was just as well for the water was painfully clear. Literally as clear as gin. Individual snails could be seen on the bottom 12 feet down in the calm lee of the lodge bank. So we elected to fish into the ripple along each side of the large island, where we expected trout to be less wary in acceptance of our artificials – a wise move. In my experience most lightly weighted patterns of imitative nymphs are likely to score in such clear water during the early season such as mayfly nymphs, stonefly nymphs, dragonfly nymphs plus, of course, leaded shrimps and corixa etc. But my first choice is usually an olive-bodied damselfly

*A jubilant Stewart Smalley displays
a colourful brace of John O'Gaunts
rainbows, taken on damselfly nymphs.*

114

nymph. I gave Stewart a 'slimline' damsel to try, and tied on to my 14 foot leader with a 5 lb point a bulkier damselfly imitation with a marabou tail. Frankly so long as we kept well back from the margins so as not to spook those following fish which decided only to grab hold at the last moment, it appeared that anything tied in olive and damselfly nymph sized, stood a chance of being nobbled, especially 'on the drop'. With some fish and all were beautifully proportioned rainbows in the 2½ - 5 lbs size bracket the slowly disappearing cast would merely 'twitch' a couple of inches, whilst others gave simply unmissable registrations on the 'Zebra' line.

I spent some time stalking a particularly large brown trout which looked all of 10 lbs plus. But he wasn't having any, having no doubt seen all the patterns a dozen times before. So to make things more interesting I scaled down to a lighter point and drifted a tiny black and orange buzzer through the surface ripple. This too brought response, though not as effectively as damselfly nymphs. Stewart tried small goldheads without a take and myself likewise with a black stonefly imitation. Those rainbows wanted olive damselfly nymphs all right and each and every one of them delighted us with several spectacular jumps following long, simply unstoppable exhilarating runs, screaming our lines out right down to the backing.

THE LURE OF 'BLACK'

Even the rainbow trout of small manmade fisheries can prove difficult to catch and show a surprising level of preference in certain conditions.

Take a recent trip I made into Buckinghamshire for instance, to meet up with tackle designer and manufacture Mick Willis at his own stillwater fishery. To start with, being a farm drainage reservoir of around an acre, nicely bordered by sedges and overhanging willows, the water had noticeably coloured up following several consecutive days of sunshine. So with depths averaging between 8 and 14 feet, a visibility of less than 12 inches was hardly conducive to hectic action and it immediately became apparent, following

Pal Mick Willis from Dunstable in Bedfordshire, heaves out a chunky 'double figure' rainbow, taken on a 'black fritz lead head' from his own still water fishery.

115

a sharp overnight frost accompanied by bright sunshine from our 10.00 a.m. start, that we would need to search the lower water layers.

With thick shoals of 2-inch-long rudd fry taking refuge along the margins I put up an olive fritz lead head and was delighted at the way it imitated these little fish upon which Mick had mentioned the larger trout feed. And with rainbows present reaching into mid/double figures, plus the occasional big brownie, I was confident of inducing pulls from short jerky retrieves once my artificial had descended to the taking level. Yet save for one fast hit when the hook point missed, after half an hour I remained troutless, despite searching all the middle to lower levels thoroughly.

Fortunes immediately changed, however, when I swapped the olive for a 'black' fritz with a confident pull on only the second cast. And as on so many occasions whilst trouting in heavily coloured water the dense colour of black outfished all others, simply I assume because as a silhouette the trout could see it more easily. Trout, remember, are looking up into the brightness of the sky whilst we are doing the reverse and peering downwards into a darkening scene.

I gently eased the fly from this first trout, a nice rainbow of around 6 lbs, following a superb tail-walking and head-shaking scrap while it lay still in the water at my feet (Mick practises a catch and release policy) and continued to enjoy some wonderful battles with Mick's larger rainbows. My best, a chunky specimen of around 14 lbs, actually ran the entire 35 yard floating line off the reel down to the backing before I could get it under control. What superb entertainment, yet within a couple of hours sport ended as abruptly as it had started. A common phenomenon on small waters due to the fact that a large proportion of the lake's trout had either seen or been fooled by our imitations. It was time for a liquid lunch!

TROUTING THAT'S SIMPLY MARVELLOUS

Narborough Trout Lakes 'Big Fish Day', held annually at the beginning of October, is a competition event many specialist East Anglian fly fishermen really look forward to and with good reason. The four, tree-lined clearwater lakes were stocked with a larger proportion of whoppers than usual, providing everyone amongst the 69 anglers who entered with a very real chance of hooking into a double-figure rainbow. Much has to do with the quality of water at this friendly day-ticket fishery enthusiastically run by the Pritchard family and situated just off the A47 road 10 miles from King's Lynn.

Fed by the pure clear water of the diminutive River Nar bordered by lush water meadows (there is in fact an enchanting 'nature walk' open to non-anglers), Narborough Trout Lakes offer superb sight casting and induced take trouting to the stealthy fly rodder who stalks individual trout through polaroid glasses, using weighted nymphs presented on a floating line. I was, therefore, rather taken aback as I walked around taking photographs before fishing myself, to observe so many anglers not wearing polarising glasses. I actually remarked to owner, Ray Pritchard, that had I driven halfway to the fishery and forgotten my fly box, I could always purchase a few imitations at the shop, but had I left my 'yellow lens' polaroids at home, I would have gone back for them. Such, in my opinion, is the importance of wearing polarising glasses. After all, if you cannot physically see the trout and more importantly their reaction to your imitation through clear water, you are at a complete disadvantage and obliged to fish virtually blind by continually casting and retrieving. As it was I managed to winkle out a 9 lb rainbow from beneath a huge willow

Russel Coulson gives a huge rainbow trout some stick. Hooked in Willow Lake at the famous Narborough Trout Fisheries, Norfolk, the monster, when finally subdued following a long battle, tipped the scales at 18 lbs 1 oz.

spanning Sovereign Lake, literally within minutes of creeping around. It inhaled a goldhead dragonfly nymph on the drop tied to a 6 lb point. I then moved on to Willow Lake where Phil Bareham, all the way from Ely in Cambridgeshire, accounted for two beautiful rainbows in quick succession. They weighed 10 and $13\frac{1}{2}$ lbs respectively. He was justifiably over the moon and took the Bruce and Walker prize rod for the highest aggregate of trout caught during the day at 37 lbs 3 ozs.

Much of Willow Lake was rippled by a strong wind making observation nigh on impossible, but at the southern end by the outlet a house-sized patch of calm surface permitted exact presentation to several monster rainbows which were regularly patrolling the area. Standing stock still beneath an overhanging willow I merely watched without casting for a good 15 minutes while a particularly deepset rainbow repeatedly ventured close into my own bank through a deep run. Upon its fifth or sixth visit I flicked out a black, leaded 'fritz' lure and obviously twitched it at the right moment to instigate an aggressive take. Weighing $14\frac{1}{4}$ lbs, this was a particularly pleasing specimen (my largest Norfolk trout ever) following a marvellous scrap. An hour later I invited a 10 lbs rainbow into grabbing hold but the largest rainbow I was to photograph weighed 18 lbs 1 oz and fell to the rod of Russel Coulson from Peterborough: a truly colossal creature which gave him an unforgettable scrap for over 15 minutes. The largest rainbow trout of the day incidentally, weighing a staggering 19 lbs was caught by Karl Miller.

FUN IN THE PUNT

Long trotting the Hampshire Avon for sea trout in the famous 'bridge pool' in the centre of Christchurch has become something of an annual October event for Leighton Buzzard tackle manufacturer Mick Willis and me. We purposefully book the 'punt' for the solitude and advantageous position it provides once we have pulled ourselves out into the middle of the fish-packed pool via a chain and pulley system. Things didn't initially go according to plan on a recent visit however. For starters, the local gardening department had freshly enriched the huge flowerbeds surrounding the pool with a layer of fertiliser made from both animal and human excreta apparently! And we nearly gagged whilst transporting our gear from the estate car to the punt. Then before we could stow everything on board, a contracting gardener started up his powerful strimmer and liberally sprayed grass cuttings over everything. There was no point in loading the punt for at least 15 minutes so I put my trotting rod together (already made up with float rig and secured at each end with elastic bands) and eased a piece of fluffy white breadflake covering a size 12 hook down beside the wall where, due to a high tide, there was round 5 feet of water over gravel. I missed the first bite but connected with the second, a nice thin-lipped grey mullet of around 3 lbs, before Mick had even threaded line through his rod rings. 'I'll get you back, Wilson', was his reply, although not in the way I'm sure he intended.

We had been finally settled in the pool for no more than half an hour when upstream came an Environment Agency maintenance boat with two guys on board, one clutching a large chainsaw. They then spent the next hour demolishing a huge tree caught against the upstream brick supports of the road bridge not 10 yards from where we sat. And, would

Long trotting for sea trout can prove both a fascinating and rewarding technique, as punt partner Mick Willis proves with a nice fish from the Bridge Pool on the Hampshire Avon in Christchurch.

you believe, amongst all the clatter a group of canoeists with their instructors paddled into the pool for a training exercise, one of them turning the canoe completely over. It was like Piccadilly Circus for a good hour at least. But they do say everything comes to he who waits and eventually the pool settled down to normality.

We first thought that there were few sea trout in the pool because our long-trotted maggots attracted nothing but dace, despite our going through the best part of a gallon to 'feed the dace off'. But once the tide had run off and started to flood again we started hooking into some hard-fighting sea trout between 2 and 3 lbs. What marvellous scraps they put up on trotting tackle compared even to mullet of the same size. And during our lunchtime break we accounted for several more nice mullet on float-fished breadflake. A great day after all.

HER LADYSHIP IS ALWAYS A CLASSY CATCH

In the past 25 years or so since I first started visiting the chalkstreams of Hampshire and Berkshire for her ladyship, the grayling, I've caught thousands of this wonderful species, which bites on the coldest of days even when dace and chub won't suck in a single maggot. When snow lays thick on the ground, when your fingertips are painful to touch, when all but the centre of the river is iced over and regardless of water clarity, the grayling still pulls

My long-time fishing buddy, the late Trevor Housby, displays a superb grayling caught long trotting a southern chalk stream during the autumn.

119

I caught this fabulous, thickset grayling of 2 lbs 11 ozs on long trotted maggots from the River Frome in Dorset - centre pin fishing at its finest.

your float under positively as it inhales a red worm or a couple of maggots. It is the one species that will bite when all else won't – regardless.

I've also fly fished, spun and worm fished in Canada's far north, in the province of Manitoba and the North West Territories in the Ferguson and Kazan River systems where 2 lb grayling are killed for shore lunch. They are that prolific. I've taken big grayling on fly, albeit whilst salmon fishing the Tweed at Kelso, and from the majestic Tay at Dunkeld whilst purpose-fully trotting for the species. But a real monster had always eluded me.

Where I live in Norfolk, not far from Norwich City, grayling these days are like rocking-horse droppings. To be honest, if my life depended upon catching a grayling locally there are a couple of fast, gravel-bottomed runs of my local River Wensum where, following some serious trotting for a few hours, I just might come up with a single grayling. But this hardly constitutes grayling fishing as I know it, or more importantly how I wish to enjoy it. And I have no problem whatso-ever in making a 300 mile round trip down south for a day's grayling fishing along the chalkstreams of Hampshire and Dorset, believe me.

When my old mate and one of the greatest British all-round anglers who ever long trotted, the late Trevor Housby, first took me grayling fishing on the River Test, I was like a boy in a sweetshop. I went like a bull at a gate at every swim. I photographed everything we caught, and I even took two large grayling home with me (they were unwanted on the exclusive trout beat of the Test we fished) for preserving. They weighed 1 lbs 10 ozs and 1 lb 14 ozs respectively and they stare down at me from their bow-fronted glass case high on my office wall as I write this. I feel proud of them because not only did I catch them, I also stuffed them. I later preserved a 2½ lb grayling that Trevor caught which still hangs on the wall in the house where his wife Ida and son Russ live. That grayling encompasses all our feelings not only for the angler we loved, but for this enigmatic species. I have caught many fish of over 2 lbs in weight since. Certainly too many by far to count, and those Canadian arctic grayling apart, which even at 3 lbs were commonly hooked, I had never landed one of over 3 lbs from an English river, not until a few weeks ago that is. So now I'm going to tell you about it.

Being a private beat of a famous chalkstream where brown trout rule OK, you'll forgive me if I decline to name this particularly prolific beat of the river Frome. Prolific, that is, in jumbo-sized grayling for the trout are nothing out of the ordinary, which is kind of strange. Now being both a chalkstream and a spate river I have always been puzzled why it throws up so many huge grayling. In looks and sheer breeding power Hampshire's River Test would seem to possess all the credentials for record-breaking grayling, dace, even roach potential, but not so whereas lesser known fast-flowing rivers, due to unidentified factors, have the ability to produce specimens of truly huge proportions. Anyway, here I was with good friends Trevor Stroud and Bruce Vaughan, enjoying a long -trotting session for grayling when the light values never climbed above a 30th at 2.8 (keen photographers will identify with our problems) throughout the entire day. Nevertheless, with the river running fast and fairly clear some quality grayling were on the cards. Despite our casual start following a late night and prolonged evening meal at a local Indian restaurant, we three systematically wandered the river the next morning trying numerous swims for perhaps 30 minutes or so at each run, before either scoring or moving on. And this, of course, is the way to treat grayling fishing. If they are having it a fish usually comes on your very first or second trot through.

On one particular acute bend, where the flow angles sharply across to the far bank leaving a defined crease on the side line along which to steadily guide the double maggot bait, an instant bite produced a superb grayling of 2 lbs 11 ozs. I expected nothing more but on the second trot through, gently holding back on the 7AA Avon float, the tip dipped positively again and when I struck the rod arched over to the vibrating pulse of what was obviously not a trout or grilse but a big grayling. It is the way they hang in the flow and twist whilst you try and force them upstream which makes you realise that on the end of your line, attached to just a 16 hook, is a specimen 'lady of the stream'. Weighing in at half an ounce over 3 lbs this particular grayling, a male, complete with splendid sail-like dorsal fin edged in crimson, was just one of four biggies taken that day. Specimens of 2 lbs 10 ozs and a brace at 2 lbs 11 ozs completed what for me was the best quartet I have ever landed in a day's fishing.

GRAYLING AND BACON

It's an open secret that in sub-zero weather it pays to concentrate upon river species such as chub and grayling which usually bite regardless of water temperatures, so you'll be pleased to know that of late I have actually been following my own advice.

It all started with a trip down south to a secluded chalkstream beat where I teamed up with an old friend and fellow angling colleague who writes for the *Daily Telegraph*, Fred J. Taylor. Fred had in fact mentioned some time back that producer-director Tony Frances fancied getting the two of us together for an episode of his *Heart of the Countryside* television series screened by Carlton, where hopefully I would catch, followed by Fred cooking the grayling out in the open right beside the river. It certainly sounded a winning formula if only we could get a fair crack of the weather, because already a prior date planned at the start of the winter had to be cancelled at the last minute due to gale-force winds and flooded rivers. But now, following a sharp overnight frost accompanied by a carpet of mist covering the river and eerily back-lit by the rising sun, we were finally treated to a beautiful day with the river flowing fast but clear. Absolutely perfect conditions for catching her ladyship, the grayling, using long-trotting tackle comprising of a lightweight 13 foot carbon rod, centre-pin reel and two maggots on a size 14 hook tied direct to 2.6 lb test line at the business end.

Long trotting is a method I personally never tire of using because exploring a river's course by probing into every nook and cranny, each sidestream entrance, every slow eddy, the lay-bys, hatch pools, long straights between bends etc., etc., using current force to trot the bait downstream presented just above bottom beneath a chunky wide-topped chubber float, offers the ultimate freshwater challenge. Normally I would return all the grayling I catch, but on this special occasion food was required for Fred's makeshift kitchen erected literally within feet of the sparkling, fast-flowing chalkstream. So while I set off downriver with the camera team to capture some action, Fred got the barbecue going.

Fortunately the grayling were most obliging and in less than an hour we had captured enough fishing footage for the programme and sufficient grayling for the cook-out from just one swim, a long glide immediately upstream from the confluence of where two carriers meet. I loose fed maggots through the middle 10 yards above the junction, hoping that by the time they sunk to the riverbed they would concentrate grayling along the crease of smooth water formed by the converging carriers. So good was the quality of sport that I would have liked to fish on and meander downstream exploring other spots, but we were after all there for television and so I returned to Fred with six goodly grayling averaging around a pound apiece and watched while he went to work.

Now the last time I ate fish outdoors was in Canada's North West Territories whilst fishing the deep, cold and unbelievably clear lakes for pike, giant lake trout and arctic grayling which appear to be the very same species we catch in Europe. And for shore lunch all three species were gutted and carefully filleted free of bones by our Indian guides and then cut into matchbox-sized chunks, rolled in heavily seasoned flour and pan fried in lard over a blazing log fire. With big-cut potato chips, onion rings and tins of beans and corn on the side, it was a meal to warm the cockles of any hungry fisherman, I can tell you.

Fred's preparation was entirely different and started with four of the grayling simply being gutted and stuffed with a large knob of butter, a little fresh lemon juice, plus a heavy dash of black pepper and salt. Two were wrapped in silver kitchen foil, two in layers of wet newspaper and all four were put on to the barbecue.

The remaining two were carefully filleted, rolled in seasoned flour and pan fried in butter along with an equal quantity of prime bacon. Boy, did it smell good. Fred then produced two bottles of Australian champagne he had been saving for such an occasion and the pair of us sat down to an 11 o'clock riverside brunch of the most delicious grayling I've ever eaten. Something which prompts me to question why trout are held in such high esteem. Strange isn't it?

UPSTREAM NYMPHING FOR GRAYLING

The most enjoyable fly fishing outfit I own comprises of a 2 oz, $7\frac{1}{2}$ foot carbon brook rod and tiny, super-light magnesium fly reel, holding a size 4 floating line. It has eventually subdued, following some spectacular battles, many a double-figure rainbow trout from southern stillwater fisheries, brownies to 6 lbs from the Rivers Kennet, Anton and Test, plus literally hundreds of fine grayling. Which prompts me to suggest that one of the most exciting ways of luring her ladyship, perhaps second only to long trotting, is presenting the upstream nymph on a super-light outfit. Even grayling of quite modest proportions will then show their mettle in streamy currents and, of course, should you hook anything of $1\frac{1}{2}$ lbs plus on such a light combo, well you have a real treat of a battle in store.

For the majority of situations found within the confines of our smaller, grayling-holding rivers, upstream nymphing should be considered a close-range technique where, through careful stalking along the riverbank, wearing polaroid glasses and drab clothing, using the cover of marginal vegetation to full advantage, you approach likely-looking runs always from a downstream direction. Sometimes you can actually see the grayling, sometimes not. Either way, be most stealthy getting into position so that an accurate

upstream cast can be made (perhaps a little across) plopping a weighted nymph in at the extreme head of the run on a 2 lbs test tippet, and allow it to come tumbling back downstream over the gravel totally unhindered, just like items of natural food delivered by the current. Your quarry will not then immediately be on its guard.

It is essential to keep your eyes glued to the leader and fly line on the surface, whilst gathering line as it is brought back by the flow, and be ready for that lightning 'snatch' as a grayling inhales the artificial. The line may simply 'twitch' heavily or as is generally the case dart forward several inches, so your response must be equally fast, by jerking firmly on the line gathered in your left hand, whilst simultaneously lifting the rod up smartly with your right, assuming you are right handed of course. Be prepared, however, for a low conversion rate.

Unlike trout, grayling won't hang on too long once they realise the nymph is not real food. And if you successfully land one grayling from, say, every three or four takes, you will be doing well. Certainly better than I've ever managed. Incidentally I prefer a weight -forward floating fly line for this really short-range casting and find that greasing the leader is only necessary when tackling the shallowest runs. I will then give the leader a rub of solid mucilin floatant to within say 4 or 5 feet of the artificial, but we are talking really shallow water here, in the 12 – 18 inch depth range. Anything deeper and the leader is not treated.

While the initial few casts in every new run may each bring a strikeable response and a chance of a hook-up, you soon come to accept just how quickly grayling wise up. So don't waste your time with repeated casting once the imitation becomes ignored. Try a change of artificial by all means, but the name of this delightful game is being mobile and moving on. So travel really light, then you'll want to cover as much water as possible.

With regards to artificials, my favourite grayling patterns are leaded shrimps and gold - or tin headed nymphs, like hare's ear, pheasant-tail etc., and it's most important they are sufficiently weighted. In my experience most popular stillwater patterns sold over the counter are too light by far for this specialised 'flowing water' technique. So for covering grayling inhabiting fast, turbulent runs, some of which might shelve down to between 3 and 5 feet, consider having a few really heavy 'Czech' nymphs tied up to order, or make them yourself. There is nothing more pleasurable. Runs through the middle of narrow rivers and especially those tight into the near bank (most commonly found along southern chalkstreams) can be most effectively worked using this technique, as there is little chance of the artificial being drawn unnaturally 'across' the flow which can so easily happen when opting to cover runs along the opposite bank.

You can even nobble grayling from ridiculously short and even quite turbulent runs really tight into the near bank by a totally unorthodox method. Simply kneel well back from the water's edge and with just a few feet of fly line out plus the leader, dunk a heavily weighted shrimp or goldhead nymph using an overhead 'flip' into the head of the run and, whilst endeavouring to maintain a slight bow in the leader (your bite indicator), follow through with the rod tip kept high, as the imitation is drawn down over the gravel bed. Short, sharp pulls are the indications to watch out for here and your reactions must be equally speedy to connect.

The nice thing about taking grayling on the upstream nymph is that unlike the technique of long trotting which, due to dense summer weed, can only be employed during the colder months, the fly rod can be used effectively all season through.

Chapter Four

GLOBAL SALTWATER GLADIATORS

CHRIS TARRANT JOINS WILSON IN THE FLORIDA KEYS

Having spent much of the last decade researching some of the most inspirational and spectacular angling locations on this planet, covering monster fish of coarse, sea and game fishing, and subsequently sending the synopsis of a new TV series plus my *Greatest Fishing Adventures* book (upon which it was based) to all five terrestrial TV channels, I was somewhat dismayed, considering that one in every 20 people in the UK enjoys fishing, that not the slightest interest was shown. Three-line replies were apparently all my 20 years as an angling TV presenter/director warranted. Which is why my 12 part *Fishing Safari* series has been enjoying a great run from December 2003 on The Discovery Home and Leisure Channel. And while I shall be forever grateful to Discovery for providing the budget to make such an international series, at the same time, I feel saddened that TV licence payers who have faithfully followed my exploits for the best part of 20 years, and who cannot afford satellite TV, were not able to watch.

So what is it that stops you the viewer from being able to watch fishing on terrestrial television having duly paid your licence fee? After all, aren't BBC2, Channel 4 and Channel 5 supposed to be providing 'niche' and 'fringe' programmes? But when do you ever see table tennis, karate, shooting, judo, archery, kick boxing, weight lifting, water sports etc. (I could go on) and of course 'angling' on these channels? Is it because most programming commissioners are leftist, anti-field sports, anti-life, vegetarians or vegans?

The only exception has been my long-running Anglia-produced *Go Fishing* series which for 18 years (featuring 108 programmes filmed in over 20 countries) was the only 'regular' angling series on terrestrial TV, albeit for the last few years available to Anglia and Meridian TV viewers only. I say 'was', because to make the *Safari* series for Discovery it was necessary for me to sever my links with Anglia Television (Anglia weren't interested in the *Safari* series either, would you believe) as I could not in the space of six months, be

Just look at these massive tarpon which gather to be hand-fed at the boat dock beside 'Robbies bar' at Islamorada in the Florida Keys. Ace cameraman Paul Bennett joins Chris Tarrant and me for a 'crew' pic having shot the intro sequence to my 2004 'Fishing Safari' TV series.

shooting two angling series simultaneously.

So unless something miraculous happens in the future, my terrestrial TV days are over. Frankly, it's all very sad. Even worse is the constant diet of football, reality shows, football, makeover shows, get me out of here dross, football and even more football, that television continues to spoon-feed us with. Really, do they want us all to become 'zombies'? There, I've had my say, now on to fishing in the Florida Keys with good friend and fellow TV presenter Chris Tarrant.

For anyone who has never experienced the gut-busting and arm-wrenching pain of fighting a 50 - lbs - plus amberjack up from 300 feet down on stand-up 50 lb class gear, it is to say the least, quite devastating, and by the tortured expression covering Chris Tarrant's usually jovial face, I could only assume he must have been enjoying the occasion. Where were we? On board 47 foot *Blue Chip Too* skippered by 'Skip Bradeen', some 11 miles off Islamorada (our base in the Florida Keys) out in the deep-blue Atlantic where the sea bed rises from 600 feet to a plateau just 300 feet deep. And it would be difficult to find such a fish-filled hot spot for amberjacks anywhere else. The top of the plateau appears to be 'paved' with lunkers in the 40 - 70 lbs bracket, plus the inevitable horde of hammerhead sharks averaging 200 - 300 lbs. And guess what their favourite snack is? Fortunately as I recall , sharks were not a problem during our session, but I have on past occasions lost as many as four or five big amberjacks in a single sitting. And there's nothing funny about reeling in a beautifully conditioned 10 lb 'amberjack's head', having risked initiating a hernia whilst playing its owner for 20 minutes. Believe me.

This fantastic, if somewhat frenzied sport happens on the drift, and is based on who can get a 'speedo' (a mackerel species caught over inshore reefs) using a pound of lead above the long, 100 lb mono trace, down to the bottom, fast enough. The savage 'hit' from an amberjack often occurring within 'seconds' of the bait's arrival. I rather think Chris slept well that night after hauling up five whoppers to around 60 lbs.

Hauling heavyweight jacks from the Atlantic however, was far from his most memorable battle.I had arranged a tarpon fishing trip out with my old mate and skipper John Rawle with whom I made several *Go Fishing* episodes out from Bradwell in Essex during the 1990s. Nowadays, from March through to the end of May however, John is based in Islamorada where from his 17 foot Maverick skiff guests can target shallow water sharks, bonefish, barracuda, redfish, snook, jacks etc. and in our case monstrous-great tarpon topping 100 lbs. And mostly all from the warm, shallow waters of Florida Bay.

In 20 years of making angling TV programmes and videos I had never tried filming during the hours of darkness. But John said our best chance of monster tarpon was from 3.00 a.m. till dawn, so after showing Chris what big tarpon looked like along at famous 'Robbies' bar and boat dock (hundereds of huge tarpon gather to be fed by hand, would you believe) we set off the following morning to film by torchlight. And very well it came out too, I'm surprised to report. Though I doubt cameraman Paul Bennett would want to film in the pitch black on every shoot. Fortunately, I managed to hook and following an hour of gut busting agony, finally bring to the boat my largest tarpon ever which John Rawle estimated at fully 160 lbs. What a superbly proportioned creature. I then managed to lose two more which within seconds both jumped off the hook, while after much sweating and cursing Chris finally brought to the skiff his best (and first) tarpon of 130 lbs. Both incidently were caught on just 20 lb test line and came to float-fished blue crabs really making our weeks filming in the Keys a most memorable occasion, as it was all captured on camera.

Mind you, as Chris said, everything he hooked turned out to be a personal best, including would you believe, no less than five permit in a single session when we motored over 70 miles out (yes 70) into the Gulf of Mexico on board skipper Randy Towes 35 foot contender. And every one topped 20 lbs. That's comparable almost to a golfer downing five holes in-one during the same session. But he nearly lost one of them because a monstrous jewfish estimated by Randy at 500 lbs, suddenly came up from the depths to grab hold. Fortunately it missed, and it was all captured on video footage. As were our exploits with sharks, both lemons and nurse sharks, plus my losing that monster jewfish following a half-hour battle. But I guess that even on stand-up 50 lb class the end was always inevitable. Though I did haul up a baby jewfish of around 70 - 80lbs as a consolation prize. What a trip.

GREAT TV FIGHT BUT MY BEST FISH GOT AWAY

Whenever I am asked about the largest fish I have caught, I can't help remembering the unseen monsters that got away. A particular encounter sprang to mind while visiting friends, Chris Sandford and Gelly Morgan, at their riverside Sussex home. Gelly reminded me of our exploits in Asia and Africa several years back when making a 12 part international series of my *Go Fishing* TV programme. One adventure I'll simply never forget, because most people still (over 10 years later) ask the same question - 'What was that monster you lost while boat fishing off East Africa?' It was certainly the largest swimming creature I've ever been connected to, but it found itself on my line by complete chance.

We were filming a sailfish programme on board Angus Paul's boat, *Tina* and trolling a couple of mounted fish baits on outriggers. We also had three middle rods out, trolling a mixture of strip and skirts, and kona head lures, using one of my outfits which included a Penn International 30 reel full to the brim with 40 lb mono and a red hardwood teaser

The 'Go Fishing' TV cameras record every second of my epic encounter with an unseen monster hooked off the east coast of Africa at Malindi. Sadly, after a strength- sapping two hour battle, it broke free. Was I gutted or what?

20 feet up the trace. On this rod I caught a small yellowfin tuna of around 10 - 12 lbs, but before we could capture its iridescent colours on tape the boat had swung round putting the subject in shadow of the wheelhouse. So I lowered the tuna over the side while Angus tried to bring the stern into the sun again. He never managed this because both the outrigger-presented mounted fish baits, which had sunk during our deliberation with the tuna, were taken simultaneously by a pair of 70-lb-plus acrobatic sailfish.

When all was calm again and the sailfish released I heard the ratchet on my own outfit clicking away with the line taut and angled steeply downwards. Something had nobbled the tuna and was heading off big time. I grunted and groaned as I heaved on the rod while the mystery fish slowly headed south along the coast keeping parallel with the Kenyan shoreline. We suspected the unseen monster to be a big shark but as it hadn't bitten through the monofilament trace within two minutes Angus stated that it was a black marlin in the 600 lbs bracket, or more. I was having to brace myself against such a powerful force, standing up because we had removed the one fighting chair for unhindered camera views. The fish was rarely more than 150 yards from our stern after three-quarters of an hour so I harnessed up to alleviate the strain on my arms.

After two hours of sweat and pain with me no nearer to landing the unseen monster than when I first hooked it, the line started to angle upwards sharply. It was going to jump. It came faster and faster towards the surface where any second we expected to see its identity, but the line fractured just above the hook and fell back limply. And limp just about sums up the way I felt too.

THE BIG ONE

At seminars, at trade and consumer tackle shows, during angling dinners or slide shows, on the bank and by letter, the question I am most often asked is, 'What kind of fishing do you like best?' and more to the point, 'Which species do you consider the world's most exciting sportfish?'. Well now, in sheer physical size and athletic, animal power, I guess that blue and black marlin would share the top honours here. But then we are talking big game boats, experienced crews , expensive trolling charters of up to £1000 a day and anything but a one-to-one situation. No-one for instance can possibly take a boat out on their own and hope single-handedly to land a large bill fish. So it is perhaps from the outset unfair to include the saltwater gladiators, which include swordfish and sailfish, amongst every man's view of what is the most exciting and fights the hardest.

Whilst bill fishing incidentally I've enjoyed some great scraps with dorado, wahoo and jumbo-sized tuna which truly never know when to stop pulling. But again into the equation come designer boats, an attentive crew and fighting chairs, etc. So let's concentrate on species hooked and played on *terra firma* or from a small skiff or dinghy. What about the salmonoids for instance, which in the British Isles have always been at the very top of the list in everyone's aspirations. Well, having caught most so-called cold water game species on fly and spoon over the years, including North American steelhead, char and giant lake trout, (although I have yet to bank a huchen or taimen salmon), all, I am sorry to say, fall way, way behind in strength and durability of most blue water adversaries. Even the high leaping golden dorado of Brazil's massive rainforest rivers can't compete on the same level.

Take the humble amberjack, for instance: average-sized specimens in the 40 - 60 lbs bracket will almost pull your arms from their sockets and battle away for anything up to half an hour despite a 50 lb line class stand-up boat rod and multiplier combination. And amberjacks are 10 a penny in the Atlantic off the Florida Keys. It's a fact that compared

Helped by Seychelles skipper 'Sydney' my wife Jo displays a high leaping, fast running 70 lb sailfish. But in my opinion this exotic gamefish does not come into the same power-league as either the tarpon or the majestic mahseer of Southern India.

to our cold water species of both fresh and salt water, tropical saltwater fish are simply in an endurance class of their own. Just ask anyone who has hooked into a sizeable bonefish of between say 6 and 9 lbs and watched helplessly in total disbelief as their fly reel empties of up to 200 yards of line and backing. And should you hook a permit, the reel empties even quicker. It is a physiological fact that due to higher water temperatures a fish's metabolic rate and its ability to fight harder and for longer increase dramatically to a point beyond the comprehension of those yet to sample exotic speedsters.

By now catfish enthusiasts may assume I have forgotten their favourite fish, but not so. In fact I rate pussies amongst the hardest fighting and most exciting of all freshwater adversaries on a worldwide basis. And amongst these I include the American Channel catfish, the European wels and the African vundu, which I personally rate one of the most durable battlers in tropical freshwater. By now you have, of course, gathered that on an international basis most popular coarse species like carp and sea fish such as cod (though pollack fight harder) simply don't rate a look in. Correct! Which is how it is with sharks which, teeth apart, are purely average fighters though they look aggressive. And the same goes for big rays, barracudas, even the tenacious conger eel.

For my money and considering the whole world over, two species stand out high above all others in their power, their strength, their durability, their difficult to catch factor and their sheer majesty. They are the saltwater tarpon and the freshwater mahseer. I caught my first tarpon way back in 1969 when I lived in a beach house on the west coast of Barbados. It weighed 86 lbs and during the hour-long battle in pitch blackness I was made to run backwards and forwards along the sandy beach using extreme sidestrain as a lever on my reverse taper beachcaster in an effort to stop this awesome creature from reaching the sanctuary of coral reefs at each end of the bay from where I cast my flying fish deadbait just 40 yards out into the surf. During the fight I honestly assumed my adversary was something approaching the 200 lbs mark. And if I think deeply I can remember the encounter still as though it were yesterday.

Similarly the mahseer I've caught in India within the 80 – 90 lbs bracket have also fought for the best part of an hour, and in a fast flowing river too, doing something like 8 knots. Here we are talking a 40 lb line class outfit and a fight where actually swimming across the river and running hundreds of yards downstream across jagged black bedrock in an effort to get below the fish, are all part of the fight. Small wonder that nausea and nervous exhaustion accompany every memorable mahseer battle. But always there has been that image of a big, beautiful fully scaled fish to behold that has urged me on to see it through despite the pain, discomfort, danger and aching arm muscle, not to mention a bruised crotch. Being fully scaled with silver scales the size of beer mats upon which details of the catch can be written as a memento, tarpon and mahseer share at least one physical similarity. Their most common denominator, however, is that they both live in warm water. The mahseer of southern India live in rivers flowing at an incredible 80° F while tarpon frequent tropical salt and brackish bays, inlets and mangrove swamps where the water is equally as warm.

Frankly, as adversaries, I am glad one lives in tropical oceans and the other inhabits tropical freshwater, otherwise, and although I've caught 100-lb-plus tarpon in the Florida Keys using the very same outfit that has subdued 90-lb-plus mahseer in India, I would have to make a comparison in their levels of strength and durability which is truly awesome. Perhaps it is just as well that tarpon do not inhabit fast-flowing boulder-strewn rivers like the mahseer. Conversely I'm rather glad the mahseer doesn't repeatedly jump like the tarpon whilst running, or I'd never see one on the bank beaten.

THE WONDERFUL SEYCHELLES

As I look out through my office window upon a lawn full of brown leaves, a lake full of frozen seagulls sitting upon cold grey water, reflecting the flat grey sky above, I cannot help but dream of the sun on my back and fishing in the tropics. Of palm trees and exotic fruits, coral white sands, powder blue skies and turquoise waters simply alive with colourful hard-battling saltwater adversaries. And if you were to push me for just one location right now above all others, not that I would need much pushing on this totally grey winter's day in Norfolk, I would have no hesitation in recommending the wonderful Seychelles.

Though my wife Jo and I revisited the islands a couple of years back to get married and to fish, of course, it is several years now since I first fell in love with this veritable angler's paradise, a collection of over 100 exotic tropical islands, most of which are coral atolls rising mere feet above sea level from an unbelievably rich and shallow plateau in the Indian Ocean, off the north-east coast of Africa.

Over 900 species of fish, from colourful reef dwellers to tail-walking gladiators like marlin and sailfish, inhabit these calm and crystal-clear blue waters. But what makes the Seychelles extra special and so unbelievably prolific is that with just 70,000 people inhabiting an area of 250,000 square miles (about the size of Spain) and geographically being so isolated from major populations who need to be fed, overfishing on a commercial scale simply does not occur. I guess you could say visiting the Seychelles is almost like going back in time. Jumbo jets can in fact land only on Mahe, the largest island, which is home to 90 per cent of the population. You then island-hop by light aircraft to land on the lush grass runways of much smaller, more intimate islands and quickly get into the Robinson Crusoe way of life. Though I experienced some magnificent sport from both the beach and trolling offshore on beautiful Desroche in the Amirantes, a 50 minute southerly

133

flight from Mahe, my favourite havens are Bird Island and Denis Island. Both you can walk around in a couple of hours and both are situated due north of Mahe, on the very edge of the shallow Seychelles plateau with quick access to a sudden and massive drop-off into a cobalt blue void over 1000 feet deep. This distinct colour line can actually be seen from the beach affording some of the world's most exciting and virginal saltwater sports fishing. And it's all mere minutes away from the shore. There is often barely enough time to get all the lines out before any one of a dozen or more powerful heavily toothed or acrobatic species grabs hold. My first sailfish out of Denis Island came so close I could still recognise the manager walking his dog along the beach.

Such is the quality of fishing. And if trolling lures or mounted fish baits on just 20 or 30 lb class outfits for bill fish, wahoo, barracuda, dorado and several members of the tuna family becomes too predictable or too knackering, which it does, well you can take is easy and drift boat fish over the inshore reefs. Here, in depths varying between 20 and 60 feet, you'll catch a never-ending variety of spectacularly coloured battlers on fish strip bait whether you wield a light boat rod or a local handline. No doubt, as I did, you'll lose count of the different species which include snappers, grunts, coral trout, trevallys, breams, parrot fish and two of the most colourful oddities I have ever seen in salt - or freshwater anywhere in the world – the moontail sea bass and the tomato hind. Both are so vividly coloured in bright tomato red, had an artist painted either you would call him a liar. Should, however, you not fancy going afloat, beachcasting can prove extremely exciting with numbers of stingrays, guitar fish and small sharks coming really close inshore, especially during the hours of darkness. There are bonefish too.

Quite apart from the unbelievable fishing the Seychelles contain a real wealth of unusual flora and fauna, including the world's largest recorded tortoise in the massive shape of Esmaralda, who lives on Bird Island and weighs in at getting on for half a ton. Bird Island also contains the world's largest breeding colony of sooty terns – over a million of them.

IN THE GAMBIA 'CAPTAIN FISH' RULE OK

Normally I'd say that it's impossible to spend a week in the Gambia as I did just recently without catching anything. But then I do have to stand back from fishing occasionally in my capacity as an angling photographer and simply capture others having their string pulled. And in the fourth Masterline International West African Shore Fishing Championship held just recently along the beautiful beaches of Tangi, some 20 miles south of the capital Banjul, most of the 75 competitors enjoyed fabulous sport and shared over £7,000 in prize money plus over £20,000 in tackle vouchers. No mean event this.

Actually the three day championship attracted shore fishing enthusiasts from Ireland, England, Holland and South Africa, with those able to hit distances of 120 – 130 yards with bait taking top honours. Captain fish in the 8 – 20 lb range and crevalle jacks in the 5 – 10 lb bracket produced the bulk of the winning catches and all to fresh prawns, 1½ kilos of which were supplied to every competitor. Numbers of heavyweight stingrays and guitar fish, unlike last year's competition, simply did not show during the three days though catfish, butterfish, rubber-lipped groupers, cassavas and ninebones etc., helped to swell catches along with the occasional small barracuda – on a five points per fish and 10 points per kilo scoring basis.

The largest guitar fish, of 18 lbs, was caught by John O'Brien from Waterford in

Left to right: experienced Gambian skipper Mark Longster, Alan Yates with his 24 lbs captain fish, and Chris Leibbrant.

Ireland, last year's overall winner. This time, however, John had to settle for third place behind Norman Message from Eastbourne who came second, top spot falling to Richard Yates whose father Alan, well known England International, not only came fourth but also won the heaviest fish prize with a superb captain fish of 24 lbs.

Organised by John Prescott in Ireland and Richard Sheared of World Sport Fishing in Bedfordshire, much credit must also go to Mark Longster and Tracey Day of Gambia Fishing who arranged fresh bait daily and ensured everything ran really smoothly. Immediately after the competition Mark arranged for one of his boats to take my daughter Lisa, her fiancé Lee and myself for a day's bottom fishing in the wide mouth of the Gambia River at Baraa, opposite Banjul, while my wife Jo played around the hotel pool with our seven-year-old granddaughter. Wilson had a day's fishing at last! Even then I couldn't help handing over the rod of those I did hook so Lee and Lisa could enjoy the spirited fights of rubber-lipped grouper, sunpats, captain fish, cassarvas and other oddities found in this angling haven called the Gambia. I might even enter the competition myself next year!

WHEN A TARPON HITS, IT'S LIKE YOU'VE HOOKED A LORRY DOING 50 MPH

If I remember correctly, the last occasion I fished with Essex skipper John Rawle was several years back on board *Donna Mary* in an uncomfortable force 7 some 10 miles off Bradwell, trying to catch bass for my Anglia Television programme, *Go Fishing*. What a difference to tarpon fishing with him in the Florida Keys just recently, when even at 3.00 a.m. the temperature was a humid 80º F and the shallow flats of Florida Bay ghostly calm as John twisted his 17 foot flat bottomed skiff around marker posts and through narrow mangrove channels, picking out landmarks every so often with a powerful spotlamp. A speed of around 25 knots was nothing to the 115 hp Yamaha outboard, but in the pitch

Believe it or not, this 80 lb tarpon held for the camera by skipper John Rawle, and caught by Dave Johnson is just a baby.

black, so necessary for ensuring sport with ultra-cautious tarpon, the 20 minute trip out to deepwater channels where these monstrous fish were laying up, though hairy, heightened sensory perception to fever pitch.

The air cooled noticeably for instance close to islands of dense mangroves which held the moisture and a pungent, not unpleasant aroma of sulphur. And when John finally cut the powerful engine to set the skiff drifting slowly with the tide two distinct sounds could be heard through the blackness: the occasional distant car or truck along US Highway 1, which links all the Keys together for a distance of 170 miles between Miami and Key West, and the distinct sounds of huge tarpon feeding on the surface. Now a 'busting' tarpon can sound as loud as someone falling overboard (we're talking fish in the 80 – 200 lbs class here) or as muffled as someone popping a wine bottle cork from a hundred yards away. It depends how aggressively they are feeding on the night, but either way expectations rise to fever pitch when the boat is drifting amongst them, with huge shapes rolling everywhere.

John rates a small blue crab presented on a size 5/0 hook tied to a 4 foot mono trace of 100 lb test the ideal rig: the reel line being 30 lb test if using a multiplier to drift the crab beneath a float directly behind the boat, or just 20 lb test on a fixed-spool reel for casting a freelined crab on either side of the boat and then slowly winding it in just beneath the surface until a tarpon grabs hold. It's true that some bites are ridiculously gentle from such a monstrous fish which resembles a giant herring, especially in the dark, but most feel as though your line has suddenly been connected to a lorry doing 50 miles an hour.

As the hook bites home the tarpon usually catapults itself completely clear of the water in a shower of spray before crashing back in again and ripping anything up to 200 yards of line from the reel. There then commences a battle that could last for up to two hours and more. The pursuit of tarpon fishing during darkness is arguably the most exhilarating, mind-blowing and nerve-racking sport anyone is ever likely to experience on rod and line. It is indeed like a drug and you sit there dripping in a mixture of anticipation and sweat waiting for the next run like a man possessed. At least those were the reactions of the eight man party I recently escorted across the Pond to fish with John Rawle out of Islamorada. All had previously merely read stories about this crazy fish, so our total week's catch of 27 tarpon weighing between 65 and 160 lbs (most topping 100 lbs) provided many memorable battles.

FROM A JACK TO A KING

How much anticipation, excitement, pain and delight can two anglers cram into a few days' fishing? Allow me to relate a session experienced by graphic display boss Pete Hazlewood and me just recently during a week's fishing vacation with four friends spent in the famous Florida Keys, and you can judge for yourself. Our base was Islamorada, situated halfway between Miami and Key West, where we teamed up with old friend and skipper, John Rawle, from Bradwell in Essex. Between March and June John jets over to the Keys to specialise in tarpon fishing out from Islamorada and 3.00 a.m., yes 3.00 a.m., is the time it all happens when John scoots his 17 foot Maverick skiff over the shallow flats towards one of the deep channels where schools of 100-lbs-plus tarpon look for bait fish during the incoming tide beneath the long bridges spanning US Highway 1.

Yes, it's drift fishing totally in the dark, presenting a pinfish livebait or blue crab on a size 5/0 hook beneath a float just 30 yards behind the boat with 30 lb test monofilament on the multiplier reel, and possibly the most exciting and electrifying sports fishing on this planet. Why? Because literally any second right out of nowhere the 7 foot boat rod could be almost pulled from your grasp as a monster tarpon inhales the bait and moves away at speed.

Nurse sharks are usually sluggish creatures, until hoisted up for a photo. This 60 pounder is giving my fishing buddy Pete Hazelwood (left) and skipper John Rawle a real workout.

My first encounter, and it was a big tarpon, ended when the line inexplicably fractured above the float. No doubt a needle fish cut it through. My second hook-up, also a good tarpon (we are talking 100-lbs-plus monsters here) stayed on after leaping but the hook fell out once it decided to go beneath the boat. My third and last hit of the morning (all in a manic hour's fishing) resulted in a huge tarpon catapulting itself out of the water so close to the boat I actually took a step backwards, lest it jumped in. Then it went charging downtide on a long 150 yard run before I heard a grating noise – John shone his torch down at my reel to show a horrific bird's nest (left and wound over, would you believe, by the previous guest) whereupon the line instantly parted at the Birmini knot above the float. A monster estimated at possibly 170-180 lbs. Yes, I swore heavily. Then it was Pete's turn. After two misses he connected with another monster and brought a superb incredibly deep tarpon of around 150 lbs to the boat. By now the sun was shining and it was all over until the afternoon when we ventured out again into the back country for some sharks. With a rubby-dubby bag over the side within minutes several sharks could be seen cruising around and in just a three-hour session Pete and I accounted for two lemons and two nurse sharks on chunks of tuna and ladyfish, the largest being a nurse shark of approaching 300 lbs to Peter's rod. Did we have a day or what?

The warm tropical waters of the Florida Keys play host to an enormous selection of exotic hard-fishing sports fish for the visiting angler to enjoy; from sharks to sailfish, bonefish to tarpon and from stingrays to crevalle jacks. One of the adversaries I specifically targeted was the incredibly strong (many would say by far the most formidable of all the jack family) and beautifully proportioned amberjack. These deep-bodied, mighty sports fish gather around deepwater humps and wrecks on the ocean (Atlantic) side of the Florida Keys and are common in the 30 – 60 lbs size bracket. Trouble is even on 50 lb stand-up gear there is a good 20 – 30 minutes of guaranteed back-breaking pain ahead in pumping one of these giant jacks from 300 feet down, up to the surface. Most anglers become ecstatic at boating just one. Me? Well I must admit to an insatiable appetite for such hard battlers and rate the amberjack behind mahseer and tarpon, third in my own personal list of gladiators and the 'king' amongst deepwater battlers.

To encounter sport with amberjacks four friends and I had chartered *Blue Chip Too* out of Whale Harbour in Islamorada with a view to visiting 'The Hump', a plateau of coral around 2 acres in size which rises from the sea floor 600 feet down to just 300 feet, situated some 12 miles into the Atlantic. But recent excursions over The hump had resulted in most jack hook-ups ending in attacks from hammerhead sharks during the fight. So we took the skipper's advice and, following a 30 minute bait-catching session over a shallow reef just a mile offshore to secure a batch of blue runners and horse eyes (favourite amberjack baits), headed 10 miles north-west along the coastline to another 'hump' where a known wreck, also around 300 feet down, promised some big jack potential. The first couple of drifts in seas approaching a force 7 (fortunately *Blue Chip Too* is 50 feet long with a 16 feet beam) proved unrewarding. I lost a big jack in the wreck whilst friends Mike Turner and Tim White both also had fish come adrift. Presenting a bait 300 feet down in seas which make simply standing up difficult is tiresome to say the least. And because I personally wanted to boat a big jack using a lightweight outfit I was purposefully putting myself at a distinct disadvantage, standard outfits on board for the tourist angler being heavyweight 80 lb class gear.

Through sheer perseverance, however, plus a couple of lost fish, one a particularly large jack, I eventually boated a magnificent 50 lbs amberjack following a 50 minute encounter using an uptide voyager rod and just 30 lb reel line. My crotch still sports the bruises to prove it. Mike Turner also beat a beautiful jack topping 50 lbs, which like mine fought for every foot of line all the way from 300 feet down. Why do we enjoy these painful encounters so much? Well even your granny can land a big bill fish, sailfish or marlin, providing the skipper continually backs the boat up on the fish. But granny doesn't stand a chance of hauling big time, believe me.

SHARKS AND A TIGER IN AFRICA

When tour operator Christine Slater asked Emap's then publishing editor Andy Benham and me if we fancied making up numbers on a research trip to Africa's south-west coast to catch sharks from the beach and then head inland for some tiger fishing along the Zambezi, we obviously jumped at the chance. And what an exciting whirlwind trip of just five days it turned out to be. In fact I can never recall cramming so much travelling and fishing into such a short period of time.

Our first destination from Heathrow, following a 10 hour *Air Namibia* flight, was to Windhoek (pronounced 'Vintook') the capital of Namibia, which incidentally is the third most underpopulated country on this planet. We then chartered a six seater Cessna 210, piloted by a white Namibian called JC, for a one hour flight heading due west to Swakopmund on the Skeleton Coast. Here we were introduced to Ottmar, a short, most enthusiastic and rather eccentric German guide, who for several years has been taking visitors shore fishing by Landrover and offshore ground fishing on board an 18 foot ski boat powered by twin Honda 90s.

As the sea was extremely rough with huge rollers crashing up the sandy beach which stretched for mile upon mile in both directions for as far as the eye could see, Ottmar drove our party of five 20 miles north to where a huge reef broke the force of the waves 400 to 500 yards out, leaving a large area of fishable water between it and the beach. He provided all the tackle and soon had us all rigged up with 14 foot South African style surf rods, multipliers loaded with 40 lb test and a simple swivelled paternoster rig combining

Namibian guide Ottmar Leipert cradles a hound shark caught from the beach at Swakopmund by Christine Slater of Tailor Made Holidays during our whirlwind tour of this fascinating African country.

a 6 oz lead with a fresh mullet head on a size 6/0 hook: his standard shark terminal rig until the big boys put in an appearance – then the mono trace is replaced with 80 lb wire and 8/0 hook. And in case you're wondering, the 'big boys' are bronze whaler sharks weighing anything from 100 to 300 lbs plus. Cow sharks of between 80 and 150 lbs also feature in everyday catches here. Trouble was, our visit being in July (the African winter) was not really conducive to these particular sharks coming close inshore. Any time between January and April we were told would virtually guarantee action with 'bronzes' as Ottmar affectionately calls them and I had little reason to doubt his words, because we caught everything else he said we would, including three black-spotted gully sharks of between 50 and 70 lbs, plus a couple of 40-lbs-plus hound sharks. Add three more lost of similar size and it's pretty impressive action for just an afternoon's sport at the wrong time of the year. When the water warms big kob, steenbrass and three species of rays are also regular captures from the shore along the prolific Skeleton Coast.

Following a night in the superb Swakopmund Hotel where we enjoyed a magnificent meal including wine for around £8 a head, we were collected by Ottmar at 8.00 a.m., out fishing on his boat and back in again by 10.00 a.m., having caught 50 or so catfish and kob to around 4 lbs on cut sardine bait at anchor – honestly. It was amazing light tackle sport and then we boarded the Cessna for our next leg of the journey. Well, I did say it was a whirlwind tour and I meant it.

Heading in a north-easterly direction, firstly over desert and then savanna, JC brought the plane down four hours later at Mpacha airport in Katima. Here our Landrover transfer was waiting to take us over the border into Zambia where we followed the course of the mighty Zambezi River upstream for 80 miles along a dusty track (a Zambian B road) to the lodge at Mazeba Bay. This bumpy route should have taken around three hours but was nearly doubled on account of two punctures, the second within just five miles of our destination which left us without a spare. So Shaun the driver had to thumb a lift and returned an hour later with another wheel. By this time it was pitch black and quite chilly, so we lit a fire in the middle of the track and huddled around it. After a warm welcome from our hosts, Andre and Janine Van der Merwe, and a much welcomed evening meal, everyone crashed out and rose at 6.00 a.m. for an early-morning session by inflatable boat up the fast-flowing Zambezi trolling for tiger fish through deep, swirling pools.

Using Rapala shad raps and CD 14 magnums, we had a dozen or so hits, but tiger fish are notorious for catapulting themselves completely clear of the water and flinging the hooks out and we boated and released just two deep-bodied specimens of around 4-5 lbs apiece. At 9.00 a.m. the sun's brightness terminated any further action from toothy predators, so we beached the boat and walked way upstream through the bush to marvel at the magnificent Ngonye Falls (a mini Victoria Falls) and one of the major attractions at Mazeba Bay Lodge. Though I am sure some guests would give me an argument in favour of Lilundu, a four-year-old year orphan elephant that has been raised by the Van der Merwes from just a few months old, and with which visitors get to share their afternoon back at the lodge - a fascinating experience to say the least. Sightings of fish eagles, hornbills, pied kingfishers, and crocodiles and breathtaking views across the Zambezi Valley, accompanied by two further tiger sessions with fish to 7 lbs in the boat and a lost beauty of double the size saying goodbye in a kaleidoscope of spray, terminated our stay. We simply didn't have time for flights along the valley in Andrew's microlight, white water rafting or game viewing through an adjacent wildlife park. Will I return? You bet your life I will.

'THOSE MARVELLOUS BRONZE WHALERS'

As anyone amongst the growing number of British shore anglers who pilgrimage during our winter to Namibia's shark-infested 'Skeleton Coast'; in south-west Africa will confirm (January to April is prime time), landing a hefty bronze whaler from the surf is one hell of an adrenalin-pumping adventure. Most have never experienced such raw, uncontrollable power before and get to know exactly what their top-of-the-range British beachcasters are actually capable of - or not capable of, as the case may be. It truly is the most awesome spectacular and spine wrenching stand-up saltwater sports fishing anyone is ever likely to encounter in their lifetime – unless they return the following year as many do - and personally I cannot ever get enough of it.

In fact, I have enjoyed so many memorable encounters along this unique coastline which stretches for close on 1000 miles between South Africa and the Angolan border, to highlight just one is not easy. These temperate seas are so full, not only of bronze whalers in the 100 – 400 lbs bracket, there are also guitar fish, stingrays, steenbras, kob and cow sharks etc., plus spotted gully sharks and hound sharks – the latter two providing fresh rubby dubby once they have been slit from vent to throat and staked out in the surf line. It is initially difficult to take in that these smaller sharks, which average 20-40 lbs, any one of which if caught from a British beach would attract neighbouring anglers like bees to a honeypot, are merely considered 'bait', their blood-filled gills topping the list of fresh hookbaits, with mullet or mackerel heads and chunks running a close second.

One particular day stands out, however, in that our guide, Ottmar Leippert, a German who runs Levo Sportsfishing Safaris from Walvis Bay, a few miles south of our base at Swakopmund, had decided that due to massive hefts of weed in the surf locally we would go north to 'mile 100'. Now can you imagine a guide working British beaches picking you up from the hotel in a Landrover completely equipped with all tackle and baits provided, including one-piece 14 foot south African carbon surf sticks and multiplier outfits, and then driving up to or even over 100 miles to locate prime surf conditions? Namibian guides like Ottmar think nothing of it and are continually speeding along the hard-packed sand immediately behind the surf line from one stretch of beach to another, studying wind direction and wave formations, dirty or brown water immediately ruling out even the

Being a 'weight-lifter' my son Lee was only too pleased to hoist this 100 lb plus bronze whaler shark up for the cameras.

141

usually most productive locations. In any event, whenever nothing materialises within half an hour all the rods are placed back in the purpose-built holders and within no time at all the Landrover is screaming along the sand to another stretch of beach.

On this particular day, however, Ottmar somehow seemed to know from the outset that 'mile 100' would produce. And it started in electrifying style. My nephew, Richard Bowler, was the first to get a mullet head out the statutory 70-80 yards (long casting is not imperative) and before his brother Martin could do likewise Richard was hooked up and his rod hooped over. And that's how it was for just five minutes until four of our six man party were all into bronze whalers with myself on the camera, while my son Lee took a break, having had his line severed across the reef over 200 yards out. The occasion was almost farcical as Ottmar ran around like a madman ensuring none of the lines were crossing or touching each other as four hefty sharks emptied 30 lb line from the reels at alarming speed. As all big game enthusiasts know only too well, one fully taut line touching another cuts through it like a cheesewire. Were all four sharks landed, do I hear you ask? Frankly I cannot honestly remember because it was one of those magical days when the ocean floor appeared to be paved with bronze whalers. Someone attempted to account for how many hook-ups we'd had on the drive back to Swakopmund, a figure of 30 seemed rather conservative. Not all were not beached, of course, due to hooks pulling, lines fracturing upon rocks and bronze whalers simply serrating the reel line somewhere between rod tip and bait. It's some 'line bite' when the rod tip knocks gently and the line falls back limp. For when you wind in the remaining few yards of reel line it looks as though a dozen rats have been chewing it.

By mid-afternoon I had experienced several lost fish due to a mixture of circumstances just mentioned, beached two sharks of 150-lb-plus apiece and was into my third of the day which felt a real 'mother'. The rigid 14$\frac{1}{2}$ ft Zziplex 'Namibia special' made for me by beachcasting guru, Terry Carrol, comprising of a 6$\frac{1}{2}$ foot butt and 8 foot tip, was taking on a bend I hadn't before seen as 30 lb mono evaporated in a fast-reducing blurr from the ABU 10,000. Within a couple of minutes I could wind the star drag round no more and there was so much line out over the breakers (certainly 300 yards plus) that from my waist-deep position, it actually appeared the line was going uphill - a strange phenomenon. With but a few turns left I wrapped both thumbs around the spool, gritted my teeth and, swearing loudly and profusely to the unseen copulating shark without a father (sharking certainly brings the animal out of us all), crabbed my way backwards slowly up the beach, my heels digging deeply into the sand. Fortunately the line held and now some 400 yards out (accounting for the 25 per cent stretch in monofilament) the shark at last started kiting parallel to the beach, as I managed frantically to put line back on the reel. This incidentally cannot be achieved simply by standing there and power pumping from the waist – with such incredible torque against the tackle it is impossible. To recover line I then ran down the beach like a madman until I reached the surf and kept repeating the process, moving back up and down the beach again until the shark decided to power off again. Something it did on several further occasions, but it never reached as far as it did on that 'blistering' initial run.

Following well over an hour of give and take I had recovered all but the last 100 yards or so of line while the shark cruised seemingly at will just beyond the furthest breaker. I just couldn't understand my inability to horse it in through the waves after such a long fight and just had to sit down in the sand for a rest, or risk a coronary, something my wife Jo is always reminding me of. Well I am nearly 60! I certainly can't remember ever sweating so profusely either before or since.

The trouble with treating yourself to a break, of course, is that the shark also takes on a new lease of life and so a further 45 minutes elapsed before I was able to finally see its tall tail and dorsal fins cutting through the second breaker – a lovely sight. Then Ottmar and fellow guide Neil Van Rooyen rushed into the surf with a long-handled gaff (these narrow gape gaffs are only nicked into the shark's dorsal fin) and I was soon to find out why this particular shark had taken so much out of me. The 9/0 hook was firmly embedded in the wide root of one of its long pectoral fins. No wonder I experienced such little control and a truly monumental battle. Estimated at around 240 lbs (on a length for weight formula used by all the Namibian guides), was I glad to see that particular bronze whaler slowly make its way back through the waves into the Atlantic Ocean. I'd never felt so knackered in all my life.

ACTION IN KENYA

What can possibly be nicer in equatorial Africa than sipping a chilled beer in a bar full of tackle and photographic memorabilia of the great Ernest Hemingway, with wonderfully preserved examples of the sea's most charismatic species like marlin, broad bill swordfish, huge sharks and warsaw groupers etc., lining the walls, and admiring stunning views overlooking the tropical blue water of the Indian Ocean. It's difficult to think of an equivalent even. Such is 'Hemingway's Resort', situated at Watamu on the Kenya, East African coastline 20 miles south of Malindi and 70 miles north of Mombasa with flights from both airports direct to Nairobi.

The three storey thatched accommodation, with all rooms overlooking a mass of colourful shrubs and two swimming pools, providing spectacular panoramic views through tall coconut palms to the ocean, is a veritable haven to blue water enthusiasts. Hemingway's specialises in big game fishing for marlin, broad bill swordfish and sailfish, with an exciting list of arm-wrenching battlers such as yellowfin tuna, barracuda, wahoo, dorado, kingfish, cobia and several species of jacks also likely to grab your trolled kona head lures, Rapala magnums, frigate mackerel or small bonito livebaits, mounted fish strip baits, or simple squid skirt jigs.

The secret with offshore trolling is to follow the flocks of birds (mostly terns) feeding upon sardines or mantis prawns pushed up to the surface by frigate mackerel, bonito, jacks or yellowfin tuna etc. Lures and baits are then trolled expectantly around the melee in a wide circle, and as kingfish, wahoo, cudas or bill fish could be lying beneath, quite

The girls have a field-day. My wife Jo and Ellen Smalley get amongst the yellow fin trevally whilst trolling out of Hemingways resort, Watamu, Kenya.

143

literally anything may be raised and subsequently hooked from a 10 lb jack to a quarter of a ton marlin.

It's exotic bran tub fishing at its most spectacular as my wife Jo and I experienced just recently during a week's stay at Hemingway's in the company of our good friends Stewart and Ellen Smalley from Aldeburgh in Suffolk. Being an East Coast skipper himself (operating out of Orford) and specialising in bass, Stewart organised a two-man trolling boat so we guys could explore in the mornings between organised all-day charter trips on board the 35 foot boats when our wives came along.

Concentrating upon the photography for a new 'Safari' book I am currently writing, it was most enjoyable capturing the agony and the ecstasy (once landed) of Jo and Ellen battling with sailfish to over 70 lbs and yellowfin tuna to 50 lbs on just 30 lb gear, plus an assortment of yellowfin trevally and bonito etc. Unfortunately, and except for a 350 lbs black marlin landed by another Hemingway's boat, marlin were conspicuous by their absence during our short stay. Stewart and I, however, were more than kept busy in the 16 foot dinghy sporting a 50 horse outboard, exploring an assortment of known banks, drop-offs and gullies with names like wahoo villa, the canyon, karambesi corner, the mountains, the nipple and the boiling pot, in depths ranging from 30 to over 300 feet. During our morning excursions to these evocative locations (back at the bar for 1.00 p.m.) we enjoyed some cracking, arm-wrenching battles on 20 lb test gear trolling size 14 CD Rapala magnums and jigs with yellowfin tuna to over 60 lbs, kingfish to 20 lbs, plus jumbo-sized bonito and several trevally species. My, how those yellowfins pulled. If there is a harder more stamina-packed saltwater species to wear down and subdue on a pound for pound basis, then I would dearly love to catch it.

The managing director of Hemingway's, Garry Cullen, is a most enthusiastic host and up at the crack of dawn every morning to ensure guests enjoy a hearty breakfast and fill their lunchboxes from the cold buffet before setting offshore to do battle. Though a pro golfer for almost 20 years, angling won through in the end when Garry started Hemingway's in 1988. Now he specialises in fly rodding for the acrobatic sailfish, which lights up and changes colour from electric blues to various shades of purple during memorable fights on size 11 or 12 weight fly tackle and pinkish coloured flies up to 9 inches in length tied on a size 6/0 hook.

The general technique however, (though guests are encouraged to try the fly rodding approach), is trolling at somewhere between 6 and 8 knots in these clear, warm blue seas, anything up to 25 miles from base. Hemingway's Resort is situated in the middle of a huge bay protected 400 yards out by a natural reef, providing a safe inner harbour to the dozen or so game boats anchored in the Watamu National Marine Park and Reserve. Established in 1968 there are over 1000 species of fish and 200 types of coral to be found here in shallow, crystal-clear water which ensures guests enjoy unparalleled snorkelling, plus trips in the glass-bottomed boat to feed the friendliest of reef fishes which take bread scraps from your hand.

Other facilities organised at the resort include horse riding and golf, wind surfing, beach BBQs scuba diving, and dhow trips along the tranquil waters of nearby Mida Creek sipping exotic Hemingway's specials called Damas. Strangely in Swahili this means 'medicine' and is a wonderful concoction of crushed ice, vodka, lime juice, sugar and honey. Seafood 'bitings' cooked on board are also served during these sundowner trips which afford interesting spotting for a galaxy of wading birds working the mangrove-lined mudflats, including curlews, egrets, herons etc., plus ospreys and fish eagles high overhead.

MADEIRA - MY BLUE HAVEN

Less than a mile offshore from the second tallest cliff face in Europe, an awesome granite feature separating landscaped terraces of fruit trees, vineyards and flowers on either side, the sea bed continues to shelve steeply downwards to over 2000 feet. Here the sea is a majestic void of warm, purple-blue water where flying fish and dolphins skip the waves. Go a mile further out to where small groups of commercial tuna boats chum live mackerel on the drift in search of big eyes, the depth more than doubles. Such is the incredibly deep and fertile habitat along the south coast of Madeira, which lies some 360 miles off the West African coast, just north of the Canaries. A truly magical island, perhaps most loved by tourists for its winding roads and panoramic views, exotic flowers and wines, yet revered during the 1990s by big game fishermen everywhere as the blue marlin capital of the world.

To do battle in the fighting chair with these mammoth creatures which average between 600 and 700 lbs, blue water fishermen come from Cairns in Australia, Fort Lauderdale in America and most places in between for one very good reason. More 'granders' (marlin topping 1000 lbs) have been caught off Madeira's southern coastline in recent years than anywhere else on this planet. Phenomenal statistics indeed when you also consider that most are taken trolling within two to seven miles of the picturesque shoreline, colourfully dotted by white painted houses with terracotta roofs for as far into the hills as the eye can see.

So after just 10 minutes from leaving the marina in Funchal, Madeira's capital, lures are run out behind the boat and the chance of a jumbo-sized marlin begins. But as my boat partner and I were to experience, such gladiators do not happen along willy nilly and towards the end of our fourth day nothing had so much as even poked its bill out above the waves to inspect the carefully arranged formation of six marlin lures being trolled at around 9 knots.

Fellow angling journalist Dave Stuart and I had been invited along by angling fanatic Frank Perry, who in addition to being a British karate champion for several years, runs Madeira Sportsfishing with two superbly equipped big game fishing boats out of Funchal marina: *Margarita,* a 35 foot Maine coaster, and *Lara Jade,* a 33 foot Cyfish which actually holds the world record for catching more 'granders' than any other boat. Frank's business was previously owned by my old mate Roddy Hays, who was responsible for putting Madeira slap bang on the marlin map a few years ago with outstanding catches of huge blues, all caught and released during the season which runs from May through to November, many exceeding that magical 1000 lbs barrier.

Regular viewers of my *Go Fishing* television series may remember that Roddy and I initially teamed up for a wreck fishing programme when he lived in Alderney, and then several years later for some big-eyed tuna action in Madeira from his old boat *Anguilla.* But the vision of sports fishing in Madeiran waters goes back further still to the pioneering exploits of another very dear friend, the late Trevor Housby, whose catches 25 years ago indicated the island's untapped potential. By sheer coincidence Islda Housby (Madeiran by birth) and Trevor's 17-year-old son, Russel, were holidaying on the island during our stay and it was like going back full circle for me, having Russ actually crewing on our boat. But Russ couldn't make those marlin move any more than Frank could.

To change our fortunes we even tried a day's shark fishing on *Lara Jade,* skippered by Anibal Fernandez and Richard Howell, our four big mackerel baits set at different depths beneath partly inflated balloons, drifting along away from the boat in a superb slick of mackerel rubby dubby. But nothing. Then we had a go at drifting for broad bill swordfish at night using large whole squid presented deep down beneath clear plastic bottle floats each illuminated from within by a different coloured light source – great fun and I especially enjoyed catching the squid for bait using mackerel tail and jigging lures. But nothing again and I could sense Frank's frustration at those big blues not wanting to play ball. He was certainly up for Dave and I sampling some 'Madeira Magic'.

On the positive side, even during our short stay (while fishing from *Lara Jade*) and four days is not nearly enough time for marlin, a monster blue of 950 lbs was taken on Margarita, skippered by Mark Ryder Haggard and Mark Ryan. So when I fished on *Margarita,* and finally that 80 lb line class reel screamed into action like a scalded cat, with but two hours remaining on my last afternoon, for an instant I thought the miracle just might have happened. As we were trolling around the commercial tuna boats, however, pulling a mixture of both marlin and tuna lures in the hope of last call action, common sense suggested that a big-eyed tuna had grabbed hold and immediately sounded deep. But I was far from complaining and into the fighting chair like a shot, quickly clicking the bucket seat straps on to the reel lugs. The fish was by now a fair way behind the boat still ripping line down in to the blue void, so I slowly increased the lever drag to slow it down before pumping the rod quickly up and down to gain line – lovely stuff. Suddenly the world was a better place. As the converted know only too well, tuna really do wrench your arms out of their sockets and for 10-15 minutes I really had my 80 lb string pulled savouring a great scrap and tug of war with what materialised into my largest big-eye ever, a klonker of 220 lbs – can't wait to get back after a marlin though.

GET YOUR STRING PULLED IN THE BAHAMAS

Following the flights from Heathrow to Miami, to Nassau and to Exuma, it was difficult to believe that over 30 years had flown by since I last fished in the Bahamas. And my mind instantly returned to those carefree, early years in the Merchant Navy when on board the P&O cruise ship *SS Oronsay* I enjoyed some fabulous battles with sharks in the warm blue waters off Nassau. This recent visit, however, was entirely different and started with an unexpected invitation from Linda Patterson on behalf of the Bahamas Tourist Office to compete in the first World Invitational Bonefishing Championship (fly only) as the UK entrant alongside anglers from Japan, Italy, the USA and the Bahamas.

As the lucky prizewinners of the competition certainly experienced, the exotic islands of the Bahamas have the largest bonefish habitat anywhere in the world. Situated in the south-western corner of the Atlantic, due east of Miami, this coral archipelago wonderland comprises of 100,000 square miles of shallow ocean plateaux from which sprout over 700 exotic islands, which incidentally were under British rule until independence in 1973. The highest point is just 200 feet above sea level and the average all-year-round temperature is in the mid 80s. A tropical paradise indeed, with unrivalled hospitality and friendliness, that sports over 20 dedicated world-class bonefishing resorts separated by coral reefs, cays and mile upon mile of sparkling white sandy beaches and mudflats where, when illuminated by sunlight, the crystal-clear sea takes on all manner of breathtaking colours from shimmering jade green to cobalt blue, and from aquamarine to turquoise or emerald green.

The World Invitational Bonefishing Championship, the first of its kind, was held in the middle of the Bahamas, on Exuma, a 90-miles-long chain of islands of James Bond fame, both *Thunderball* and *Never Say Never Again* were filmed on location here. Exuma has 365 separate cays (pronounced 'keys') offering a wide diversity of bonefish habitats, from the classic wide sandy flats to dense mangrove inlets, swamps and lagoons where goliath herons, sandpipers, egrets and even ospreys are daily sightings. The local Bahamian guides have unbelievably sharp eyesight plus a vast knowledge of their particular patch and whilst wading, drifting or poling you along they are continually pointing out barracuda and any one of several species of sharks which also hunt bonefish along the same shallow flats. Except that unlike the fly fishermen, these predators don't practise catch and release. Huge stingrays are also regularly encountered sometimes in mere inches of water and on one occasion I was treated to the exceptionally rare sight of a huge sawfish, fully 12 feet in length, digging aggressively into the bottom mud for crabs using its tooth-laden saw.

The competition was exceptionally well organised and run over four consecutive days from the Club Peace and Plenty by the enthusiastic team from the Ministry of Tourism. Every entrant was allocated a different guide and a different observer (to see fair play) each morning which ensured that the same ground was never covered twice. Indeed, as only specimen bonefish measuring more than 22 inches from nose to tail fork counted for points in the competition (we are talking of bonefish weighing 6 lbs and upwards here), the guides were continually searching for schools or pods which contained the odd sizeable fish, or were on the look-out for those single, lone bonefish which generally averaged a larger size. This hunt necessitated continually zapping across the flats and reefs at speeds approaching 40 knots from one favourite hot spot to another, and covering anything up to 40 or 50 miles during a day which started with lines in at 7.15 a.m. and lines out at 3.15 p.m.

Now the reason bonefish are held in such high esteem by international fly fishermen is that they not only accelerate faster from a standing start than any other light tackle sports fish but scream your entire 30 yard fly line out in a matter of seconds followed instantly by anything up to and over 150 yards of braided backing. Their power is truly phenomenal and combined with the fact that in these crystal-clear shallow waters you must track, stalk and then systematically sight cast individual fish, often over distances of 25 yards plus, in a stiff breeze, they are indeed a most challenging adversary.

To combat the prevailing windy conditions I used a 10 foot Avantage Venom rod and a WF9 floating line joined to 300 yards of pro micron backing. Competition rules dictated a tippet strength not exceeding 8 lbs, and my choice of adding around 8 feet of fluorocarbon to the upper half of a big butt leader helped turnover enormously. I tried all the favourite local fly patterns, and the acclaimed 'gotcha' special tied with a pearl glitter tail and body, long pink throat hair and chain eyes (to imitate a shrimp) really did the business. Whether being stripped in using slow even pulls, or allowing it time to sink, those bonefish inhaled it like the last shrimp in the sea, so hook-ups were no problem. It was landing them all that proved difficult. Trying to stop a bonefish, for instance, from winding your line through an entanglement of mangrove roots when it's doing 30 miles an hour is not easy, believe me. The classic time for hunting these wily speedsters is at low tide on the mudflats in water mere inches deep where their tails and dorsal fins stick out above the surface, as they search nose down for crabs. As the tide floods then you swap location and drift along the edge of the mangroves into which the bonefish eventually move for the rich pickings and to evade the capture by sharks – and it's all simply wonderful fun.

How did I do? Well the list of lost fish and hard luck stories would, I am sure, bore you sick, but included losing a real monster literally on my very last cast on the final day, one reason why I just cannot wait to get out on those flats again. But everyone experienced the same problems and I did in fact manage to get amongst the prize money by finishing in third place behind Buck Buchenroth of Jackson, Wyoming and Henry Roberts of Grand Bahamas (both bonefishing guides incidentally) which for a self-confessed bream basher, is better than I had ever hoped.

A FLY FISHING HAVEN

Kamalame Cay (pronounced 'key') is a boomerang-shaped tree-covered island of some 100 acres situated just off the north-east coast of Andros, largest of all the islands in the Bahamas. To those seeking total peace and tranquillity, five-star accommodation, a sumptuous cuisine and the most exciting fishing on this planet, Kamalame Cay is indeed the epitome of paradise – and it's just one of a whole range of bonefishing lodges available to the visiting angler. The management also offer guests shooting for pheasant, quail and duck, in addition to scuba diving, snorkelling, offshore trolling in blue water aboard a 36 footer, and my reason for being there as guest of the Bahamas Tourist Board, fly fishing for bonefish.

It was great to meet up again with friends Terrie Yamagishi, the Japanese editor of *Fly Fisherman*, and Florida sports fishing writer Walt Jennings. For the past three years we three had exchanged numerous stories about the vast geographical differences in our day-to-day fishing during events organised by the Ministry for Tourism, and here we were again along with fellow writers Bob Sterns, Taylor Gordon and Martin James from BBC Radio Lancashire, all bonded strongly together by our love for catching bonefish on the fly.

To the uninitiated it would perhaps seem impossible that a fish of between just 3-5 lbs (the average sized bonefish) can rip off your entire 35 yard floating line within five seconds, followed by most of the backing at equal speed. Suddenly the bonefish has travelled over 100 yards across the shallow coral-white sandy flats and is still going, despite a firm setting on your reel's disc drag. Such is the fight from every silver-sided missile you hook. Battles are made all the more memorable by the fact that individual fish are stalked and sight cast to, either by wading or from a shallow-bottomed skiff, poled stealthily along by your guide. Quite simply bonefish demand the skill of the chalkstream dry fly fisherman, yet pound for pound outfight the strongest of Atlantic salmon.

As I arrived too late in the afternoon at Kamalame Cay to arrange a guide and one of the 10 skiffs that operate from the Lodge, assistant manager Bruce accompanied me on a short wading trip across a wide series of flats between the Cay and mainland Andros. With barely an hour's serious fishing at our disposal we both hooked into specimen bonefish, having seen pods of fish tailing beside the mangroves. Bruce accounted for an eight-pounder whilst I lost one even larger through giving it too much drag when my backing was getting seriously low. Even when over 150 yards out that fish still had running power left to snap my 8 lb tippet like cotton. Another week in heaven had only just begun.

Seriously, if you own a fly fishing outfit, get yourself out to the Bahamas – fast!

Assistant manager 'Bruce' shows a magnificent 'Kamalame Cay' bonefish.

THE BOYS FROM BRAZIL

Swanning off to warmer climes every now and then gives me the opportunity not only to learn fresh techniques, but also to find ways of fishing that can be applied to certain locations back home. A classic example is a trip I made a few years back to Brazil's awesome Parana River near Foz, just below the famous Iguacu Falls – arguably even more breathtaking than Africa's Victoria Falls. The technique in question is drift fishing from a moving boat using live and dead fish to catch the legendary golden dorado, a colourful high-jumping voracious predator with immensely powerful bone-crunching jaws.

Now if I tell you that the Parana River varies between 300 and 700 yards across, with a centre channel depth seldom less than 100 feet including a heavily boulder-strewn bottom, you must realise that to the newcomer it is somewhat intimidating. Especially as it speeds along at somewhere between 6 and 8 knots sending up huge vortexes of water to spiral on to the surface. As the Parana cuts for thousands of miles through a tropical wilderness of rain forest, bordered on steep-sided banks by tall bamboos and vines, the chatter from crickets and colourful finches never ceases. Every now and then the river rises as much as 30 feet overnight due to sudden surges of water from hundreds of miles upstream. The Parana is second only to the Amazon and flows for more than 2,500 miles before entering the River Plate system. It also boasts the largest hydro-electric power dam in the world, 120 metres high, and 18 working turbines at the southern end of Lake Itaipu providing about one-third of Brazil's electricity.

To combat such a powerful river I found an 11 foot stepped-up $2^{3/4}$ lb test curve rod coupled to a multiplier holding 20 lb test mono was perfect. I cast just half an ounce of lead plus wire trace, 6/0 hook and bait 20-40 yards upstream as the boat drifted (side on to the flow) over the rockiest ledges (called corridors locally) which harbour the largest concentrations of dorado. These are thick-backed, yellow-flanked beauties weighing anything from 10 lbs to more than 60 lbs.

The technique revolves around paying out line until the morenita livebait (a 6-10 inch scaleless eel-like fish) bounces back over and along the tops of the corridor of rocks where the dorado are holding station, at current speed and no more. Obviously, as the surface layers invariably move along at a faster speed than down below, you need to be forever feeding out a little extra line to compensate but not so much that the bait becomes snagged in the rocks, as it unfortunately does with frustrating regularity. Nevertheless, thanks to the fact that dorado are born acrobats and upon feeling cold steel insist on zooming straight up to the surface where they repeatedly fling themselves clear of the water, a reasonable proportion of savage hits are converted into dorado in the boat. If they had any sense they would dive and sever the line over the rocks within seconds. Fortunately most don't. It's all great fun, brought to a wonderful climax every now and again by enormous tropical jau or pintado catfish (which grow to more than 200 lbs) grabbing the bait and setting off. Unfortunately these monsters are seldom landed on such light tackle, though they are caught commercially by locals on 400 lb test dead lines at night.

Naturally this specialised form of 'back-drifting' is a technique where you simply dare not put the rod down for a moment and one that with a few changes I now use for catching pike from my local deep and fast-flowing tidal rivers in Norfolk. The best conditions I've found are during the winter months at the bottom of low spring tides when the normally coloured tidal rivers like the Yare, Bure, Waveney and Wensum are at their clearest. I then cut the outboard motor at the top of a potentially productive reach, having positioned the boat sideways on to the flow, and drift merrily along in a world of my own. I cast back upstream working a mounted deadbait close to the bottom with between two and four swan shots on the line (depending on depth and current speed) immediately above the trace swivel in order to get it down quickly. Then start twitching it. Sometimes I need to pay out extra line in order to keep the deadbait working away in that taking depth band within two feet of the bottom. Sometimes the flow is such that this is not necessary. It really is a most fascinating way of working a river for pike. Try it and see.

JUST WILD ABOUT THE KAISER'S GIFT

I've fished in some wild and woolly places in my time but none more dangerous, breathtaking and game rich than a remote area of Tanzania called the Selous. Opened by the Germans in 1905 and said to be a birthday gift from the Kaiser to his wife (some present), this 30,000 square mile game reserve is the largest protected wildlife sanctuary in Africa, probably the entire world, yet it is inhabited by fewer than 200 people. What a place to go fishing.

Bordering The Selous and gathering strength and stature from an amalgam of wild, sandy rivers like the Kilombero, Great Ruaha and Luwegu is the mighty Rufigi, creating the largest river basin in Africa. My fishing companion was fellow angling journalist and old friend Dave Lewis from Swansea in South Wales, our final destination being the Sand Rivers Camp on the Selous at Kiba, an hour's flight by light aircraft from Dar es Salaam – a truly fascinating journey in itself. The comfortable lodge perched on stilts directly over the river was managed by an English couple, Alex and Harriet Edwards, and under the experienced supervision of Alex, who had 'second to none knowledge' of the local natural history, we explored the exotic freshwater fishing of this pristine wilderness, comprising woodland, grassy plains, swamps and marshes interlaced with natural lakes and the fast-flowing Rufigi river, for several totally fascinating days.

All manner of species are on offer here, including several types of catfish, barbel and the tooth-laden tiger fish. At some of the more remote upriver locations rarely fished by anyone, some weird and wonderful tropical catfish came our way on both fish strip and luncheon meat baits. In fact the Rufigi is simply paved with bottom-feeding predators from spined and armoured cats called squeakers, to monsters of over 5 feet long. Tiger fish strike everywhere and I would dearly loved to have stayed connected to two huge specimens which like so many tigers stay on the hook for but a few seconds only before literally 'jumping' right off. Presenting huge chunks of ledgered buffalo meat in the hope of big quarry certainly produced screaming runs on my 30 lb outfit, but fish were not to blame. It seemed quite bizarre to be standing there playing crocodiles, though usually they bit through our 50 lb wire traces post-haste. I have in fact fished in few rivers around the world containing as many crocodiles and particularly hippos as the Rufigi, and we were on constant guard from mock attacks by hippos in our aluminium punt through all the shallow parts of the river. These particular hippos definitely hated the whine from our outboard engine and were forever charging across shallows and banks towards us. Should our lightweight punt have been overturned, and taking into account the average hippo grosses two tons, making it to the shore with so many huge crocs about would have been doubtful to say the least! Talk about fishing on a knife edge, but it sure got that old adrenalin pumping.

Dave and I also enjoyed exciting sport in one of the many lakes along the river's course. In addition to numerous tiger fish in the 5-6 lbs size range, mostly on lures, we took similar-sized sharp-tooth catfish using freelined deadbaits, plus a snapping turtle that wasn't much pleased about his adventure. He hissed and spluttered but was returned, seemingly none the worse for grabbing a fish fillet.

If all this leaves the impression that when fishing in the Selous you never know what's going to grab hold next, you have got it in one. This is indeed a place of spectacular sports fishing (though we personally failed to boat anything large – monsters are undoubtedly present) and unrivalled game viewing where elephants, buffalo, giraffe, wildebeest, birds of prey and colourful bee-eaters are everyday sights, and the sweet smell of wild jasmine fills your nostrils.

TIGERS BY THE TAIL

This strange 'bottlenose' was caught by guide Steve Maartens whilst filming my 'Safari Series', October 2003.

Following a long-haul BA flight from Gatwick to Zambia's capital Lusaka, plus a three hour road transfer and finally an hour's speedboat ride down the mighty Zambesi River from Gwabi to Chiawa, my wife Jo and I were so happy to be back in Africa. Our target species was the legendary vundu catfish and the high-leaping voracious tooth-laden tiger fish which dominate the predatory food chain in these fascinating lower reaches, which are up to a mile wide and bordered by dense riverine forest along both banks.

Accompanied by friends Dave Watson and Christine Slater of Tailor Made Holidays, who arranged the safari, we stayed for the first two days at Mvuu Lodge, known as 'the place of the hippo'. Then for the remainder of the week we moved to the Royal Zambezi Lodge which offers superb, luxury riverside tent and thatch chalet accommodation set beneath a towering canopy of hardwood trees, adjacent to the Lower Zambezi National Park where the Chongue River enters the Zambezi. And a more evocative, scenically stunning location would indeed be difficult to find anywhere on this planet. In fact the river here encapsulates all that is wonderful about Africa, with a myriad of wild animals on view. There is even a friendly hippo called 'Henry' who after dark emerges from the river to nibble the grass in front of your chalet. Guests can canoe the river, go on walking safaris or drives by Landrover by day or by night. It is a veritable twitcher's paradise containing over 300 different species of birds, while huge crocs, hippos, baboons, buffalo, elephant, impala, waterbuck etc., are daily sightings to anglers exploring the river by boat. I ask you, where else can you drift downstream with the current presenting a small whole fish or fish strip freelined behind the boat, and wait for the electrifying hit of a tiger fish while enjoying the antics of hippos and elephant at surprisingly close range?

Owning a total of 18 huge interlocking triangular razor-sharp teeth (10 in the top jaw and eight in the lower) tiger fish make a wire trace mandatory. And to maximise on the ratio of fish landed to those hooked (many fling the hook clear when they jump) our experienced local guide Steve Maartens suggested we use wide gape size 5/0 hooks to hold freshly cut strips of fish fillet with a swan shot on the trace to keep it down near the river bed. The favoured 'bait fish' is the chessa *(Distichodus schenga)*, a bream-like bottom-feeding species. These we easily caught ledgering using small worms and size 10 hooks from slacks close into the bank, especially beneath and alongside overhanging trees. Chessa reach 3-4 lbs in weight and fight really hard. A similar species, the nkupe *(Distichodus mossambicus)* reaches weights over 10 lbs and is also good bait for tiger fish when filleted in 3 inch strips, 1 inch wide. Small tiger fish also provide excellent strip bait

and are easily caught using small spinners.

Using 6500 multipliers our reel lines were either 20 lb monofilament or 30 lb braid which I found much better for setting the hook, really sharp, strong hooks being essential. Our rods were strong 10 foot carp rods. In the fierce currents (tigers are best located in the rapids below drop-offs) we enjoyed some memorable, more exhilarating battles with this unique predatory species, taking several 'doubles'. The largest of close on 14 lbs was taken by my wife, Jo.

Having taken along several tins of luncheon meat with vundu catfish in mind, I was rewarded with a 60 lbs specimen from two chances. The second run I missed. These extremely powerful catfish, the largest freshwater African catfish incidentally, provide marvellous battles. They can also be caught on the drift and are often caught on tiger fish baits. But for best results it is better to anchor the boat on the sand bar immediately upstream of a drop-off and ledger static baits on the bottom – then wait. In addition to a large chunk of luncheon meat other baits guaranteed to catch vundu *(Heterobranchus longifilis)* are ox heart, liver and believe it or not, a ball of blue soap the size of a chicken's egg. Yes – soap, and the standard cheap blue soap sold in Africa works best because it is manufactured from attractive animal fats. Small whole fish of up to $1^{1}/_{2}$ lbs are also good, but are likely to be pecked to bits by many weird and wonderful smaller species such as squeaker catfish and electric catfish etc. – not recommended.

For vundu use a powerful 'uptide' sea fishing rod and multiplier reel holding either 50lbs braid or 35 lb monofilament with a 4 foot monofilament trace of 50 lb holding a 6/0 hook. A 2 oz bomb above the swivel is usually heavy enough to hold bottom in the quieter reaches frequented by vundu. Big slacks adjacent to where hippos muddy the water are particularly good spots. These catfish can reach proportions in excess of 100 lbs, so going too tight is foolhardy. Had we concentrated more on vundu instead of tiger fish I am certain more would have been caught, but we will most certainly be back.

A ZAMBEZI EXPERIENCE

Whenever sport is slow whilst trolling in freshwater I'm apt to daydream and pay perhaps more attention to the flora and fauna than the rod tip. Consequently I was studying the marvellous camouflage of a large crocodile sunning itself on a reeded sandbank mere feet from the boat when quite suddenly the rod was violently wrenched over. The reel screamed like a stuck pig as yet another big tiger fish leaped high into the air flinging my artificial lure from its tooth-laden jaws. Yes, I was back in Africa again from where I have recently returned from enjoying the antics of the world's most difficult sports fish to keep on the hook. Tiger fish are also arguably the most fearsome predator in freshwater, with no less than 18 large, triangular razor-sharp teeth and the majestic Zambezi River is full of them. But you do need to accept that even a six to one ratio of fish lost to those landed is about standard – that's tiger fishing.

Our party of 10 stayed at the Inchingo Chobe River Lodge on Impalila Island in Namibia where the Chobe and Zambezi Rivers meet. Here the unique safari-style accommodation comprises well-aired tented sleeping quarters joined to traditional African thatched en suite facilities with stunning views over the river. The lodge runs four 16 foot customised boats with 75 hp engines to purr you along at 30 miles per hour to explore a variety of locations from exciting rapids in both rivers to wild places far upstream in the Zambezi. Pools with names like Mirandi, Golden Pond, Jo Jo's and Nantunga Island,

A big tiger fish hooked by Keith Dellard from the Zambezi at Nantunga Island is safely netted by Impalila Island guide Christopher.

where the river varied anywhere from 100 to 300 yards across, all contained concentrations of tiger fish in the 3-15 lbs bracket ever eager to chomp away at our Rapala lures trolled at somewhere between 3 and 5 knots. Everyone in the party caught tigers over 8 lbs, with no fewer than eight specimens over 10 lbs recorded, the two most productive lures being Rapala's shad rap and 11 cm magnum shallow diver, due to much of Zambezi averaging just 4 – 8 foot in depth. And when you fancied a change from trolling the guide would pull over to the river's edge and simply drift with the flow just a few yards out from the dense marginal covering of tall reeds and papyrus amongst which live at least eight species of predatory bream in the 2 – 5 lb class. We then changed over from fast tip rods, braided trolling lines and multipliers to light telescopic spinning outfits, and size 4 or 5 Mepps-type spinners cast into gaps between the reeds. I also used my little 5 foot American baitcasting stick to good effect. And didn't those beautifully coloured bream pull. Every now and then a sharptooth barbel (really a catfish) in the 8 – 12 lbs range would add variety. And along the river's course hippo, elephant, giraffe, buffalo, waterbuck and huge monitor lizards were all to be seen. It was truly marvellous sport in an evocative environment so incredibly rich in exotic bird life.

This area of the Zambezi where the countries of Namibia, Botswana, Zimbabwe and Zambia all meet is in fact a twitcher's delight, with over 400 species to be seen throughout the year. We saw good numbers of fish eagles and yellow-billed kites were always visible searching along the river valley often casting a watchful eye at our shallow running lures. Huge flocks of the strange open-billed stork could regularly be seen working the thermals high overhead and again at close quarters when they came down to roost in the trees at dusk. Both the giant and the tiny and unbelievably coloured malachite kingfisher were daily sightings as were pied kingfishers along with egrets, many species of herons from tiny night herons to the giant grey heron, plus gulls and cormorants which were everywhere. The river is indeed an incredible food source. We also saw the extremely rare African finfoot.

Close to the Mambora rapids whilst trolling for tiger fish an awful stench suddenly filled our nostrils. The answer was the result of ivory poachers from across the border in Zambia who had crossed the river and shot three elephants on a reed-covered island. The carcasses were almost picked dry and covered in maggots and in the huge trees above were hundreds of vultures and marabou storks, their bellies full. The sights of Africa can sometimes be very harsh. I was, however, extremely impressed with the average size of the tiger fish, and shall return again in the hope of landing a 20 pounder. That they are present is beyond doubt.

THE MYSTERIOUS VUNDU

The building of a concrete dam across the deep gorge at Kariba back in the 1950s which flooded plains and forests for 170 miles along and up to 30 miles across the valley of the Zambezi River's middle reaches between Mlibizi and Charara, created not only one of the world's largest manmade lakes but an unbelievably exciting freshwater wilderness. Lake Kariba's 4000 square miles of fertile blue water fringed by mountains and rolling plains has become one of the greatest wildlife havens in Africa, and along with Victoria Falls, one of Zimbabwe's and Zambia's biggest tourist attractions.

Protruding above the surface all along the lush tropical shoreline are the now petrified treetops of past forests (called 'sticks' by the locals) bleached silvery white by the sun and providing perfect habitat to over 40 species of tropical freshwater fish from the aggressive high-jumping tiger fish whose teeth would shame the piranha to the giant vundu catfish. And the quite unique charm of fishing Kariba is that while out afloat fishing the wildlife actually comes to you in the form of elephant, buffalo, zebra, wild boar, waterbuck and numerous smaller animals which graze close by with hippos and the most enormous

Lifting a big 'vundu' catfish of 60 lbs plus for the cameras, was about all I could manage following a two hour battle, having hooked the beast on tackle intended for tigerfish.

157

crocodiles in the marginal lagoons amongst floating rafts of the purple-flowered water hyacinth. The ever chattering baboons in families of up to 20-30 strong are always within sight, be the shoreline of grass or rock, as are the most beautifully coloured birds including red-billed hoopoes, bee-eaters, kingfishers, plovers, storks, herons, egrets, Egyptian and spurwinged geese, fish eagles, kites and ever circling high up in the thermals above are the vultures.

So it will come as no surprise to learn that Wilson chose to swap freezing his 'wotsits' off on the Norfolk Broads just recently in exchange for guiding a party of 12 anglers on a 10 day fishing safari to Lake Kariba. Well someone had to do it, didn't they? Now a fishing safari 'Kariba style' means exploring all those mouth-watering spots you fancy for as long as you fancy. You then simply move on to another during the heat of the day when it's too hot to fish, though game viewing as you cruise along is a continual pleasure. At the disposal of our party were two 60 foot luxury cruisers complete with three crew and each with twin fishing tenders complete with engines, plus an extra fishing boat and engine. I could then rotate every morning and evening session to fish with different anglers in order to put them on the right trail.

Despite water levels at their lowest since the dam was first built, our party of anglers, all couples incidentally (Kariba is the ideal location to suit the Mrs), enjoyed some hectic action with the fearsome tiger fish amongst the sticks. Lures worked well but it was the local freshwater sardine called kapenta, freelined two or three up on a size 1/0 hook to a wire trace, which really sorted them out. We also caught bream, squeaker catfish and barbel and I had an electric catfish slip the hook at the boat – fortunately. Our most electrifying action, however, occurred in the Sanyati Gorge when after the legendary vundu catfish for which as bait you use soap – yes soap. A chicken egg-sized lump of local blue soap seems best, probably because it contains animal fat and oils which ooze out and attract only vundu. It is, therefore, a very selective bait because if you use a lump of meat or fish everything from the tiniest-toothed tropical aquarium fish up to a crocodile is liable to grab hold. So soap it is, covering a forged 6/0 hook on a swivelled 3 foot mono trace of 40 lb test which resists the abrasive teeth of the vundu. A heavy spinning or light uptide rod and multiplier filled with 25-35 lb mono completed the outfit.

The actual technique revolves around drifting along with the tender side on to the wind, preferably with a drogue out the side to slow the boat down, and literally to bump the soap gently and slowly along the bottom. And when a vundu grabs hold the line usually evaporates from the reel at alarming speed. So it pays to keep the spool out of gear with the ratchet on. After several yards have been taken you then slam the reel into gear, allow the line to fully tighten, and lean back, at which point the vundu does a runner taking up to100 yards of line out against the clutch in several unstoppable bursts. When it finally slows down it's an arduous fight bringing it up to the top for netting because when it finally sees daylight this mysterious armour-headed catfish power-dives down to the bottom again and you are immediately back to square one.

From three vundu sessions the party accounted for no less than eight fish averaging over 60 lbs with three lost due to inexperience more than anything. My brother and I both boated vundu over 70 lbs and a real whopper of 95 lbs was finally landed after a tremendous hour-long battle by Ruth Taylor from Huntingdon who weighs only 5 lbs heavier herself.

THE DEVIL'S CAULDRON

Isn't it amazing these days how quickly we can be fishing in another continent? A couple of weeks back I drove from my Norfolk home in the afternoon to meet up with fellow angling journalist Dave Lewis from Swansea at Heathrow's Terminal 1. By 8.00 p.m. we had boarded an Air Alliance overnight flight direct to Entebbe and $7^{1}/_{2}$ hours later (there is a three hour time difference) we arrived in central East Africa in Uganda. Our guide, Jonathan Wright of 'Semliki Safaris' loaded all our tackle into his 4x4 and just a few hours later we were overlooking one of the world's most awesome freshwater locations at famous Murchison Falls. Here the entire might of the River Nile, the world's longest river, is channelled through a narrow gap in the rocks, mere yards wide, amid a maelstrom of thundering white water to fall over 100 feet into a churning pool below aptly named the Devil's Cauldron. I doubt we could have been salmon fishing in Scotland any quicker.

But our quarry was the legendary Nile Perch. The following morning we were joined by local expert Marco Magyar, whose personal best perch from Murchison Falls weighed a staggering $237^{1}/_{2}$ lbs – a world record had it been ratified. Our accommodation at the Nile Safari Camp situated below the Falls necessitated a 20 minute boat journey up the Nile which averages between 200 and 400 yards wide bordered along both banks by dense tropical vegetation. A fascinating trip in itself where families of hippos, huge crocodiles, buffalo, fish eagles, kites and a myriad of other colourful birds were everyday and all-day sights. These equatorial upper reaches of the Nile are so vastly different to the desert landscape of the Nile in Egypt where I had previously fished.

To catch bait we used light spinning outfits and size 00 Mepps and soon accounted for small tiger fish and colourful oddities like alestes and awaka of between 1 and 2 lbs - perch baits supreme. These were then trundled from the boat on two hook rigs to 30 lb reel lines around the slow, deep back eddies on both sides of the river about a mile downstream of Murchison Falls. I lost a good perch of around 60 lbs just when I was getting the better of it and Dave caught his first ever Nile Perch of around 30 lbs so he was happy. We each also caught hard-battling bagrus (sementendu) catfish of around 30 lbs apiece, a species which reaches weights of 80 lbs plus. Vundu catfish called 'mali' locally are also present but how they are landed from amongst such an entanglement of rocks and white water I just don't know.

The boat was then tied up half a mile below the pool and we walked along the banks via steep narrow pathways up to the Devil's Cauldron itself, a most intimidating fishing spot. Fall in here and you will be carried downstream for half a mile to where huge crocs patiently wait on the sand bars. Again it was my misfortune to pull the hooks from a good perch which grabbed a tiger fish of fully 2 lbs, before landing one of around 30 lbs on an orange Rapala, and what spectacular fights these gladiators put up in the fast turbulent water where depths can vary anything from 10 to over 50 feet. It is the lure fisherman's consummate challenge, believe me. Incidentally, due to the heavy rains which make fishing in the Nile at Murchison Falls an impossibility at certain times of the year, the period between December and March is best by far.

All too soon we had to leave the Falls for the next leg of our whirlwind tour of Uganda's spectacular freshwater fishing: a trolling stint on famous Lake Victoria around the beautiful Sesse Islands just 20 miles offshore from Entebbe.

THE SESSE ISLANDS

Wild Frontiers guide Paul Goldring assists Christine Slater display a 70 lb Sesse Islands Nile Perch caught trolling on a Rapala super shad rap.

Fellow angling journalist Dave Lewis and I enjoyed some fabulous fishing for catfish and perch in the River Nile at spectacular Murchison Falls in Uganda, before travelling overland to Kampala and then on to Entebbe which overlooks the shores of massive Lake Victoria. This, the second largest lake on our planet (behind Lake Superior), really does look like the ocean and is in fact the source of the Nile. There are over 1000 islands on Lake Victoria and our final destination, the Sesse Islands, which contain no fewer than 84 of them, was but 20 miles and an hour's boat trip away.

Jonathan Wright, our guide, introduced Dave and me to skipper Paul Goldring of G&C Tours, whose 20 foot trolling boat, sporting a pair of 60 horse outboards, was soon whisking us across the waves. Naturally my thoughts drifted back to when I had first fished for perch on Lake Victoria some 10 years ago, whilst filming one of my *Go Fishing* television programmes. Our base then was Rusinga Island over on the eastern side where just 15 per cent of the shoreline is owned by Kenya, the rest being shared equally between Tanzania and Uganda.

My boat partner during filming was good friend Andy Davison, who a couple of years later, whilst on honeymoon, would you believe, trolling a gold Russellure, caught a $191\frac{1}{2}$ lbs Nile perch which held the world record for eight years until it was eclipsed by a 213 pounder from Lake Nasser in Egypt. Just a couple of years back, however, though it has not been ratified by the International Game Fishing Association, Mr Savel Du Plessis caught a massive perch of 251 lbs trolling a Rapala CD18 off Entebbe from a boat called Isabella. That Lake Victoria wants her Nile perch record back there is little doubt and few locations offer more promise than the densely forested Sesse Islands, the best period being from August through until March. It is only the largest island which has any substantial development, the rest remain unspoilt tropical havens full of exotic birds and monkeys where dense canopies of vines and tall hardwood trees overhang the steep shorelines as you troll lures along the drop-offs, sometimes mere yards from the dense vegetation.

With fish eagles, kites and buzzards circling overhead here, on a diet of freshwater crabs, tilapia and their smaller brethren, Nile perch abound and are never far from sunken rocky drop-offs. And we were soon into them – a good dozen small fish to 20 lbs came our way trolling Russel lures, Rapalas and the Depth Raiders, before Jonathan took a fine 45 pounder. Dave Lewis then followed up with a 57 pounder and I hooked into a fish which fought far harder than its 88 lbs. What with several more modest-sized fish landed plus a couple of lost biggies which threw the hooks, our short stay which barely amounted to a day and a bit's trolling, made me think about one thing only – when I'm going back.

MONSTER PUSSIES ON THE EBRO

Exactly one year had elapsed since catfish conservation group stalwarts Keith Lambert, Simon Clarke and myself visited Spain last March. Yet the drive from Barcelona airport travelling due west through fast mountainous roads bordered by blossom-covered almond and peach trees was just as beautiful. Our destination was the town of Mequinenza where the Rio Segre joins forces with the mighty Rio Ebro, which rises in the Pyrenees and meanders in an easterly direction for over 700 miles before entering the Mediterranean through an immense delta in the region of Catalonia. A river which without question throughout its lower reaches is Europe's most carp, zander and catfish packed fishery.

Fishing here is all made possible by the Bavarian Guiding Service which provides excellent accommodation, boats, tackle and experienced guides. One such fellow is jovial

Gary Allen from St Albans who really knows how to put his guests on to those jumbo-sized wels catfish. And as more than one in every three catfish caught locally weighs in excess of that magical 100 lbs figure, I can think of no other location so relatively close to home (less than a two hour flight from Luton to Barcelona, followed by a drive of the same duration) which offers such incredible and accessible big fish potential.

As last year, our first task was to quiver tip sweetcorn along the margins to catch carp livebaits, and this in itself is great fun. The Ebro is simply stuffed with common carp to well over 40 lbs and at times it's difficult to tear yourself away from bait catching, especially when double-figure fish grab hold and provide a lengthy tussle. My sensitive telescopic Nomad Avon quiver tip never received such a battering. But big pussies were our target species after all, however, and on the second evening the largest catfish to be landed from five runs weighed a huge 110 lbs to the rod of Keith Lambert. But it was nowhere near the largest wels catfish we saw caught during our week's stay. German angler Torsten Stejmann from Hamburg landed a monstrous 7-foot-long specimen weighing 154 lbs. And what an incredible fish it was – stunningly coloured in green and grey spots and mosaic patterns, overlaid on a yellowy, greeny brown body.

The entire area around the confluence of the Segre with the Ebro is now so prolific in big cats, visitors have a choice of several effective techniques in addition to the normal ploys of float fishing or tethering carp or eels in choice lies. More and more pussies nowadays are being caught on soft plastic lures, shads, twintails, twister tails, bulldawgs and the like and on sporting 30 – 50 lb class outfits. These lures are particularly successful in the faster, shallow parts of the system where the cats lie up beneath feature lies just as chub or pike do. And of course if you ever get bored with the catfishing there are enough zander about in the 5 – 12 lbs range to make even lighter lure fishing most enjoyable indeed. Roll on next year.

*Torsten Stejmann (left) is helped by Peter Obshlager to display his massive
154 lbs Rio Ebro catfish.*

SLUGGING IT OUT WITH GIANT STURGEON

Where do fishing dreams become reality? In British Columbia in Canada, that's where, in the mighty Frazer River which boasts the largest runs of salmon on this planet. Coho, chum, sockeye, pink and chinook salmon are so incredibly plentiful, that failing to catch is simply not an option.

Having just returned from the Frazer valley at Chilliwack which is 70 miles due east of Vancouver and overlooked by the snow-topped Rocky Mountains, it is indeed difficult to think of a more exciting and prolific freshwater location. Because catching salmon to over 20 lbs each day is only half of what's on offer. Our party of six Brits were more interested in doing battle with the enigmatic white sturgeon, arguably the world's largest freshwater species which attains weights in excess of 1000 lbs.

Fishing from fast 20 foot jet boats, using powerful boat rods, multiplier reels loaded with 100 lbs braid and extra strong 6/0 hooks, monsters of this size are occasionally hooked but rarely landed. Those in the 100 – 200 lbs bracket are, however, considered attainable everyday catches which bite readily to lamprey heads or sections ledgered on the bottom in the strong flow of the Frazer River. The most productive bait, however, is a golfball-size wodge of fresh salmon eggs wrapped up in a section of nylon tights or stockings - honestly!

In depths of between just 10 to over 50 feet the bait is hoovered up by the white sturgeon with surprising finesse. Upon seeing the rod tip nodding it pays to drop the tip to encourage a more positive indication before slamming the hook home. At which point all hell usually breaks loose in the form of a blistering run which can rip anything up to 100 yards from a tightly set clutch, immediately followed by a spectacular polaris-style leap. There then follows a powerful and - should the sturgeon prove to be a whopper - a long and incredibly strength sapping fight. Two such leviathans came our way during the week's fishing. The first came off unfortunately but the second gave David Chesterman from Fleet in Hampshire the battle of his angling life. The mighty fish eventually being beached over a quarter of a mile from where it was first hooked, measured close to eight feet long and weighed over 300 lbs.

HIGHEST JUMPERS HARDEST TO HOOK

I'm often asked which fish fight the hardest, but as there are so many variables involved covering coarse, sea and game species in both still and running water, not forgetting tropical speedsters which, because their metabolic rate is far higher, probably perform best of all, I always find myself stuck for a one-fish answer. If, however, I was asked which are the most difficult species to hook and which jump the highest, then instantly I could narrow it down to just three fabulous, acrobatic fighters: one from the sea and two from tropical freshwater. Tarpon, tiger fish and the golden dorado. Each leaps high into the air upon feeling the hook in a fabulous show of gill-flaring acrobatics and for one reason or another particular to that species, provides no small amount of uncertainty about its eventually being landed.

Built like a giant herring with an equally bony, fully expandable mouth, huge silver scales and unbelievable stamina, the tarpon, which has a potential maximum weight exceeding 300 lbs, can be caught in many top tropical saltwater locations around the world, including the West African coastline, the Bahamas, the Caribbean, the Gulf of Mexico, the Florida Keys and in both Central and South America. Its incredibly bony mouth always makes setting even the sharpest of hooks uncertain, especially when tempting them on artificial lures or with the fly rod. But then most fly rodding tarpon enthusiasts are content merely with 'jumping them'. Seeing a tarpon grab their fly, enjoy that first, maybe even the second leap before they literally jump off the hook. Those who float fish live mullet or fresh crab usually enjoy a much improved hook-up rate but no one ever goes on to enjoy the fight of every tarpon they hook. Overall most are happy if they get to land one out of five.

With the fearsome tiger fish, which owns an even more impressive set of jaws than most sharks, the landing to hooking rate is even less. This unbelievably acrobatic and aggressive freshwater predator with distinctly bright red fins, lives in several of Africa's major river systems including the Nile and the Zambezi and in the lakes through which they flow. Double-figure specimens are common and the species grows to weights in excess of 30 lbs.

In the democratic republic of the Congo (formerly Zaire) in the Congo River lives the truly enigmatic goliath tiger fish which, believe it or not, has been caught on rod and line to over 100 lb with inch-long teeth to match. Without question the most awesome predator in freshwater anywhere in the world. Whether trolling or casting artificial lures, hooking any tiger fish is usually much improved by swapping the rear treble for a large wide-gape single which more easily finds purchase behind the 18 large canine teeth which are set 10 in the top and eight in the bottom of its strong jaws. Treble hooks all too easily become caught between these teeth and are flung forcibly out on the tiger fish's first exhilarating leap. They literally catapult themselves out of the water. Losing 10 tigers straight off from 10 hits is not unusual.

Last but not least comes the golden dorado of South America's mighty Parana River system, which in the distinct colour pattern of its swallow-shaped tail is not totally unlike the tiger fish. The dorado, however, is bathed in yellowy gold and has much smaller teeth. Its jaws however have extra strong crunching power which instantly flattens even strongly forged treble hooks fitted to the very best quality lures. Capable of reaching weights topping 60 lbs this formidable predator has enormous jumping power and will instantly come zooming up even from 20 to 40 feet down when hooked amongst rocks to leap high into the air in a glittering shower of spray and fling the hook. For sheer speed, cussedness, acrobatic jumping prowess and their ability of shaking the hook out, I find it very difficult to choose between the tarpon, tiger fish and the golden dorado. They are each crazy, crazy fish.

MAHSEER MAGIC

Several years have elapsed since my wife Jo and I visited the wonderful jungles of southern India where goliath mahseer live among the boulder-strewn rapids of a truly awesome river, the Cauvery. India is indeed a land of bizarre extremes in both wealth and poverty and this time Jo stayed at home while I perilously (don't question this until you drive in India) manoeuvred the jeep along 60 miles of pot-holed roads shared by chickens, monkeys, ox carts, goat herders, auto rickshaw (a three wheel taxi) and India's favourite car, the Ambassadeur, none other than what was once our own old Morris Oxford – yes, you can still buy a new version in India!

Enjoying the drive south from Banglaore down towards the valley I have come to love so much were my brother Dave, the late Len Head, and Jason Davies, who had each successfully sweet-talked me into sharing India with them. India has entered my soul and the mighty mahseer lived up to its legendary expectations as the world's most powerful and enigmatic freshwater sports fish. It's a species of barbel that grows to over 100 lbs, has scales the size of beer mats and pharyngeal (throat) teeth the size of a child's hands. Like no other fish it swims effortlessly among the white water rapids in excess of 10 knots where it dines on most species of fish, including its own kind, and upon river crabs.

Throughout the dusty drive in temperatures well above 100°F my mind wandered back to when old mate Andy Davison, and I first spent an arduous five weeks at the river with few provisions. As the road started to descend towards the river valley around hairpin bends, I pondered whether all the stories I had heard recently were true and if our fishing would be affected. Poaching through illegal netting was apparently now commonplace along with more dynamiting than ever. To cap it all, overfishing by parties of foreign anglers along my favourite stretch was even keeping the locals away from their

Assisted by Martin Founds of Anglers World Holidays, I am still having trouble lifting this 80 lb Indian 'golden mahseer' for the camera, following an epic, hour long battle.

own river. How sad that commercial interests always overtake spiritual reasoning. Then we were merrily bumping along the track which cuts through dense thorn scrub towards our final destination where I had planned to make camp.

Due mainly to the previous year's monsoon rains that had left the river running too cold and too high by far we perhaps didn't catch as many mahseer as I'd hoped for. Our tackle consisted of 11 foot 3 lb test curve rods and multipliers loaded with 35lb test mono and size 6/0 hooks tied direct, with just an ounce of lead strip wound around the line 20 inches above to deliberately catch in the rocks and hold our baits steady in the fierce currents where the biggest mahseer prefer to hold station. Standard bait for mahseer is 'ragi-paste' made from the locally grown and ground millet flour which has been moulded into chicken egg-sized balls after adding water, and then boiled for 20 minutes to bring out the natural gluten. This makes a fabulous 'rubbery' paste-cum-boilie which withstands the fast flow and the constant 'pecking' from smaller species.

My favourite bait for mahseer, however, is a deep-bodied bream-like fish called a 'petagara' and once my guide, Suban, had procured one in his cast net and I'd lobbed it upstream and across the flow to bounce along attractively in the white water between huge boulders, it wasn't long before something grabbed hold and slammed the rod tip hard over. This leviathan, however, could not be budged (usually a big mahseer immediately belts off downriver) because the line was trapped among the rocks. So it was into the coracle post-haste and over to the opposite side of the river so that a more direct line of pull could be achieved. Trouble was there were but 30 yards of turbulent water remaining between the unseen monster, which was still on and attempting to pull my arms out of their sockets, and a steep drop over into fierce rapids where a maelstrom of white water crashed over massive car-sized boulders for several hundred yards downstream. I had the choice of piling on maximum pressure and possibly risk losing a monster due to line abrasion, or taking things easy and following the mahseer down through the rapids. A route it could have easily taken simply with a flick of its vast tail. For when a mahseer does turn side on to the flow no fishing rod and line combination in the world has the credentials for stopping it.

Fortunately, as it turned out, I chose the former option, gritted my teeth and started to pump heavily while leaning back from a position high up on a rocky ledge to achieve maximum torque. And although the great fish made numerous gut-wrenching runs, it never quite made those rapids. Consequently, after an unbelievably tiring battle lasting 30 minutes – short for such a big fish – I finally managed to guide its bulk into the edge and into the arms of a grinning Suban. It was a noticeably long thickset specimen which pulled the spring balance down to exactly 91 lbs – it looked much heavier.

These phenomenal creatures are truly majestic fish. It was in fact my second largest mahseer ever and though our party accounted for others of 78 lbs, 68 lbs, 52 lbs and many between 20 and 40 lbs, it proved to be the best of a most memorable trip.

MAHSEER MAKE US WAIT

To be successful when fishing the Upper Great Ouse for specimen perch and chub you need to be always alert and concentrate as though you have just missed a bite and are expecting another. Well, strange though it may seem, Mahseer fishing in the rock-strewn rapid water of Indian rivers is no different – only the climate and location. With buttocks perched uncomfortably around jagged black bedrock and one knee raised to support the rod butt against the unbelievable force of the current, you patiently wait with a ledgered chicken egg-sized ball of ragi-paste or a 6 oz deadbait cast downstream and across, conveniently caught with a small spiral of lead amongst the rocks in the fastest deepest pools. You wait for perhaps 20, 40 or even 60 minutes for those thick rubbery lips of the mahseer's cavernous mouth to vacuum up the bait and belt off downstream, thus tearing the lead coil from the rocks and in the process virtually hooking itself, not in an dissimilar fashion to the way in which our European barbel bites. Only a mahseer bite is like attaching your line to a runaway lorry, and in the meantime whilst you wait your eyes greedily observe all the wonders of the river valley.

You hear the distinct 'did-de-do-it, did-de-do-it' of the red wattled lapwing as it mobs an eagle or crow venturing too close above its nest amongst the dense marginal vegetation. You smile whilst watching the inquisitive antics of the Indian otter at play, or an elderly woman cow herder (women's lib really works in India) scold her buffaloes as they graze upon coarse grasses provided by the lifeblood of this charismatic country – the monsoon rains.

Eleven years had passed since buddy Andy Davison and I first visited Southern India and the state of Karnataka to do battle with the mighty mahseer. Yet just recently here we were again camping beside the Cauvery River marvelling at its rich diversity in natural history. On our first evening we were treated to the kind of experience that still might not happen were you to spend a month of Sundays birdspotting in Scotland. We watched for fully 20 minutes as an osprey searched the shallows along the opposite bank from where we sat fishing not 60 yards away. Every now and then it would hover in that strange wing-flapping leant-back stance with talons outstretched, not unlike a goose coming into land, before plummeting down in an attempt to grab its prey, which eventually turned out to be a mahseer of around $1\frac{1}{2}$ lbs. What a truly majestic sight. It then circled directly overhead as if to say, 'Well I've got my dinner,' before flying away down the valley to its nest.

We had to admit that the osprey which we observed most evenings was far more successful than us. Due to the river running higher than we would have liked for the end of March, and noticeably a little colder, the mahseer were not concentrated in the pools where past experiences suggested they should have been, neither were they biting. We should have perhaps arranged a longer stay than just seven days at the river, to allow for the fluctuating water levels, because for the first three days not a single bite came our way from prime pools which for over a decade had produced countless hour-long fights with monster mahseer weighing between 60 and 90 lbs. In fact never before had we visited without catching mahseer over 70 lbs.

A marker stone placed in the margins suddenly revealed one morning that the river had gone down a measly inch. Now we are talking here of a river hundreds of miles long, which in parts widens to between 300 and 400 yards across and increases in depth to over 30 feet during the monsoon rains. So why on earth one inch should suddenly make the mahseer bite I cannot imagine, but they did, though in temperature and in clarity the river appeared the same.

From three sessions we caught just five mahseer before the river started rising again which instantly put the kiss of death upon further sport. Using deadbaits I took a real baby of around 5 lbs followed by others of 30 and 35 lbs respectively whilst Andy had two, one of 30 lbs and the second a superb golden mahseer of exactly 70 lbs, which led him and guide Bola a merry song and dance up and down the river in the coracle. By some miracle the river had rewarded our efforts with the stamp of mahseer for which it has become famous, on our last day.

CARRY ON UP THE NILE

Lake Nasser, created by the building of a high dam at Aswan in the 1950s which flooded more than 300 miles of the Nile Valley, is not only Egypt's largest sheet of freshwater – this former desert, now a wildllife haven, is also one of the largest manmade lakes in the world, with a surface area of 2,500 square miles. As far as you can see the shoreline is one of sand, interspersed with tall rocky outcrops and hills. It's a harsh and seemingly barren land but scorpions, giant spiders, lizards, snakes, crocodiles, jackals, gerbils, foxes and numerous birds of prey, plus egrets, herons, plovers, Egyptian geese, bee-eaters, pelicans and occasionally flamingos share the watery wilderness of a lake which has a unique if somewhat strange spiritual beauty.

Most tourists make the long pilgrimage by light aircraft or by coach from Aswan to Abu Simbel at the south-western end, to marvel at the temple and formidable sculptures of the pharaohs. They were built by Rameses II to impose fear among the Nubian

On Lake Nasser, perch exceeding 100 lbs, like this beauty displayed for the camera by top guide Mohamed, are called 'buffaloes'.

population. However, anglers exploring by boat actually get to see very much more, as is often the case.

The entire sports fishing operation on Lake Nasser, called 'The African Angler', is the brainchild of Tim Baily, a genial softly spoken and farsighted Kenyan. He decided to explore the fishing potential several years back after watching one of my *Go Fishing* television programmes about the Nile perch fishing of Lake Victoria in Kenya. This I consider a wonderful compliment because, while Lake Victoria has to some extent declined through the ill management and overfishing, Baily's catch and release policies will hopefully preserve what I consider to be the world's most exciting and challenging stillwater fishing. That's not just for Nile perch but also the tooth-laden tiger fish, plus vundu catfish and large tilapias. Where else can you stand on the shore – rock-hopping is perhaps a better description – and on artificial lures using a 20 lb reel line and a heavy spinning rod have the opportunity of slamming into freshwater gladiators of between 10 and 100 lbs, or believe it or not, monsters of even twice that size? Lake Nasser's Nile perch record over 200 lbs to the rod of Wilma Mcdermid was rocked recently by a German visitor's report of a 260 lb monster. Nasser is quite capable of throwing up very much larger leviathans still.

Proof came a few weeks back while I was escorting groups on safari by boat throughout the lake's middle reaches between Garf Hussein and Khor Mariya with English guide Will Wragg. I was having a wonderful time casting along the shoreline taking some real scrappy perch to close on 70 lbs. Then I hooked a comparatively small one of around 15 lbs close to the bottom in 20 feet of water. I couldn't understand why it zoomed straight up to the surface and propelled itself high into the air like a polaris

169

missile. But when it came close in amongst the rocks only a few feet out all was revealed. Immediately below, breathtakingly visible, was a Nile perch the size of which one only dreams about. My 15 pounder was to have been its next meal or 'snack'. For several minutes this monster followed my hooked fish around, allowing me to estimate its incredible bulk. I put it at 6 feet in length, 18 inches across the back and about 24 inches in depth. It was that close I could have tapped it on the head with my rod tip. That perch could not have weighed less than 200 lbs. Although I have caught and witnessed the capture of numerous other Nile perch plus mahseer and tarpon all of between 90 and 160 lbs this monster took my breath away. It's a memory I shall never forget.

For the trip Normark Sport kindly provided me with a whole range of their incredibly strong Rapala artificial lures with the most effective patterns proving to be shad raps over shallow, boulder-strewn water around the shorelines and the CD sinking Magnums for deeper water. My favourite is the CD 14 cm (in blue mackerel), CD meaning countdown. This allows you to count the lure's 'nose first' descent at about a foot per second. They are a particularly useful feature for exploring deep troughs and gulleys well out from the rocky shoreline. Our party accounted for several huge perch between 80 and 95 lbs while trolling using the 18 cm Magnums and deep-diving 'depth raiders' which come in both sinking and floater/diving formats.

Even more medium-sized specimens came while shore fishing. Something I really enjoy about Lake Nasser. That's a sentiment shared by John Jarvis, a retired builder from Hillingdon in Middlesex. His first ever Nile perch, which took a shad rap cast just five yards from the rocky ledges of a small island, weighed a staggering 90 lbs. What a baptism.

No doubt we shall be back again next year to feel the heat of the Egyptian sun and marvel at how a desert has become a feature-packed habitat playground for both man and beast, and battle with those incredible monsters in the land of the pharaohs.

A MONSTER AT LAST

For many many years now it has been my personal ambition to catch a freshwater fish weighing in excess of that magical 100 lbs barrier. I've certainly done my time over the years and enjoyed some fabulous sport in the tropics, coming close with giant vundu catfish to 95 lbs from Zimbabwe's massive Lake Kariba, and I've beaten no fewer than three mahseer over 90 lbs from the fast-flowing Cauvery River in southern India. From both Kenya's Lake Victoria and from Egypt's Lake Nasser I've also caught numbers of Nile perch between 75 and 88 lbs. But try as I might, and this has included a few lost monster perch, particularly from Lake Nasser, that ton-up specimen just wasn't going to happen and seemed like a pipe dream, until just recently that is.

It was my third trip since January, escorting anglers who like me want to get their string pulled by a whopper. And with several giant perch topping 200 lbs already having been caught from this 300 mile manmade lake, which covers what was once the Nile valley between Aswan and the Sudan, expectations of a big fish are always high. For me, however, the magic started the evening before, which due to the antics of a group of jackals turned into an unusual experience. Upon seeing a jackal within 50 yards of the shoreline where our supply boat was tied up for the evening, someone decided to walk ashore in the dark and deposit their left-overs from dinner on top of a mound not 40 feet away to see if these normally inquisitive but naturally timid animals would come closer.

Having taken my Samalight HD 200 lighting unit along, should just such an occasion present itself, I positioned the powerful beam of light on top of the mound and went ashore to set up the video camera on the tripod in case the jackals played ball. Which I'm glad to say they did. At one time no fewer than five were captured in the torch beam and by using maximum gain the digital camera recorded this truly memorable occasion of wild animals feeding upon leftovers – seemingly oblivious to more than a dozen humans staring in wonderment. You could have heard a pin drop.

Jackals and the desert fox are in fact regular campsite visitors around Lake Nasser during the quiet hours of darkness once everyone has turned in, as their footprints seen in the sand on the following morning testify. But rarely do you get the chance of actually seeing them at such close quarters, let alone recording the occasion. It was a privilege indeed. Our encounter with a noisy frog, however, was entirely different. Once all the titbits had been cleared and the jackals moved on it was time for everyone to resume drinking before thinking about getting their heads

Helped by Tim Baily (left) and faithful guide Mohamed (below), I finally get to cuddle a monstrous Nile Perch. 120 lbs to be exact. I was one happy bunny.

down. But not five feet from the bows of the boat upon which I slept there was a large frog squatting in the mud, puffing its cheeks out every few seconds and creating the loudest most irritating 'RIVET' you've ever heard. He didn't seem to mind me picking him up and depositing him in the reedy margins fully 50 yards away, and I walked back to the boat making sure there were no snakes in the torch beam, to resume some serious drinking. It was a sultry, warm intoxicating evening, the kind where your mind is truly at peace.

Ten minutes later, in exactly the same spot to the inch, I swear, sat exactly the same frog which, of course, brought a hail of disbelieving laughter from everyone who thought I was batty anyway moving the frog in the first place. Up I got again and this time I walked fully 100 yards before dropping him into a dense bed of marginal reeds and again returned to the boat. Yes – you've guessed correctly. Twenty minutes later (a determined frog this one) a loud indignant 'RIVET' told everyone that he was back again. And I suffered in silence while everyone laughed themselves silly. Actually I think the jackals and the perch were an omen because on the following morning I finally struck gold. First, however, one of my guests, John Smith from Birmingham, hooked into a whopper trolling a silver Russel lure in deep water beside a steep-sided island. Following a spirited fight of almost half an hour John's bottom jaw dropped open when he saw the sight of a giant Nile perch wallowing on the surface and tail walking. All 111 lbs of it.

It's a fact and something I tell all my guests who come to Lake Nasser, that most catch their largest freshwater fish ever during their first week on the lake. Few return home without boating perch of at least 50 lbs. Now it was Wilson's turn as something feeling like a turbo-charged wheelie bin crashed directly for the bottom in over 50 feet of water, pulling my powerful uptide rod into an alarming bend and making the 35 lb mono sing in the wind like a canary. Five feet long with a 42 inch girth it was exactly the big one I'd hoped to capture on film whilst putting the finishing touches to an hour-long safari-based fishing video all about this unbelievable lake. Was I a happy bunny. It pulled the scales down to exactly 120 lbs.

A 'NASSER' BUFFALO BONANZA

Due to the swollen waters of Egypt's River Nile which feeds massive Lake Nasser, levels during the past few months have risen to the highest point ever recorded since the lake was created by the construction of the high dam across the Nile valley at Aswan in the early 1960s. And whilst this meant actually fishing over the very same now sunken rocky islands and hilltops where I had camped and shore fished for Nile perch more than six months previously, whilst escorting a party of perch enthusiasts, the phenomenon offered enormous potential. At least that's how Tim Baily read the situation when he greeted Andy Davison and me at the boat moorings following our flights from Heathrow to Luxor and Luxor on to Aswan. Tim's plan was to ignore all our favourite hot spots like shorelines and sheer-sided drop-offs which had produced previously, to concentrate upon totally unfished areas created by the lake's extra depth. And how right he was.

Andy Davison brings a 100 lbs plus Nile perch to the surface for a tail-walking display.

Under the banner of the African Angler, Tim has with the help of local guides successfully run specialised boat fishing trips on Lake Nasser for close on six years now, in search of both tiger fish and the giant Nile perch, and his knowledge of this enigmatic watershed is second to none. Add the fact that my buddy, Andy Davison, for eight years held the IGFA world record for Nile perch with a $191\frac{1}{2}$ lbs monster from Lake Victoria (until it was beaten by a 213 pounder from Lake Nasser) two years back and you can see I was in the very best of company for a week's serious fishing safari after big perch.

Tim had thoughtfully installed my favourite guide, Mohammed, on board our 25 foot trolling boat and within just a few hours we four were heading through the centre of the lake where deep down in depths exceeding 300 feet lies the original riverbed and the ancient mysteries of the Nile. We, however, were more interested in depths of between just 15 and 30 feet where sunken islands of large boulders provided a galaxy of new ambush points.

Trolling combinations of large plugs both sinking and floating divers including Rapala CD 18s and 22s depth raiders, russelures, reef diggers and nilsmasters etc., on 30 lb class outfits, we struck gold on only our second location. Andy banged into a good perch of around 80 lbs which unfortunately dived under the boat and severed the line around the prop. This necessitated having the engine up, removal of the propeller and installing a new sheer pin to unwind yet more old fishing line. The old pin was about to disintegrate. During this operation we had drifted into slightly shallower water where dense beds of new weed growth sprouted from between the boulders. An area we normally wouldn't have associated with huge perch, but when Mohammed restarted the engine and I dropped my lure over the side it hadn't travelled but a few yards before the rod tip was wrenched over savagely and line started to evaporate from the multiplier.

Following several of those marvellous head-shaking lunges across the surface so characteristic of the Nile perch and a super fight, we hoisted my buffalo on to the scales in a weigh sling. All perch over 100 lbs are called 'buffaloes' by Nasser regulars due to their distinctly humped backs. This beauty took the needle round to 135 lbs, beating my previous best by 14 lbs. What a start. But there was more to come and the most prolific catch of big fish in which it has ever been my privilege to share. In just three days concentrating upon two different areas, though both possessing the same features of weed and boulder-strewn sunken islands, our boat accounted for no less than an unprecedented 10 perch of over 100 lbs.

Andy took four 'buffaloes', the best at 139 lbs, I also took four, the best 141 lbs; Tim caught one at 129 lbs and Mohammed ironically accounted for the heaviest at 162 lbs using Tim's rod while Tim worked the engine. In all we accounted for a combined weight exceeding 2500 lbs with 35 perch averaging around 75 lbs apiece during our week. Tim rates it the best catch ever recorded on the lake and is convinced the fishing is actually progressively getting better.

'IN PRAISE OF MAIZE'

In these days of pre-made and bubble-packed aggressively marketed designer baits, available in all colours of the rainbow and produced in every conceivable flavour known to man, it is rather nice to get back to basics every so often. Take maize for instance; the nicest, cleanest and arguably the cheapest bait you could possibly ever choose to use, which is especially effective during these warmer months for a whole variety of cyprinid species like roach, rudd, bream, tench bream, chub, barbel and carp. A 25 kilo sack of whole (also called 'plate') maize will set you back less than two packets of cigarettes. So if talking in terms of pints, a day's fishing can be measured quite literally in pence.

Prepared maize is yellowy-orange with an attractive, nutty-wheaty-popcorn aroma (popcorn is, of course, simply exploded maize) which swells to twice the size of even a large kernel of sweetcorn. Two maize kernels fit perfectly on a size 8 hook or you can hair rig three kernels to a size 6. On a size 10 hook just one maize kernel is sufficient – and each is totally impervious to the attentions of small, nuisance species. Maize, however, does require careful preparation. Start by soaking the hard grains in water for a few days. Then either pressure cook for 20 minutes in reasonable quantities or prepare a few handfuls at a time in the microwave in a shallow bowl with water. If you cannot be bothered simply purchase a large prepared tub at your local tackle shop. I can thoroughly recommend the 2.2 kilo plastic tubs of maize marketed by Dynamite Baits, which are actually cooked in their own juices. You can get hooked on the smell alone! Unlike many baits your prepared maize can, of course, be taken home at the end of the day and popped into the freezer in a poly bag for use in future sessions. Quite frankly I cannot think of a more versatile bait, whether river or lake fishing.

DRIVE 'EM NUTS WITH A SWITCH TO PARTICLES

Whilst summer carp and tench fishing is still in full swing you may by now find that on stillwater fisheries, constantly bombarded with boilies, bites are becoming less regular. It is in fact a common occurrence because quite simply fish refuse to be fooled repeatedly on the same old baits. And very often a changeover to a smaller, completely different offering will totally revitalise your sport with these two species. My suggestion would be to switch over to particles: peas, grains, beans, and nuts etc., all of which can be easily prepared and coloured if desired. The secret of fishing particles is that bottom-feeding species like carp and tench become so confident grubbing about and hoovering up numerous small food items (as opposed to large single baits) because this is the way in which they feed naturally. Consequently they become far less suspicious of your hookbait lying amongst countless others – until it's too late.

Hair rigged particles are great baits for carp, tench, bream, chub and barbel.

Sweetcorn is perhaps the best example of how particle baits can score, but there are numerous others which work with equal effectiveness, such as stewed wheat, tick beans, maple peas, peanuts, black-eyed beans, soya beans, chickpeas, butter beans, red kidney beans, etc. A trip along to your local pet stores or corn merchants will I am sure provide you with still more ideas. The best way of preparing all these 'hard' particles is first to pre-soak them in cold water for two days in a large plastic bucket, preferably one with a rip-off airtight lid, because the next stage, after first straining off the water, is to cover them with boiling water by at least several inches before firmly putting the lid on. After two days remove the lid, drain the excess water (most will have been absorbed by the particles during this 'stewing' stage) and separate into poly bags for immediate use or pop into the freezer. This is why it makes sense to prepare your particle baits in bulk. Purchasing by the sack load is very much cheaper too. Incidentally pale particles such as black-eyed beans, chickpeas and soya beans, etc., can easily be coloured and even flavoured during the stewing process when you cover them with boiling water. Simply add a spoonful of powdered carp bait dye, plus a spoonful of flavouring (if desired) and stir thoroughly before sealing the airtight lid. The results will amaze you. There's no mess or grief from the woman of the house, whose saucepans you just might have been tempted to use. I can vividly remember many years back when a teenager trying to explain to my mother why the kitchen stank of burnt stewed hempseed – because I had left it to boil dry on the gas ring whilst watching football on the telly.

There is really no need for kitchen preparation – even when stewing hempseed. It can be prepared in exactly the same manner I have described. And if you allow it to remain in its own juices for a few days before straining off the excess liquid, so much the better. Don't worry about the increased 'fermenting' smell and milkiness in the liquid. It will drive carp, tench and barbel incidentally, not to mention bream and chub, absolutely wild. Stewed hempseed is unquestionably the most effective loose feed attractor by far. Although I rarely use it on the hook, a liberal carpet catapulted out to lay on the bottom is the perfect partner to float-fished or ledgered particle baits. Carp especially become almost incensed by its introduction and will forage and root amongst the bottom silt for hours sucking up the tiny seeds, often creating enormous craters in the process. On occasion they seem totally preoccupied by hempseed and whenever this happens use small dark-coloured particles for hookbait. Tares, black lentils, black beans and maple peas are highly recommended and should be presented off the hook (a size 10) on a short hair.

WHY I'M JUST ITCHING TO GO SNITCHING

During these summer months one of the most effective of all natural baits for species like bream, tench, carp, chub, barbel, eels, catfish and especially perch, is the humble worm. You can, of course, talk local farmers or riding stables into letting you fork through their manure heaps (the ammonia level may even be beneficial to asthmatics) to gather a supply of brandlings, or look for redworms in well rotted piles of leaves stacked beside the roadside from County Council lorry sweepings. But should you require a supply of our largest earthworm, better known as the lobworm, then obtaining your own is the answer. All three species of worm are, of course, readily available pre-packed from most specialist tackle shops but in the case of the lobworm there really is nothing like 'snitching' your own. And by 'snitching' I mean collecting them off the lawn at night by torchlight when they leave their burrows following a good downpour to mate.

Now even without rain there will always be a few lobworms poking their heads out above ground once darkness falls. But take my advice and resist the temptation for this only encourages frustrating tug-of-war battles with you on one end and the worm on the other. It results in either rather 'stretched' worms which won't keep for long, or a broken lobworm (the head end only) which you refused to allow back down its burrow. So be wise, hope for a period of prolonged rainfall and wait for it to stop. Then once darkness

Lively lobworms produced these jumbo-sized perch for (L-R) brothers Martin and Richard Bowler, from the Upper Reaches of the Great Ouse. The smallest scaled 3 lbs 10 ozs, and the largest, 4 lbs 2 ozs.

has fallen you can enjoy superb 'snitching'. Why? Well because then all these silly worms come completely out of their holes to meet each other, have sex, lie there totally uninhibited etc., but more to the point they can easily be picked up. Incidentally, I find the best way of collecting is to hang a one-gallon plastic bucket on a strap around my neck at chest height. I then have one hand free to point the torch and the other for picking them up.

The very best evenings of all are following days of persistent rain which eventually stops to leave a smell of fresh moisture in the air. Then, and only then, will you find harvesting lobworms an absolute doddle. Now don't go thinking you need half an acre of lawn behind the house to go 'snitching'. If you do own a large well kept lawn of short grass (you can't catch lobs in long grass) then fine. If you don't, simply walk or drive along to your local cricket pitch, where someone conveniently keeps the grass down to 'snitching' length for you.

Now at this point I must admit to several rather strange and even embarrassing situations that have occurred due solely to my gathering lobworms for bait. If only the chub in my local River Wensum knew to what lengths I go in order to catch them. One dark night, for example, due to concentrating purely on pulling worms, I suddenly fell headlong over a bicycle and straight on top (honestly) of a courting couple taking Billy Jo Spier's advice of putting a 'blanket on the ground'. How a 17-year-old Wilson with purely chub baits in mind didn't end up in hospital with some broken limbs from the owner of the Raleigh Roadster I'll never know. Fortunately he believed my story of collecting worms for fishing. After all, who would have been daft enough to fill a gallon bucket full of worms as an excuse or an alibi for a peeping tom?

Then there was the night PC Plod just wouldn't have it that I was not out to relieve the cricket club pavilion of its funds. Apparently he had been watching my torch beam wavering erratically all over Drayton cricket pitch (six miles west of Norwich) for an hour or more, before leaving the warmth of his Panda to make an easy arrest. Even half a bucket of lobs, my torch, sopping wet trainers etc., were barely enough to reverse his suspicions. Then the penny dropped and he said, 'You're that geezer who laughs all the while in that fishing programme on the telly aren't you?' Fame at last, I thought.

OK, now allow me to give all of you potential lob collectors a few important tips. For starters, don't use a quartz halogen torch. A wide-beamed, soft light is far less likely to send worms scurrying back down their burrows. Strong, direct light really does scare them, which of course is why they come out at night. Over on the other side of the Pond Americans actually call lobworms 'night crawlers'. Don't scrape your feet along the ground when walking as the vibrations will send the worms back down their burrows post-haste. Literally creep along like a chicken, lifting one foot in front of the other. Think about it. If chickens scrape their feet they don't get to eat.

For those who live in the country there is actually an alternative (daytime) method of obtaining lobworms. When the ground is soft simply watch how hundreds of seagulls suddenly appear from nowhere behind the tractor when fields are being ploughed. But don't just go plodding across a farmer's field. A simple 'May I?' does no harm at all. You'll then never be without what I rate as the finest of all freshwater baits – lobworms.

BAKING YOUR OWN FLOATERS

It may well be the end of September but there's still time enough for catching species like carp, rudd, golden orfe and, of course, chub on floating baits. Such delicacies as floating trout and carp pellets, Chum mixer biscuits, cat treats, breadcrust and even floating boilies are all well known, well used and easy to obtain pre-packed. So if following a long summer of attention the species you have been after are by now rather wised up and you are looking for a new alternative – well, why not bake your own floaters? It's easy.

If you already make your own high protein pastes or boiled baits, you are halfway there, because virtually any pliable paste mix with the addition of a few more eggs can be baked in the oven and cut into cubes for use as floating baits. You simply need to obtain a 7x11x1$\frac{1}{2}$ inch deep baking tray and a good supply of eggs, plus a selection of various ingredients to use as the base of your floating cake, which ideally should turn out really rubbery to thwart the attentions of pecking and nibbling nuisance species and stay on the hook well.

My favourite base ingredients are trout and carp pellets (both sinking and floating) ground into a fine dust with the aid of a food or coffee grinder. You can, however, make do by using a mortar and pestle but be sure to grind the pellets literally into a fine powder. Rabbit pellets, chicken pellets, pig pellets, etc., all can be used as a base, as can flavoured cat and dog biscuits. Pre-packed powdered, specially formulated bird foods and conditioners such as Sluis CLO, Robin Red, Nectarblend etc., also make super base mixes. If you already make your own high protein pastes and boilies, to bake the same mix as a floating cake, remember that you will require at least twice as many eggs. If it's all new to you then assemble the following ingredients and have a go.

Obtain 2 ozs of sodium caseinate (specialist tackle shops sell this milk derivative which provides buoyancy), 4ozs of ground pellets, dog or cat treats, or bird foods etc., 3 ozs of semolina, 1 oz wheat gluten (specialist tackle shop) which acts as a binder, 1 teaspoon baking powder and, if required, 1 level teaspoon powder colouring (yellow, red, green etc.) and/or 1 level teaspoon liquid flavouring, plus one dozen large eggs.

Now, start by whisking the eggs thoroughly (together with any liquid colouring) in a large bowl to produce lots of air bubbles and then add to all the dry well mixed ingredients previously mentioned, including any powder colouring. If the mix still appears on the dry side add a few more eggs until it reaches a thick, soupy consistency. Whisk gently before pouring into the well greased or oiled baking tray to a depth of around $\frac{3}{4}$ inch, no more. Now smooth the top over and put straight into the middle of a pre-heated oven set to gas mark 4 (180° C) for 30 minutes, whereupon it can be tipped from the tray and left to cool. With a sharp long-bladed knife your decidedly 'rubbery' floating cake can now be cut into the size of cubes desired, divided into portions sufficient for a day's fishing and popped into the freezer in poly bags until required. Alternatively you can freeze the entire cake in a sealed poly bag until needed.

As you will discover, this rubbery floating cake will last for ages against the attentions of small nuisance species, quite unlike good old plain breadcrust which disintegrates within a very short time. You can present your designer floater side hooked, or on a short hair for extra spooky fish with the aid of a small floating controller, or over short distances simple freelining tactics should suffice. Either way you'll be offering a completely different kind of floating bait which due to the ingredients selected is certain to be one the fish haven't been tricked into accepting before. So catches are bound to improve.

PASTE MAKING THE EASY WAY

In these times of pre-made, pre-packed and unmercifully marketed freshwater baits like boilies and pellets etc., concocting your own paste does, I suppose, sound a bit old hat. But then as every other angler won't be using the paste you are using, species such as tench, chub, carp and barbel have little reason to become suspicious. Whereas in some of our more popular carp fisheries for instance, where the hard, round form of boilies distributed amongst the same old spots immediately puts wary fish on their guard. I can just imagine a big old fish sideling up to a carpet of pre-mades and saying, 'Oh no, not tutti fruiti again'. Now let me say at the beginning, there is, of course, nothing to stop you from subsequently rolling up and making a batch of boilies (as deterrent to the picking actions of nuisance species) from all of the pastes I am going to mention. Indeed, boilies first came about from boiling a ball of paste in water to form a skin and thus make it impervious to the attentions of small fish. Many of the old angling books written around the turn of the century about the British rule in India and servicemen angling for the mighty mahseer, contained a simple recipe for turning the locally grown and ground millet flour called ragi into a rubbery ball the size of a chicken's egg. The grey-coloured flour is mixed with water and kneaded into balls of stiff paste to which strong aromatic spices are added such as asafoetida and hing, before the balls are boiled in water for 20 minutes. And the formula still works today because boiling simply brings out the natural gluten in the flour to form an elastic skin around the bait.

But let's make some simple pastes (whether you then boil them is purely academic) and to start there really is nothing easier than sadza paste. This rubbery hookbait is concocted from white maize meal which is a staple food throughout southern central Africa. However, the yellow maize meal available from your local tackle shop will do nicely. You

simply add three cupfuls of maize meal and a cupful of plain white flour to 1½ pints of boiling water, plus a couple of beaten eggs, and your choice of colouring and flavouring, a teaspoonful of each being quite sufficient. Once all the ingredients are in the saucepan (procure an old one specifically for the purpose of making baits), reduce the heat to a slow boil and with a long-handled wooden spoon stir and work the mix firmly for a couple of minutes, which is all it takes for the ingredients to form a ball of wonderful rubbery paste the size of a coconut. It is so ridiculously quick – honestly! Then remove from the saucepan and place in a 3 pint plastic bait box and leave to cool. A little extra kneading is usually required after it has cooled prior to using, and that's it.

Even without colouring sadza is an attractive pale yellow paste that really stays on the hook well for species like chub, tench, barbel, bream and particularly carp. In African lakes, local spices are used to enhance its flavour and colour, a teaspoonful each of curry powder and turmeric being the most popular for all cyprinid species.

With the same summer species of tench, bream, chub, barbel and carp still in mind, how about trying bird food paste? My favourite base, which contains various cereals, milk derivatives, oils, fats, vitamins, seeds and vegetables etc., is Sluis CLO which is actually a food and conditioner combined, blended specifically for canaries and other cage birds and is available pre-packed in 100 gram bags from your local pet shop. Simply empty 2 cupfuls of CLO into a large bowl together with 3 large eggs plus a teaspoonful of powdered or liquid carp bait dye and knead the mix firmly into a smooth paste something like the consistency of soft plasticine. Without colouring the paste will turn out an attractive golden yellow.

Trout and carp pellet paste – any of these pelleted fish foods can easily be made into a creamy paste for all the previously mentioned species. Firstly use a coffee grinder, food blender or a mortar and pestle (the hard way) to reduce 2 pints of pellets to a fine dust. Put into a large mixing bowl and knead in 6 large raw eggs (more if necessary) until the resulting paste is of a creamy plasticine like consistency. Incidentally not only trout and carp pellets make great pastes. A visit to your local pet shop or corn store will reveal all kinds of goodies in the way of rabbit pellets, pig pellets and chicken pellets, etc., etc., of various types and sizes. And all once reduced to a fine dust and bound together with raw eggs, produce attractive paste baits for very little cost.

Due to their consistency soft protein pastes are amongst the most effective for catching tench and carp and are easily made from the same high-protein ingredients from which boilies are produced. Into a large bowl put equal parts of calcium caseinate, semolina and wheatgerm and mix well. Then add water to which a teaspoon each of flavouring and colouring has been dissolved and knead thoroughly. To make the paste 'super light' so it rests attractively upon aquatic vegetation, add a couple of ounces of sodium caseinate to the dry mix. It is a sticky business working and kneading milk derivative ingredients, but the resulting 'rubbery paste' is well worth the effort.

One last word about the actual colouration of all the pastes I have mentioned is, I think, quite relevant. Be sure to make the past darker than would appear necessary because the bottom of the lake or river is invariably darker than you think. And drastically contrasting baits can spook wary tench and carp so very easily.

IT'S TIME FOR COCKTAILS

When the going gets tough because fish start to wise up, then try ringing the changes by using what would initially seem an unlikely combination of baits. There is, for instance, no way under natural conditions that bread and worms stick together. Yet for presenting a couple of gyrating brandlings enticingly above bottom weeds to summer species like tench, you simply thread a small cube of breadcrust along the hook shank before adding the worms. And the inherent buoyancy in the crust does the rest. You can also use floating sweetcorn (available only from specialist tackle shops) as the buoyancy aid, or a mini marshmallow. These highly visible baits produced specifically for angling come pre-packed in screw-lid plastic jars and are available in three sizes and several fluorescent colours with most pungent flavours. They can be used with great effort to pop up virtually any small bait above bottom weeds or debris, or to ensure that small non-buoyant baits can be presented in the surface film.

Size for size these mini marshmallows are exceedingly buoyant. Natural baits both terrestrial and water borne also go well together as cocktails providing extra attraction from additional smell, movement, shape and colour. And as it's always difficult to predict what is going to be the winning combination on the day be prepared to try anything.

How about cocktail variations like maggots and a brandling on the same hook? Or casters and a dendrobena, mealworm and casters, casters and wasp or hornet grub, wasp grub and lobtail, lobtail and waxworms, shrimp (boiled or natural) and brandling? Then there's freshwater winkle (out of its shell) and maggots, caddis larvae and redworm, bloodworm and squatt, grasshopper and redworm, cockle (sea) and dendrobena, lobtail and mussel chunk (from a swan mussel). This list is truly endless. Spend some time thinking about previously untried combinations.

Naturals also team up well with and give that extra zing to manufactured freshwater baits, especially those which are presented on a hair off the hook, like boilies, luncheon meat or cheese cubes etc. Simply sleeve a small attractive natural like a brandling, maggot or a mealworm on to the hook bend. The extra 'movement' from this cocktail can really swing things around when fish are feeling dour.

But it's not just the freshwater angler who can benefit from cocktails. Sea fishermen are far more likely to be adventurous especially with frozen bait such as cuttlefish and squid. For 'cocktails' both should be cut into long strips as the main offering which is then spiced up by tipping the hook with a slither of herring, mackerel or king ragworm. Baby squid tipped with a large ragworm work well too and provide a good mouthful. Alternatively add a strip of squid for its toughness and added attraction to soft fish fillets of frozen mackerel or herring that are perhaps past their sell-by date. Though it's impossible to better the attraction of fresh mackerel strip or fillet, there is no harm making a cocktail by adding a fresh sandeel or a big ragworm or two. In fact a side of fresh sandeel is a wonderful addition to any bottom-fished seabait, especially attractor spoon rigs which sport strings of coloured beads to interest large flatfish such as brill and plaice etc. Of course, British mullet enthusiasts already know that tipping the treble hook of a small bar spinner with harbour ragworm is the best way of tricking this enigmatic super-crafty fish into grabbing hold. Actually instigating a lure cocktail by adding fish flesh or bait to the hook of an artificial is something the British freshwater angler could well adopt from his

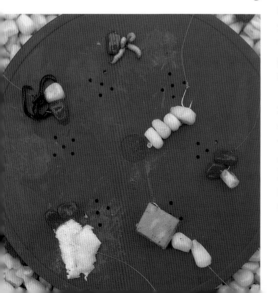

saltwater counterpart. My introduction to this clever ruse came several years back when downrigger trolling in depths down to more than 100 feet for the giant lake trout inhabiting the cold clearwater lakes of Canada's North West Territories.

Setting the large barbless hook of the heavy 6 inch spoon proved frustratingly difficult due to the colossal amount of stretch in monofilament line when trolling in such deep water. But adding a strip of fish gut to the size 7/0 hook made those big lakers hit with such aggression, the ratio of fish hooked to those lost on the strike immediately improved tenfold. Today, of course, I would use a non-stretch braided reel line to alleviate stretch.

I have since used 'lure cocktails' when seeking predatory freshwater species in other parts of the world and it works everywhere. Yes, with our own perch, zander and pike too. I do think however, that due to their extra aggressiveness brought about by increased water temperatures, tropical freshwater species respond best of all. Take the legendary tiger fish and the species of predatory bream inhabiting Africa's Zambezi River for instance, both are noted for slamming hard into artificial lures but, and here's the secret of 'lure cocktails' with fish strip or gut or worms on the hook, they hang on that much longer. Consequently the hook-up rate is greatly improved especially with tiger fish most of which seem, by hook or by crook, to jump off the hook anyway.

CHUB AND MASH

Round about this time of the year with winter chub fishing in mind it makes good sense to start saving those stale bread scraps. I hang an old keep net up in the garage, well away from the mice for this very purpose. It matters not whether the bread is brown or white, sliced or uncut, it just has to be older than five or six days, because new doughy bread is next to useless for making a batch of quick-sinking 'mash', the chubber's groundbait attractor supreme, which separates whilst sinking into a million tiny fragments. So it actually attracts without overfeeding if used sparingly. A most important factor when considering species like chub and roach in rivers, when water temperatures have reduced their metabolic rate to an all-time low, is that fish move about a lot less and consequently feed less aggressively less often but most important of all consume smaller particles of food. Remember the same chub that in seconds swam several feet through clear water to intercept a falling slug or lobworm freelined into the head of the swim back in September, and pulled the rod round in a zonking bite, will now take several minutes to browse over the same piece of riverbed. And in severe cold may even take several minutes to actually approach your bait before sucking it in. But back to our mash.

Once a good quantity of stale bread scraps has been collected I empty the entire lot into the sink, having first put the plug in, and cover with warm water. Then I leave for an hour or so until the bread becomes well and truly soaked before pulling the plug and mashing it all up between my fingers. The remnants from at least several loaves can all be mashed together provided you have a large enough sink, and once squeezed tightly to remove most of the water, is best divided into batches sufficient for a day's chub fishing and popped into strong poly bags. These are then stored in the freezer until required. So on the evening before an early morning session I simply take a bag out and leave overnight in a couple of inches of hot water in the sink to thaw out.

There are no freezing cold fingers early on a frosty morning unless, like I once used to (and this really is self-induced masochism), you opt for taking old bread along to the river and dunk in the landing net before mashing, for not only will you be wasting precious minutes at a potentially productive time and possibly disturbing spooky fish, the consequences could stay with you throughout the day. Indeed, I can remember times when my fingers never recovered and remained painfully cold throughout the entire session, but I've since learned and now prepare well ahead of time. Incidentally, should I quickly require a bag of mash for an impromptu session when conditions suddenly look promising in the afternoon with just a few hours of daylight remaining, and I cannot resist a trip along to my local River Wensum, simply immersing the frozen bag in a saucepan of hot water for a few minutes soon defrosts the contents.

Breadmash really is a most convenient attractor when using bread in one of its many forms as hookbait or soft pastes concocted from cheese or ground-down carp or trout pellets etc., etc. Breadflake taken from the inside of a fresh white loaf is, however, my first hookbait choice, followed by a small cube of breadcrust. Large compressed bread pellets from a wide-headed punch (4-6 mm) also work effectively, particularly if long trotting. Punched pellets stay on the hook so well, but don't wind them, or any breadbait for that matter, back upstream as this looks decidedly unnatural and may deter wary chub from biting. Strangely, pike have a liking for white bread travelling fast upstream against the flow and predatory aggression is not something you wish to instigate unintentionally. Simply execute a hard false strike at the end of the run through to dislodge the bait, and like as not every once in a while you'll even be pleasantly surprised by a bonus chub hanging on the end.

For both long trotting and ledgering sessions my favourite ploy is to pre-bait the head of any likely looking swim with a couple or three handfuls of mash whilst walking upstream to the top-most point of the fishery before meandering slowly back downriver, searching each in turn. In fact it has virtually become standard practice wherever I fish these days and has consistently produced bumper days in cold conditions not only from my local Rivers Wensum, Bure, Yare, Wissey and Waveney but from stretches with which I am not that familiar on rivers like the Dorset Stour, Hampshire Avon, the Upper Great Ouse and Berkshire's River Kennet.

You just need that presence of mind at the start of the session when it's tempting simply to plink down in a known favourite or the first good looking swim you come to. But be patient and content in the knowledge that every group of chub (or roach) in your selected swims will have sampled the mash long before your hookbait is presented to them. Consequently, without the slightest disturbance they will have fed confidently on your mash and be suitably aroused, on the look-out for more bread feed by the time you arrive. Instant bites in several of your baited swims will therefore result. Try it and see.

It is imperative to use scraps of 'stale' bread when making a good 'mash'.

FREEZING DOWN DEADBAITS TO ORDER

If like me you'll be using both fresh and saltwater deadbaits for pike and zander this winter, don't for goodness sake wait until a few days before your first trip to start organising those batches of freshly killed and frozen baits. These are, of course, available pre-packed from specialist tackle shops but the cost compared to obtaining and freezing down your own is quite considerable, quite apart from the freshness aspects. The secret is to keep a sharp eye out on the wet-fish stalls at your local market for recent landings. And buy up in bulk those herrings, smelt, and mackerel as they come in. Another excellent source comes from trout farmers, some of whom are only too pleased to sell off small disfigured fish that will never be required for stocking. And as trout are reared by the thousand all of a particular size you can sometimes even obtain baits of exactly the length required.

Pike fishermen who also enjoy the occasional sea trip can also think well ahead by taking home all the small fresh mackerel caught on feathers. And don't throw away those bony horse mackerel better known as 'scad'. They make great pike baits.

Now if you cannot bring yourself to kill small freshwater species like dace, roach and skimmer bream, etc., which other anglers enjoy catching, then capitalise on collecting eels for deadbaits wherever you see a dredger working. As the bottom mud is picked up beside the riverbank walk along with a bucket and collect them as they wriggle out. Eels of 12-14 inches long make great half-baits while longer, thicker specimens are best cut into 5-6 inch sections.

With all the baits I've mentioned here don't simply bung them into the freezer in one big lump. Spare a few minutes by wrapping each individually in clingfilm, before popping into the freezer in batches of so many fish. When presenting static deadbaits for instance six to nine baits may be sufficient for a morning's session, whereas wobbling small whole deadbaits for much of the day could consume 12-15 baits.

THE DELIGHT OF MINI BAITCASTING OUTFITS

Why on earth 5 – 6 foot long American-style baitcasting rods are so called I know not. They are in fact the perfect example of a contradiction in terms because their distinctly stiffish action, so crucial for working 'life' into artificial lures, would, upon casting, make most baits fly off the hooks. But that's what fishermen over on the opposite side of the Pond call them and so we are stuck with the terminology.

There is another strange anomaly here in that American sports fishermen also choose to partner short, baitcasting rods with right-hand baby multiplying reels instead of left-hand models. And as these reels are always used on top of the rod, having used his right hand for casting, the angler must then swap hands for retrieving the lure. Whereas this simple job is surely best performed with the left hand (assuming the angler is right handed of course) as indeed everyone fishes on both sides of the Atlantic with all other types of freshwater reels.

As changing over hands really does ruin fluidity between casting and instantly commencing the retrieve, I am tempted to suggest here that American fishermen are in fact cack-handed, which is surprising when you consider that they actually invented the technique of lure fishing using these lovely little outfits in the first place. Unfortunately, and as a consequence, today most manufacturers of suitable baby multipliers naturally

During the summer months chub are a delight to catch using a mini baitcasting outfit and surface 'popping' plugs.

target the huge (cack-handed) American market, thus producing right-handed reels only. It really is a frustrating situation for the would-be British baitcasting enthusiast because sadly there are only a handful of suitable left-handed models currently available. Most baby multipliers are fitted with magnetic braking systems to minimise overruns and single-action tri-bars for casting which puts the reel into free spool simply by pressing down with the heel of the thumb.

As these lovely little reels also come fitted with level wind mechanisms for neatly laying the line back and forwards across the lightweight, narrow spool, smooth and extremely accurate casts can be repeatedly made using little more than an overhead flick of the wrist. It really is single-handed efficiency at its most enjoyable, matched only perhaps by that of the fly rod. What's more, baitcasting outfits can be employed to catch chub, perch and zander in addition to pike, our most popular predatory freshwater species. So there's plenty of scope in the types of lure that can be worked. Indeed all but the very lightest of spinners can be directed accurately over short distances into all those awkward spots and choice lies such as gaps between weed and reedbeds, beneath low bridges, under overhanging trees, alongside lily beds etc., etc. You simply keep moving around the lake or pit or along the river using your enquiring mind to search out predators from all the prime feature lies in a completely mobile fashion carrying the absolute minimum of tackle.

OK, so if you are out in a boat why not take the entire lure collection along, and if it's anything like mine which includes a dozen or more large flat boxes, plus a huge four-section cantilever tray box full, then you'll probably need a boat. But generally speaking a small box containing say a dozen or so different lures, plus unhooking glove, a pair of forceps and a few spare wire traces, will all fit easily into a fishing waistcoat and is literally all you require for a wandering session. That's the beauty of these baitcasting outfits. By 'travelling light' you will cover more ground. My lure choice would contain at least one large spoon such as a 28.35 gram Landa-pikko for counting down into deep holes and gullies, with pike in mind, and a shallow diving plug like the Mugger in bright silver. This lure casts like a bullet and seems to draw out perch, chub and pike from their lies and into an attacking mood like no other. Being a floating diver that will only dive a few feet it can be trotted down a river on the surface with the flow over weed beds and extreme shallows and then retrieved when actually over those deeper, choice lies. Chub adore it.

Actually with chub in mind, and if you haven't as yet searched for them with artificials, a real treat is in store – I simply love to work those mini lead-headed spinning jigs adding an imitation plastic or jellyworm, fish, frog or newt etc. It opens up a whole new exciting field of thought and a whole pile of fun.

WHICH LURE?

My enormous collection of freshwater artificial lures, comprising of spinners, spoons, plugs and jigs, is generally sorted into groups or types and orderly stored in large flat plastic boxes to suit various situations. That is until I start swapping patterns around by putting a small selection from each into a single box for those research trips into exotic, unknown locations where I never know what's required and so consequently must be geared up for any eventuality. And over the past few months species like tiger fish, barracuda, arctic char, predatory bream, lake trout etc. and numerous other toothy predators resulted in so much lure swapping from box to box, that my entire collection was in one hell of a mess.

In fact, I got to the point where I couldn't stand it any longer and in one mad moment tipped the contents (over 200 lures) of no less than 15 boxes on to the bonnet of the car (my wife's car I hasten to add) for a grand sort-out. Whereupon, would you believe, the skies immediately clouded over and it started to rain. But that's life. I simply reached for the can of WD40 and gave the contents of each box a good spraying once it had been filled with lures of the same type, such as top water churners, surface poppers, shallow floating divers, mid-water divers, deep divers, sinking shallow divers, sinking deep divers, large spoons, small spoons and spinners, spinner baits and buzz baits etc., etc. Finally after almost an entire morning's frustration which included some lure husbandry in the way of replacing rusty or misshapen trebles and split rings, my entire lure collection was all neatly separated once again into various categories. It was a job that had to be done but which also highlighted the importance of knowing the action of each individual lure and the depths to which it can be worked effectively. For at no time is this more important than right now as another winter of predatory action with perch, chub, zander and pike gets under way.

You see it's not just the artificial which catches predators but the angler who is working and retrieving it: at the correct speed in an attractive, irregular manner to simulate a wounded fish and thus an easy prey and, most important of all, at the correct depth. This, remember, becomes all the more critical in the really low water temperatures (that we shall be experiencing over the next few months) when a fish's metabolic rate slows right down. The very same pike, for instance, which chased a surface popper or even your empty swim feeder for several yards through surface greenery in August, may now show not the slightest interest in your choice of artificial lure, regardless of its pedigree, action, or however much it cost, unless you virtually bump that pike on the snout. This is why depth bands and the level at which a pike is lying are so important to the winter lure fisherman

who is after consistent sport. Fact is, in low water temperatures pike spend much of their day actually lying on or within an inch or two of the bottom detritus. A profusion of those tiny, double-sucker leaches stuck to the gill plates, pectoral, pelvic and anal fins only confirms this, and indicates exactly at what depth your artificial needs to be worked in order to induce predatory aggression. In really clear water my advice is to go for presentation within two feet of the lake or river bed. In heavily coloured water, let's say no more than a foot of clear visibility, then halve that distance and endeavour to work your artificial no more than a foot above the pike's head.

Now everyone has their favourite types, patterns and makes of lure, and I'm certainly no exception. So working on the 'layer cake' principle and visualising the water in cross-section with depth divisions of say two feet, let me outline a few of the patterns which I think are more likely to score. I purposefully won't go into colour, which is too lengthy a subject, simply the type of lure and at which depth it will most effectively work.

Starting with exceptionally shallow water of just two feet deep I put enormous faith in a large but light (20 gm) spoon, which can be worked really slowly without fouling bottom. In plugs go for floating divers like Heddon's meadow mouse, Mann's 1 + minus, ABU's Hi-Lo minnow, arc minnow or Heddon's zara gossa. In depths of four feet my instant choice would be Masterline's mugger, Heddon's big bud or Normark's shad rap shallow runner, in addition to a plain large spoon of around 25 gm or a Toby salmo.

Going down to depths of six to eight feet, once again I personally rate spoons very highly, like Kuusamo's Professor, ABU's atom, Uto or Big Wiggley in sizes 20/35 gm or the Lauda Pikko Fatta 35 gm. In plugs go for floating divers such as lazy-ike, invincible or a magnum tad polly which can be worked really slowly. Due to their strong vibratory pulses, spinner baits also start to become effective within this depth band, particularly in heavily coloured waters where to many predators sound is perhaps more crucial in their hunting than sight.

Going deeper still, say 10-14 feet down, both heavy (30-40 gm) spoons and slow working spinner baits will really produce. But they need to be accurately counted down and retrieved slowly. In floating-diving plus do try the magnum hellbender, monster shad or Rapala's big-lipped deep divers such as the shad rap deep runner and Risto rap. In big format plugs try the swim wiss which has two points of attachment (to vary the angle of dive) and the excellent Shadling deep diver. In these depths of 10 feet plus sinking divers really come into their own because just like big spoons certain models can be quite accurately counted down (at around a foot per second) to the 'taking zone' before commencing the retrieve. And for this I thoroughly recommend Normark's rapala CD (countdown) Magnum range in 9, 11 and 14 cm sizes which all have wonderfully strong hooks and a tantalising side-to-side wiggle. Also worth trying is the Yo Zuri range of jointed sinkers and ABU's jointed Hi Lo. Finally for those who like a really large plug try the famous creek chub (jointed) pikie which can be retrieved really slowly without loss of action.

IS IT A HYBRID OR NOT?

There will always be controversy in the angling press about the stocking of F1 carp hybrids into commercial fisheries. Those first-generation hybrids which could be either common carp/crucian crosses or common carp/brown goldfish crosses are valuable to commercial fisheries because they rarely top 7 lbs and so alleviate the constant need for netting out king carp once they grow too large to be successfully landed by pole anglers. The bottom line here, however, is that due to the prolific manner in which carp species interbreed if all mixed together, our native stocks of crucian carp will be at risk. It is indeed now difficult to set off for a day's crucian carp fishing with the certainty that your catch will be a true crucian and not a first - or second-generation hybrid of either common carp or brown goldfish parentage, or simply a brown goldfish.

The British Record Fish Committee must rate the 'hybrid syndrome' as their most common problem because their consultant biologist, Alwyne Wheeler, has suggested there now could be a mere handful of stillwaters throughout the British Isles still actually containing true crucians. The current British record crucian of 4 lbs 8 ozs came from one of those safe waters, the RMC Summer Pit at Yately on the Surrey/Hampshire border.

Personally I should hate the strain of true crucians to disappear because since I was a six-year-old child I have enjoyed catching this cheeky, often frustratingly difficult to tempt little carp coloured in buttery bronze with distinctly rounded fins. And my advice to those uncertain of whether the carp they catch are crucians or not, is to study the species' unique colouration. Fish which are greyish or dark brown without the slightest hint of buttery bronze and especially those sporting tiny barbels are all guaranteed to be hybrids.

Our most common hybrids are, of course, roach/bream and roach/rudd, though in much of southern Ireland where huge shoals of both rudd and bream share the same spawning areas of vast loughs, the beautiful and extremely hard-fighting rudd/bream hybrid is extremely common. This particular hybrid, so obvious due to the golden colouration of the rudd mixed with the shape of the bream, is quite rare in England. In 50 years of fishing I doubt I've caught more than a dozen. Yet just a few weeks back whilst sharing a morning's Norfolk estate lake tench fishing with Scottish angler Kevin Patterson, I was delighted to put the landing net beneath a real beauty hooked by him. Weighing around 3 lbs this rudd/bream hybrid was a rare catch from a Norfolk water and a fine specimen. Isn't it a pity we don't have record status for hybrids? Then again who would want to take on the task of defining 'which' is 'what'?

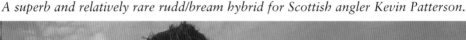

A superb and relatively rare rudd/bream hybrid for Scottish angler Kevin Patterson.

190

STARTING 'EM YOUNG

Why Bola, our West Highland terrier, and my five-year-old granddaughter, Alisha's, cabbage patch dolly 'Rebecca' have to be in the boat every time we enjoy an hour's fishing together I just don't know. But just like her mother before her, my daughter Lisa, who was equally adamant about what we should take (like sandwiches and flask of coffee, even when fishing within 50 yards of the house), she gets her own way. And her granddad revels in it of course.

I guess 'starting em young' has been a kind of ritual in our household. My dad ensured that I visited ponds and brooks to net for newts, frogs and sticklebacks when I was a nipper, so it seemed only natural for me to educate my own small children in the delights of natural history. Sadly today, what with computerised games that keep kids indoors glued to the monitor or TV screen and the media insisting there are now more abductors, molesters and rapists around to the square yard than ever before on this island of ours, small wonder the majority of children do not experience nature in a hands-on way during their adolescence. Add diminishing ecosystems within our small rivers due to water abstraction, not to mention the dreaded cormorant which still defies any sensible legislation from the government and which continues to ravage the ever reducing population of silver shoal (children's) fishes and it doesn't take a university degree to understand that children who would be anglers have access to few locations where they can experience the gentle art. What's that saying? We are merely the caretakers of the environment for tomorrow's children. We of my generation should collectively feel ashamed for what is happening to our natural history and the dismal legacy about to be passed on.

But let's return to the boat. Alisha is now knocking out small, glistening, silver-sided roach and golden-bodied rudd as fast as granddad can rebait the size 16 hook with pieces of breadflake and she is having a whale of a time. There are a dozen or so in the bucket and she keeps looking through the water at them totally fascinated. As indeed I first did half a century ago. Her rod is actually made from 10 foot two-piece fly rod blanks to which a slim cork handle and sliding reel fittings have been added. Those short monstrosities, wrapped in bubble-packed kit form and sold on cards are great for bashing down stinging nettles but not for children to learn fishing and stand any chance of hitting a bite when the float disappears. Hence granddad insisting she uses a longer rod which is quite manageable because it is light.

Her reel is an old Mitchell 308, a really small yet still perfectly serviceable tool, filled with 3 lbs monofilament. Her tiny hands certainly couldn't manage anything larger. The end rig is simple and geared to the hungry horde of roach and rudd that exist in my two lakes, ever willing to bite boldly virtually regardless of weather conditions. There is little need for complicated shotting patterns which tangle easily or fine-tipped floats. I have simply pinched on the line a couple of BB shots half-way between hook and the peacock waggler float, fixed top and bottom which is set at mid depth. And fortunately as yet (over several hour-long sessions) Alisha has failed to create a tangle that granddad could not unravel. Sorry, it's time to go back in. Alisha now wants to make a birthday cake for her nanny, Jo. Just when I was getting into it all too.

SIZE DOESN'T MATTER

I'm often asked how it is that after hour-long battles fighting the mighty mahseer, weighing close on 100 lbs, from the rock-strewn, fast-flowing rivers in southern India, and Nile Perch well in excess of that weight from Egypt's Lake Nasser, I can return home and enjoy catching roach or dace weighing mere ounces. But the fact is, when all things are relative, size really doesn't matter.

Take an impromptu session after tiddlers I made a few weeks back for instance in sub-zero temperatures. It was one of those days when loyalty was divided between penning my regular angling columns and popping into the lounge every so often to catch up on how England's cricketers were faring in Durban against South Africa during the Third Test. Whenever I returned to my office and dutifully picked up the pen again my eyes instantly wandered through the window to lakes completely covered in ice. And I really felt the need to get out fishing. Sadly river sport was totally out of the question, my local Wensum being over the banks with freezing cold dirty brown floodwater. What's more, following three consecutive nights of clear skies and heavy frosts, temperatures had plummeted to between minus 3° and 5°C. So I couldn't even fish my own lakes to catch some fresh pike and zander baits for the weekend. Ice covered everything.

By lunchtime I could stand my indecision no longer. I went outside to the wood store, found a heavy log (with a convenient hole in the middle) then raided the garden shed for a length of rope. In no time at all I had cleared a car-sized hole in the ice in the smaller, deeper of my two lakes in a swim where just a rod length out the bottom shelves down to around eight feet. I used a long handled landing net to remove the half-inch-thick pieces of broken ice and threw out a couple of handfuls of maggots. Then I returned to the

After breaking a clearing in the ice I was more than pleased, accounting for a netful of small roach and rudd on a freezing cold day.

cricket for half an hour to give the swim a rest.

The sun was bright and as high as it was going to get when I rigged up a 13 foot float rod with a small insert waggler, locked with bulk shot to present the bait just above bottom. I fixed just two small shot down the line with a tiny size 10 dust shot within 6 inches of the size 20 hook and nicked on a single maggot. The dust shot dotted the float's fine tip down to a mere blip on the surface, providing instant bite indication. In super-cold water small fish won't pull an inch of float tip under. It's a point worth remembering.

To my joy bites came almost immediately and after a dozen or so sprats I changed the 20 for a size 16 hook to present two maggots or a single caster in order to deter the 2 – 3 inch roach from biting and encourage a slightly larger (pike and zander sized) stamp. Which it did. On two occasions the rod tip arched over heavily as something very much larger grabbed hold, but sprang back just as quickly, the small hook pulling instantly free from what I took to be carp. But it was a bite a chuck from rudd and roach in the 2 to 4 oz bracket plus a couple of gudgeon. Just what I wanted.

Every so often a robin arrived on the scene to share the contents of my maggot tin as they do, whilst a treecreeper continually hopped up and down the trunks of tall birch trees to my left. Though cold it was one of those wonderful moments in fishing when it was sufficient and indeed a privilege just to be sitting there. Just before I packed up after two hours of most enjoyable sport, a kingfisher came zooming through the conifers behind me at such speed I thought it was going to take my head off. It missed my right ear by 18 inches, I swear, with an audible 'whoosh'. I must have coincidentally been sitting in the middle of one of its regular flight paths. I felt compassion for this the most strikingly colourful and handsome of all our winter birds. For here was one fisherman which wouldn't catch from the lakes until the ice thawed.

What was the final tally? Around 30 well earned fish. Like I said earlier, size really doesn't matter. Different challenges are all relative.

As far back as the 1980s, when my hair was still dark brown, I knew that cormorants were up to no good. So I took my stuffed cormorant along wherever I went pike fishing, just to piss the others off.

WHY THE CORMORANT 'BLACK PLAGUE' MUST BE STOPPED

I have said it before and, because it's an odds-on certainty, I'll say it again. If overnight the cormorant miraculously changed into a four-foot-high rabbit and started munching its way through fields of cabbages and carrots, there would be an immediate Bill passed in Westminister to cull its numbers. After all, isn't the Ministry of Agriculture, Fisheries and Food (MAFF) there to protect our farming and fishery interests? Well you would think so wouldn't you? I am referring of course to the long awaited, recently issued, government funded study which took £1 million of taxpayers' money and four long years to find out what every freshwater angler could have told them in the first place. That increasing numbers of cormorants now residing inland, throughout the British Isles, are quickly raping their way through many of our inland waterway fisheries, both publicly and privately owned. Yet following this MAFF contracted survey, which proved inconclusive although it was acknowledged that cormorants have caused damage 'for specific fisheries', anglers have little cheer because research failed to provide any practical means of deterring cormorant predation or controlling bird numbers. Apparently MAFF is content only for fishery owners to 'scare' the black plague (as it surely is) away to give someone else the problem. And not deal with the problem directly.

Unfortunately all this has arisen due to yet another 'sovereignty reducing law' in the form of a European Community Directive on the conservation of wild birds (EEC/79/409) in 1979, which listed 74 species considered rare, endangered or vulnerable to be given greater protection. The intention was to include the pygmy cormorant, an uncommon species, but in a mistake which remained uncorrected for 17 years, 'sinensis' sub-species of cormorants (those which are eating our silver shoal fish) were included. However in 1996, when 10,000 anglers attended a lobby of the European Parliament in Strasbourg, because European fish farms had been decimated by more than 50% of their stocks by cormorants, a resolution was passed for 'sinensis' to be removed from the EU directive.

This came into effect in 1997 when EU member countries were required to downgrade the protection afforded to 'sinensis'.

All of this must be seen for what it is, bureaucratic lunacy, because prior to 1981 cormorants in the UK could be and were shot without the need for special permission or a licence, just like other pests and vermin such as rats and rabbits. Because neither of the two main cormorant sub-species 'sinensis' were ever endangered throughout the UK or Europe.

It's a great pity that the RSPB, renowned for keeping its head in the sand (except when encouraging members to cull the North American ruddy duck, which dares to breed with a Spanish white-headed duck, not even in this country would you believe, but in Spain), hasn't put a favourable oar in. Because there are dire consequences for our indigenous waterbirds like kingfishers, great crested grebes and herons, once cormorants have laid the cupboard bare of small silver shoal fishes. Surely the food source of indigenous birds is more important. But believe me there is a more sinister stage still - as I have witnessed in a lake next to my house which during the last few years has been emptied of its once prolific stocks of roach and rudd. What do you think the pike now prey heavily upon in the spring once their fish diet has all but dried up, when young coots, moorhens, mallards and yes, even greylag and Egyptian goslings first leave the nest? Exactly! Rules for obtaining licences to legally shoot cormorants and restore our waning water ecologies must be relaxed at once. The past 10 years have indeed been bureaucratic lunacy! It is totally inconceivable to me that in Britain we can shoot pheasant, mallard and, believe it or not, even golden plovers but not cormorants.

REVEALED – SECRETS OF MY ULTIMATE SEX GUIDE

Few anglers would argue that differentiating between the sexes of our freshwater fishes has always been a puzzle, apart from the obvious that is. Take the male three-spined stickleback which from childhood we have affectionately called 'red throat'. A proud, aggressive little fish with turquoise blue eyes that bullies egg-laden silver-bodied females into a nest built entirely by himself from strands of soft-rooted weeds. So there is absolutely no confusion who wears the boots (or flippers) here.

With most other species, however, it's not so easy deciding exactly which is which. But let's first consider some other mini species which might well share a pond or brook home in close proximity to sticklebacks. And down there amongst the bottom strata live both bullheads and stone loach, neither of which can be easily identified as to their sex. With the humble minnow, however, we start to see light at the end of the tunnel, in that being a member of the cyprinid or carp-like family of fishes, all of which have pharyngeal (throat) teeth amongst other similarities, all male cyprinids also during propagation of their kind, develop tiny white spawning tubercles over their heads and shoulders which are used in a sandpapery way (and 'sandpaper' is exactly what they feel like to the touch) to stimulate female's eggs by bumping into her swollen flanks.

So you can also expect to find these tubercles on male gudgeon, dace, roach, chub, bream, rudd, carp, barbel and on tench during their respective spawning seasons. Consider the beautiful golden orfe which is also a cyprinid, because the only time to differentiate between male and female is also during April when they spawn and the males not only sport tiny white tubercles but also feel decidedly rough to the touch in the process. While the female orfe, just like female dace – being pigeon chested and decidedly soft to the touch – also has more rounded features. Just a few weeks after the spawning ritual, however, it's back to square one again and impossible to tell the difference between mum and dad.

Now some cyprinids, tench in particular, actually have very distinct, physical differences. The male's large pelvic fins, for instance, are decidedly 'crinkly' and spoon shaped compared to the noticeably slimline pelvis of the female. What's more these huge fins when flattened to the body virtually cover the vent. And this goes for both the common or green tench and the highly decorative banana-coloured golden tench. With carp a noticeable feature of adult fish is that the males have much larger pectoral fins compared to females, a characteristic which incidentally is more obvious in long lean wild-carp-type individuals than the short and thick-bodied, pot-bellied Italian strain of carp.

Eels of course breed in the Sargasso Sea in mid-Atlantic nowhere near freshwater, whilst predators such as perch, zander and pike are in visible terms almost indistinguishable. However, female perch are noticeably shorter and deeper in the belly than the longer, leaner males immediately prior to their springtime spawning ritual, while male pike lovingly called 'jacks' are all head and lean in the body. It's easy to be clever when observing them spawning as several smallish males often attend a big plump female. But throughout the rest of the year a small female pike looks very much like a small male pike. Males incidentally are said rarely to exceed between 12 and 13 lbs in weight.

Out on its own, and a fish which there should really never be the slightest confusion in sexing, is the colourful grayling. Apart from being somewhat darker, the longer leaner

Just like dace, and several other cyprinids, the only sure way of sexing golden orfe is during their spawning cycle when the females have egg-swollen bellies and are smooth to the touch, whilst the males are covered in tiny tubercles and feel sandpapery. I caught this 5 lb beauty on a small floater.

male grayling is blessed with a huge and exceedingly colourful sail-like dorsal fin which, when flattened along its back, almost covers the tiny adipose fin. Whereas the female's dorsal fin is noticeably smaller, being square in shape even when spread open between thumb and forefinger.

Oh, I nearly forgot the trout, which again like the grayling is not difficult to sex. Adult males, for instance, in both brown and rainbows have inordinately large mouths compared to females and darken considerably when spawning time approaches. Male brown trout especially, apart from squirting their milky white milt all over the place, develop a hooked lower jaw for gripping the females and for warding off competitors.

FISH *ARE* GETTING BIGGER

Due to chronic water abstraction and being over-eutrophic, due to run-off from farming chemicals, and not forgetting, of course, the decimation of silver shoal species for which cormorants are largely responsible, many of our major river systems, particularly the clear -flowing upper reaches, now contain far fewer fish. And as fewer fish invariably means that there is more grub to go round (natural food in the way of aquatic insect life etc.) as a consequence, the remaining fish just keep getting larger and larger. An over-simplification of what is a complex subject? Well, that's as may be. But I assume you know where I am coming from. Why, 25 years ago the thought of Mr Average catching an 8 lbs tench, double-figure barbel and bream or a 30 lbs carp, would have seemed impossible. Yet today fish of these weights are featured each and every week in the angling newspapers and many of them landed not by enthusiastic or eccentric specialists who have given up work and dedicated their life to putting big fish on the bank with the help of secret rigs and special baits, if there are such anglers. And I for one think it's a great trend if everyone gets their string pulled by klonking great fish. But I am concerned about the future and river systems which, though currently famous for catches of big fish, have precious little in the nursery coming through to become the big fish of tomorrow. Inverted pyramids with small numbers of adult whoppers at the top but few shoals of small to medium size fish at the lower end of the scale are neither natural nor healthy. But today they are becoming all too common and we tend to lose sight of this fact. Obviously what worries me is what happens when all the big old ones have died off. This is the $64,000 question. Mind you, not all species are increasing their weight potential.

Take dace, roach and rudd for example because a 1 lb dace, and a 2 lb roach or rudd are as difficult to catch and as special today as they have always been and the yardsticks by which we judge specimens of these three species. A 2 lb grayling, a perch of 3 lbs and a 20 lb pike also fall into the same category. They are all specimen target weights to aim for that have stood the test of time. To celebrate an angler's achievements, the bottlers Williams & Humbert used to give a bottle of their dry sack sherry to anyone who managed to catch a 2 lb roach, 5 lb tench or a 20 lb pike. And a young Wilson felt enormously proud at the tender age of 15 catching his first 2lb roach from the River Waveney at Bungay in Suffolk, and sending the details off to claim a bottle of plonk for his dad. And that was over 40 years ago.

Today, however, it's a strangely different climate because tench, bream, barbel and carp have now escalated in their weight potential beyond all comprehension. As all four are bottom feeders many anglers attribute the phenomenal weight increase of these four species to the amount of high protein bait they are fed in the form of boilies. And with

I caught this near 14 lb bream on a slider-float, fishing a deep Norfolk lake. It accepted a lobtail and would have smashed the British record during the early 1980s. Now specimens of this stamp are commonplace.

regard to certain stillwaters I think this is fair comment. But then how do we explain the double-figure tench which come from massive Tring reservoirs where they feed upon natural foods like zoo planktons and midge larvae, and not boilies. Remember way back in the 1950s the tench record was just 8½ lbs, now it is over 15 lbs and eight and nine pounders are so commonplace most specialist anglers don't even both to report them, because they know much larger tench will dominate the headlines.

The tench phenomenon really is a mystery but with both bream and barbel I simply think it's a case of there being fewer fish in smaller shoals, with a glut of food available, including the pre-baiting of specialist anglers, and little in the way of competition species to limit their growth potential. In 1982 I witnessed Mike Davison catch the then 'new' record bream of 13 lbs 9 ozs from Beeston Lake in Norfolk. It put just 1 oz on the then record of 13 lbs 8 ozs caught from Chiddingstone Castle Lake way back in 1945. The carp record of that time, believe it or not, was just 26 lbs. Now it's over 60 lbs. Nowadays bream of 13 and 14 lbs are almost weekly catches from gravel pits, meres and estate lakes up and down the country. I've even bettered the old record myself on several occasions from stillwaters, including multiple catches, and taken double-figure river bream. An almost unheard of occurrence 20 years ago. Where will it all end?

WHY TEST CURVES?

Most of the specialist-type carbon fibre Avon, carp or pike rods produced today all have one thing in common, they are rated in test curves, with a figure of somewhere between 1 and 3 lbs clearly marked together with the rod's length and manufacturer's logo immediately above the handle. Yet I'll wager a very small percentage of anglers indeed actually know why and to what purpose these test curve ratings were invented. Actually we have the late Dick Walker to thank for this extremely useful guide as to which line strengths will marry nicely with a rod's test curve, and therefore how powerful it is. Dick applied a basic rule of thumb during the early days of carp fishing way back in the 1950s, when designing his specialist-built cane rods, such as the famous MK4 carp and Avon rods, and as yet no-one has improved upon the test curve principle. Incidentally, the words test curve, simply relate to the strain (in lbs) required to pull the rod's tip round into a quarter circle using a spring balance. To ascertain the rod's overall line strength you then simply multiply that figure (its test curve rating) by 5. Therefore a test curve of, say, $2\frac{1}{4}$ lbs will result in an ideal line strength of approximately $11\frac{1}{4}$ lbs. To find the rod's safe lower limit multiply by 4. This gives a line strength of $9\frac{1}{4}$ lbs and for its safe upper limit, by 6, which allows lines of up to $13\frac{1}{2}$ lbs to be used. So in short, a $2\frac{1}{4}$ lbs test curve rod is best matched with lines from $9\frac{1}{4}$ to $13\frac{1}{2}$ lbs breaking strain. But I must stress that such figures offer only a general guideline, because far lighter and heavier lines may be used with the same rod in experienced hands. Remember that the test curve rating method was designed for rods constructed of built cane which had a parabolic action, and nothing like or nowhere near so versatile as the carbon fibre equivalents of today. But it is still an extremely useful way of instantly gauging the power of a particular rod and calculating a strength of line so that both rod and line stretch simultaneously like one gigantic elastic band. There is no safer, more enjoyable way of subduing the biggest adversaries.

TACKLING HABITAT HIDEOUTS

Nowhere is the art of 'reading the water' (and it is indeed an art that needs constant practice), more important to success than when river fishing. You can opt for a 'chuck it and chance it' approach on large lakes and pits when in search of predators by whacking out a deadbait as far as you can, cast for pike or a ledgered lobworm if perch are your quarry, and every now and again even be successful, but when considering running water accurate location is of paramount importance. Moreover the smaller the river the more precise your swim selection and casting needs to be.

Let's take a shoal of specimen-sized perch or chub which live in the subdued light beneath an overhanging willow or alder along a small habitat-rich river for instance, because even during the winter months without leaves on the branches light values directly beneath will still be noticeably lower down on the bottom of the river. The best haunts, of course, are where the lower branches have collected debris during flooding to form dark, cavernous 'rafts' which completely cover up to several square yards of the surface. Such swims are both home and point of ambush from which to attack shoals of small prey fish, such as bleak and dace, plus a lair into which the occupants retreat during bright sunshine and in clear water conditions. Casts, therefore, need to place the bait close beside the hideout or, better still, if the overhanging tree is on the near bank, to work it actually well beneath the raft. This is easily accomplished by using minimal shot on the ledger link –

just enough to touch bottom, and casting several feet along the outside edge of the raft. Then with the rod tip held low hold back hard on the bait so the current bumps it inwards beneath the raft to where the perch or chub will be lying. So expect and be ready for an immediate response.

When the river is up and coloured the occupants will confidently explore the area immediately upstream of their hideout so don't put that first cast straight into the hot spot. It could actually scare and disperse the occupants. Simply work progressively downstream from several yards above the raft until bites materialise. It goes without saying, I hope, that fishing from well above the swim is imperative. Sit right on top of it and you can expect perhaps that first bite with nothing to follow thereafter.

Next to rafts my favourite haunts for the two previously mentioned species are where dense beds of brown decaying sedges line the rear or opposite bank. Thick beds produce numerous hideouts, where perch in particular use their vertical stripes in wonderful camouflage against the stems. Beds situated along both banks create some marvellous hot spots though you cannot always be sure where the shoals will be holding station. I particularly favour cutbacks where slightly slacker water exists behind clumps which jut out into the flow. A bait quiver tipped into the slack might produce, particularly when levels are up, or you can long trot close beside, literally brushing the leading stems with the float during low, clear water conditions when a moving bait like a gyrating worm will often induce an aggressive response. Either way keep introducing fragments of broken worms close beside the sedge stems on a regular basis to keep the swim active and maybe you can attract two or three good fish before having to move on. It's a great mobile way of producing the very best from these intimate diminutive rivers.

IT'S WORTH KNOWING YOUR LILIES'

Now that May has arrived the stalks, pads and flowers of water lilies will be pushing their way to the surface first in stillwater and a little later in rivers, all over the country. It is a time of the year that I particularly love and very much look forward to. Not only as a prelude to summer but because with the increased water temperatures that stimulate growth of aquatic plants comes the first real visible movements of our summer species like rudd, tench and carp in particular.

As I sit here writing this in a cedarwood summerhouse overlooking a shallow bay in one of my own lakes, already the carp are moving about with purpose and getting ready for their annual spawning ritual which I feel will take place earlier than usual this year. Every so often a great bow wave shatters the tranquillity of the surface where immature lily pads are multiplying literally by the day. And in this particular bay no larger than a tennis court I have planted a dozen or more colourful varieties including James Brydon (a striking deep red), Chromatella (a creamy yellow) and Helen Fowler (a pastel pink). Other varieties include your bog-standard white water lilies such as *Nymphea alba* and *Nymphea carnea* (which has a pinkish flush) which are most commonly and cheaply obtained from garden and aquatic centres.

Now although the earliest form of lily cultivation does in fact date back to Egypt and the XIIth dynasty, 3000 years BC, we must pay homage to a Frenchman by the name of Joseph Bony Latour Marliac who, from the 1860s, started cross-pollinating hardy nymphaeas, many of which form the bulk of coloured varieties that grace our ornamental ponds and fisheries to this very day. Unfortunately Marliac took the secrets of hybridising lilies with him to his grave in 1911. But his work lives on and always will. In fact over 70 hardy varieties were created by this veritable genius and the next lily you purchase at an aquatic centre is more than likely to bear the 'Marliacea' label.

There is, however, rather more to a lily as far as the angler is concerned, than its colour. And being aware of a particular lily's sub-surface structure could mean all the difference between landing a goodish carp hooked amongst dense lilies and losing it. For instance, all the previously mentioned cultivated lilies do not have sub-surface leaves, merely flowers and surface pads. And so a tench or carp is more easily extracted from amongst their entanglement of rather weak stalks than from the robust common yellow water lily *Nuphar lutea*. Also called the 'brandy bottle' due to the shape of the seed pod once its yellow petals have rotted away, the common yellow lily is found all over the British Isles in both running and still water, easily recognisable in addition to the tight yellow flower on erect stalks, by its profusion of sub-surface soft lettuce-like leaves more commonly called cabbages. In slow-moving river systems plagued by boats, particularly turbid waters where

Nymphaea alba, the original white waterlily from which many of today's colourful and hardy hybrids originated.

light cannot penetrate, few pads and flower stalks ever reach the surface and those which do are soon hacked off by propellers, but down below the bottom is nevertheless carpeted in thick cabbages, much frequented by tench, bream and roach.

To many this would seem an entirely separate aquatic plant but it is the common yellow lily none-the-less which has tremendously thick turnip-like rhizomes, the diameter of a man's leg. So when hooking carp amongst dense beds of yellow water lilies in stillwater fisheries it's well to appreciate this fact by keeping the rod up high to stop getting its head down and threading your line through a maze of rhizomes from which extraction is virtually impossible. This is why powerful all-through action rods, coupled to a stretchy brand of monofilament line are imperative for these hit and hold tussles, where you often need literally to bounce your carp over and through the pads whilst calmly walking backwards.

Playing a fish in the accepted manner of lowering the rod and pumping upwards to gain line is a nicety you simply cannot afford when fishing in the thick of lilies. Animal determination, coupled to a knowledge of the fish's habitat always puts more specimens on the bank – believe me.

A lovely little plant called the dwarf pond lily *(Nymphoides peltata)* can also prove quite a handful when attempting to extract a fat tench or carp from its impenetrable mass of two to three inch round pads. This rampant plant is easily recognisable by the tiny yellow, buttercup-like flowers, which cover the surface in bright profusion during full sunlight. The dwarf pond lily shares the ability of the common yellow lily in being able to reach the surface from depths of at least eight feet. But fortunately, as each stalk rising from the lake bed may divide into several flower-holding plantlets at the surface, there is never such a mass of greenery lower down as you might imagine. Care must nevertheless be taken when trying to heave a good fish up to the surface actually through the dense surface canopy of pads and flowers. So don't bottle out at the last minute and slacken off, or you'll never get to net your quarry. Be prepared to heave and haul, bouncing your carp or tench up to the top, through the jungle and across the surface up to the waiting net, all in one powerful movement. The secret is keeping the rod bent into a powerful curve throughout.

MAKE YOUR OWN 'REED' FLOATS

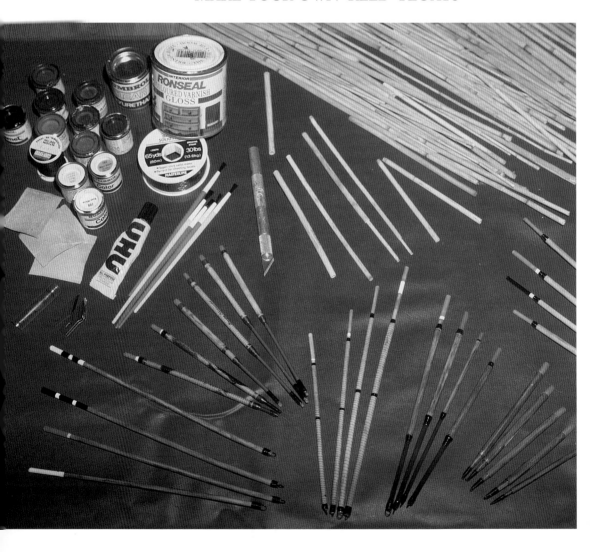

During the winter months our common reed *Phragmites communis*, also called Norfolk reed because it is used for thatching (not to be confused with reed grass *(Phalaris arundinacea)* which grows in thick beds along the margins of rivers, dykes and lakes all over the country), will turn in colouration from olive green to parchment brown. Then, and only then, once free of moisture, it should be cut just above the waterline (using a sharp rape hook) to provide the very best float-making material for the DIY enthusiast. And as commercially made floats cost anything upwards from 60p each, what about making your own for free, other than the cost of some waterproof glue, paint, thread and sharp modelling blades?

Traditionally reed is harvested between January and April then staked beside the water in bundles until required for thatching. So if you cannot personally be bothered securing a supply (I usually gather a batch whilst out boat fishing for pike on my local Norfolk Broads), simply obtain a bundle from a reed cutter.

Now the reason that reed is so suitable for float making, apart from costing absolutely nothing, is that it has buoyant airtight chambers between each knot, just like bamboo. In addition, immense personal satisfaction and pleasure can be gained from using homemade floats. And there is nothing which looks more natural or is less likely to spook wary clearwater fish than a simple reed stem. So whether you like to fish waggler style or use a stick float, even stret-peg in flowing water, an evening's entertainment this winter at the kitchen table will result in an entire armoury of these lovely floats. But first things first.

Start by selecting straight stems and flex each gently to test for resilience, immediately discarding those which break or feel spongey or do not instantly straighten after bending. Now, to make a simple straight waggler float cut on the outside edge of both end knots, whatever the intended float's length. Remember that as reed stems vary enormously in diameter each will have a different shotting capacity. Reed takes approximately two-thirds of the shotting capacity, for instance, of an identical length of peacock quill. Prior to painting and whipping on a bottom ring, use a small square of glasspaper to smooth over each end.

To make a tipped, or what is often referred to as an 'insert' waggler make a clean cut on the inside of the uppermost knot to reveal the hollow chamber (into which the tip will sleeve) and prepare a slightly smaller diameter insert which then becomes the tip. Ensure the tip end is smoothed over (at the knot) with glasspaper and cement firmly into the larger diameter stem using a clear waterproof glue.

Using fly-tying thread whip over the join and at the float's base whip on a small loop made from 15 lb test monofilament. Incidentally, if you prefer coloured floats, reed can easily be stained in green or brown by applying a coat of wood preservative. Looks really effective this but frankly I like the natural reed and usually enhance its attractiveness by running a continual whipping (with a $1/16$ th inch gap) along the entire float from immediately below the tip down to the bottom ring. A cosmetic addition which actually does increase the float's durability. To make stick or trotting floats, simply prepare a hollow main stem of 3 – 6 inches for the body, into which both a tip and a stem are glued once their knot ends have been nicely smoothed over.

Lastly, give your floats two coats of clear or matt varnish except the tip which should receive one coat of matt white followed by the fluorescent colour of your choice. My overall preference is fire orange.

My wife Jo took this early-season tench using a thumbnail-sized piece of white breadflake presented 'lift-style'.

HOW THE LIFT METHOD WORKS

Whether you search for midsummer bream or tench using a 13 foot waggler rod matched with a 3 - 4 lb reel line, or step up to an 11-12 foot Avon-actioned specialist rod, coupled to an 8lbs test line for subduing carp, few terminal rig tackle set-ups match the effectiveness of the 'lift method'. Yet many coarse fishermen are still rather mystified by its simplicity – so let me explain.

For starters the plain stem of peacock quill float or a commercial waggler is always attached bottom end only with a silicone band, as opposed to being 'locked' on the line through the bottom ring with shots on either side. Then if a carp or tench goes ploughing through dense weed beds or lilies, all you lose is the float, not the fish, due to the line fracturing at the shots. The entire shotting capacity of the float, concentrated in a single AA or swan shot, is pinched on the line somewhere between 3 and 5 inches from the hook. Which I suppose does seem rather insensitive initially, yet because the buoyancy within peacock quill actually helps support the shot while it is 'lifting' (hence the terminology 'lift method') when a fish stands on its head and sucks the bait in it feels minimal resistance until the float keels over and lies completely flat. During which time the strike should, of course, be made because once the float lies flat the fish itself is then supporting the shot and not the float. So it is liable to eject the bait post-haste. Therefore get used to striking hard and fast 'while' the float is actually 'lifting'.

If, however, the fish moves along the bottom with the bait directly away from the rod, the float tip will sink positively. Since the lift rig has a built-in plummet because of the way in which the single shot is fixed on the line close to the hook, not only does swim depth immediately become apparent when casting around different areas, extra bites are initiated by gently lifting the rod tip every so often and winding the bait in a few inches closer over a clean bottom. Now I know the bait isn't supposed to crawl along the bottom, not offerings like sweetcorn pastes or breadflake etc., anyway. But no-one has told bream, tench or carp this. So a 'snatchy' bite is quite likely when the meal looks as though it is getting away. With animal baits like prawns, shrimp, cockles or lobworms etc., bites are invariably most aggressive.

It goes without saying that when 'lift' fishing the rod should be held at all times. Put it down on a pair of rod rests and you'll miss 50 per cent of all bites, maybe more. Being right handed I find the most comfortable position is with my forearm on top of the rod handle, supported across my right knee. Try it and see. I also favour hooking the line over my forefinger as a precaution when I'm daydreaming or looking around enjoying our natural history and my eyes are not on the float. That gentle 'twitch' as the line tightens across the sensitive ball of my forefinger without me seeing the float disappear has on many occasions earned me a bonus tench or carp.

Now while the occasional side or overhead cast may be needed to reach distant spots, the lift method is really a close-range technique. By far the most effective and accurate way of casting, therefore, is to make an underarm pendulum swing of the bait, followed by a flick of the rod tip. Remember, with the 'lift method' you are casting the weight of the large shot and bait together, which allows you to fish in the tightest, narrowest gaps between bushes and trees, even with branches overhead. The underarm 'flick' has no equal. Believe me.

When specifically seeking 'bubblers' which give away their position from small groups of bubbles rising to the surface, do not cast right on top of these feeding fish and spook them. Cast several yards beyond the bubbles and feather the line down gently with your forefinger against the rim of the spool, so the bait lands softly. Then immediately wind the rig back to alongside the feeding bubbles and tighten up to cock the float. You need to be quick when doing this for two reasons. You might drag the bait along over the bottom debris or snags and bites often occur within seconds of winding down to the float tip. Try it and see.

ONE OR TWO RODS

Whilst it is accepted nowadays for freshwater specialist anglers to use three and even four rods at a time, particularly those involved with ledgering for carp on huge gravel pit complexes where stocking density is extremely low and thus bites are infrequent, I personally find attending to a couple of rods consuming enough, and for the greater part of my own fishing use just the one.

Naturally it all depends upon the technique being employed. No-one, for instance, could possibly manage to float fish with three or four rods. Yet ledgering with between two and four lines linked to electronic bite alarms is easily accomplished. Actually there have been times when fishing with just two float rods has proved impossible and decidedly detrimental to sport. A session that springs to mind here became a most memorable day for me several years back and even spawned a unique video. When using slider float tackle at a Norfolk lake I accounted for no fewer than nine double-figure bream to close on 14 lbs in a morning session. And all captured through the lens, fish after fish. I did in fact start fishing at dawn in thick mist using two identical float rod outfits, but bites on lobtails were so fast and furious for half an hour at least, I missed more than I managed to connect with, quite literally not knowing which float to hit first. So I packed the second rod away and concentrated on just one. It was a lesson I've never forgotten.

Some anglers, extremely successful ones at that, like Bob James of *Passion for Angling* TV fame and co-ordinator of the ACA, effectively ledgers in rivers simultaneously using two identical quiver-tip ledger outfits. With the two tips positioned on rod rests alongside each other any kind of registration, no matter how slight, is immediately seen whether in daylight or after dark when the tips are each fitted with a luminous light source.

Martin Bowler from Dunstable who just a few weeks back made angling history by catching two huge barbel of 14 lbs 3 ozs and 15 lbs 6 ozs respectively in a single session, then the best brace ever taken, also fishes simultaneously with two quiver-tip rods. So the effectiveness of presenting two baits at once within the same area is beyond doubt. Funnily enough, throughout last winter whilst perch fishing the upper reaches of the Great Ouse upstream from Bedford, I did on most occasions fish with two rods and as it happened to good effect. With bites proving to be spasmodic on really cold days it was indeed rather comforting to know there were two big lively lobworms on the bottom waiting for a perch to happen along, instead of just one. Now being a smallish river throughout its clear-flowing habitat-rich upper reaches, averaging less than 20 yards wide and often only half the width, the Great Ouse usually confines its perch to those choice feature swims such as deep holes or gullies on the bends, areas of diffused light beneath overhanging willows where rafts collect around the lower, trailing branches, and runs alongside or gaps between beds of tall dark-green onion-like bullrushes. Weir, mill and overshoot pools are, of course, also well worth exploration and invariably contain a shoal or two of resident adult perch.

And my two-rod approach is as follows: Either I trot a worm downstream beneath a

float with one rod and present a ledgered bait with the line clipped on to a ledger bobbin on the second; or I present two ledgered baits, the first is via a quiver-tip rod, the tip of which draws my concentration, while a bobbin indicator set up on the second rod is positioned close by just a couple of feet away. Whilst concentrating upon the finely tapered quiver tip I have no difficulty whatsoever in striking when a bright-red, ten-pin ledger bobbin starts to fall or rise on the second rod. Generally I quiver tip at mid-range and use the bobbin indicator rig for close-range work. Then if a big perch is hooked on the former, I can simply lift the second rod off the front rest and sink the tip so tangles are avoided. Conversely, should a fish gobble up the close-range worm, I immediately angle the quiver-tip rod up high, supported by the front rest only, which lifts the line above the surface, permitting a wide playing area without the two lines tangling.

CATCH YOUR BASS ON THE DRIFT

While many of our once prolific sea species are now nowhere near so thick on the ground as they once were, at least there is one success story upon which we British saltwater fishermen can capitalise and have our string pulled. In fact, due to some excellent spawnings and subsequent fry recruitment during the past few years, bass are now really taking over as 'the' fish to catch virtually regardless of actual size. Although around the southern half of the British Isles there is even the choice of going for schoolies over the banks and in the mouths of estuaries or plundering wrecks for those specimens of 10 lbs and over.

What I like most about the prospect of bass fishing is that you can catch them from many different locations using a whole variety of techniques. You can ledger small whole squid or peeler crab from the shore into rock gullies, troll artificial lures, spin from an anchored or drifting boat, or chum over known inshore features like wrecks and rocky pinnacles from an anchored boat with chopped mackerel or other oily-fleshed fishes and then drift half a mackerel or a flapper downtide on the most sporting of tackle. You can float fish using crab, a large worm or small livebait, or work a heavy pirk deep down over really rough ground amongst huge overfalls of water where bass prey upon small shoal species disorientated by the sheer force of sub-surface currents. You can also take them by working a leaded jig or pirk, artificial eel or even a whole live mackerel deep down over wartime wrecks in up to 200 feet of water. Or, and this is my favourite method, you can bump your bait slowly along over steep sandbanks behind a drifting boat using really light tackle.

I think the freshwater angler in me really takes over when drifting for bass, hence the preference of using an Avon-style rod coupled to a reel line of just 8 lb test, instead of what is considered standard sea tackle. As most schoolies weigh in the region from 1 to 3 lbs why not have some real sport with them? And the Avon combo does exactly this. The choice of a baby multiplier or fixed-spool reel is purely personal, but either way remember to thoroughly rinse in cold fresh water after each trip. Overall, due to the way in which the reel can instantly be clicked into free spool for allowing the bait to drift further downtide, a small multiplier has I think the edge over fixed spools. As indeed they do in most branches of sea fishing. But the clutch must be silky smooth otherwise when a bass runs off ripping several yards of line from the reel in a matter of seconds, either the line or the hook hold will go. The take from a bass is that vicious, though you do have the all-through action Avon rod to absorb and cushion the strongest of lunges. The end rig is quite simple with a bomb of between $1^{1}/_{2}$ - 3 oz (depending upon tide flow) fixed to a snap swivel running on the 8 lb reel line above the trace swivel with a cushioning bead between. The trace itself is 5 – 6 feet long and made from 12 lb test and sports a size 2/0 long-shank, round-bend hook to accommodate the bass bait *par excellence* - a fresh, live sand-eel.

A really large ragworm hooked through the head only is second choice if sandeels are not available. Having located a potentially productive bank on the sonar screen where the bottom shelves acutely upwards with a distinct ridge on top (around which species such as large sand-eels, mackerel and bass often show up on the sonar) the skipper will motor well uptide of the bank and cut the engine so that you can cast out with a gentle lob and drift your bait along quickly over the hot spot.

Distance between rod tip and bait should be continually varied, giving it just that extra little bit of attraction created by the odd jerk and pull. You can, of course, simply cast 30 yards uptide and once the lead touches bottom, rest the rod down against the gunnel with

East coast skipper and good mate Stewart Smalley is justifiably happy with this beautiful, big, double figure bass. Note the dangling sandeel which it took.

the clutch set light to stop the rod from flying over the side should a bass grab hold. But you will enjoy the session far more by holding the rod throughout, working the bait by dropping it several yards downtide every so often, then bumping it along the sand in expectation of a hit.

Where the chance of a real whopper exists, and you'll need to accept the skipper's advice based upon local knowledge here, a step up to 15 lb reel line and a pike or carp rod would be a prudent move. But always err on the side of sport rather than size and what's generally caught from a particular mark. So don't base your outfit on the monstrous weight of a particular specimen caught several years back. Besides, so long as there are few snags about and sandbanks are usually smooth and snag free, should you be fortunate enough to hook into a double-figure bass on 8 lb test, don't panic. Just relax and enjoy the ensuing fight which I doubt will pull your string any more than a carp of similar size anyway.

A final word here if I may be so bold. For goodness' sake don't take a sackful of school bass home. One or two sizeable fish for dinner, yes, but think about helping to preserve a healthy balance in the sea which has far from an infinite source considering the amount of commercial fishing pressure imposed upon it.

A BASS TO REMEMBER

Where Suffolk's River Alde enters the North Sea, south-west of Orford, for the last few miles it changes name to become the River Ore and haven to a myriad of wading birds. Curlews, avocets, oyster catchers and others (it's a twitcher's paradise) were all working the mudbanks as local bass expert Stewart Smalley and I left the river and headed due east in his 20 foot boat, *Aldeburgh Angler*, towards a series of rips over sandbanks some 20 miles out.

Stewart, who runs specialised light tackle trips for bass between June and October was on a mission to catch some sizeable bass for CEFAS (the Centre of Environment, Fisheries and Aquaculture Science) and to bring them back alive for study in their tanks at Lowestoft. Over 2000 bass have been tagged recently by CEFAS and members of the Bass Anglers' Sports Fishing Society as part of a wider study of the species, which is being supported by MAFF.

Naturally Wilson was only too pleased to be invited along and once we were over the rips where depth sharply rises from over 60 feet to less than 30 at the very top of the

You don't whack into too many big bass in a lifetime, which is why I am over the moon with this fine 12 pounder caught on the drift over an east coast wreck.

211

sandbank, Stewart was into a 4 lb bass on the very first drift. It had gobbled up a large ragworm on a size 3/0 hook and being in pristine condition was put straight into the livewell. A good start.

Stewart turned the boat around and we motored uptide again to drift back over the same sandbank; Stewart fished ragworm and I persevered with a frozen sandeel, both of us with 8 ozs of lead above our 10 foot traces to keep the baits close to the sea bed. Suddenly the remains of a wreck came up on the fish-finder screen, 'Crank your bait up John', says Stewart, 'or we'll pull into it, then if you're quick lower it straight down again on top of it and crank the lead up a couple of turns'. This we did and I was just on the point of lowering my sandeel down again when the rod was almost wrenched from my grasp. 'You're in the wreck', says Stewart, but the chugging rod tip and vibrations transmitted via my braided reel line told me differently and I put on maximum pressure from stopping what was obviously a big bass reaching the rusting ironwork. Following a marvellous tussle the great fish finally surfaced 30 yards behind the boat – certainly my biggest bass ever. Stewart bundled it into the net and there it was, 12 lbs exactly of streamlined majesty, coloured in metallic shades of white, silver, slate grey and blue.

This old fellow, and it looked old, though scale and fin perfect, was returned immediately, though we kept others of between 3 and 6 lbs in the livewell for our return to the quay at Orford where a tank and vehicle were waiting to transport them to the laboratories at Lowestoft. Incidentally, if anyone catches a tagged bass, please return the tag to CEFAS (Tel: 01502 524526) with details of capture location area and the fish's weight.

PROTECT YOUR BASS NOW

While many sea anglers including myself have been enjoying a renaissance in bass fishing all around the British Isles during the past few years, due to climatic changes and nursery areas providing good numbers of adolescent bass, a recent press release from the National Federation of Sea Anglers warns that commercial overfishing has now led to mass slaughter of our most exciting saltwater adversary. It is, therefore, vital that we anglers take action before the next season commences.

A group who are in the process of changing the way our Government and the EU look upon sea anglers and their needs is The Bass Anglers' Sports Fishing Society (BASS), who have been in action on our behalf for the last two and a half years working through the National Federation of Sea Anglers, by sending a resolution to the European Anglers' Alliance general assembly held in Oslo earlier this year. B.A.S.S. want the bass to be made Europe's first marine game fish which will give it protection from commercial overfishing and provide anglers with their fair share of stocks.

BASS also want the minimum size limit raised (in stages) to 55 cm which should result in the availability of more decent-sized fish. Their first demand, however, is that the annual winter slaughter of the adult spawning stock is ended. Each winter bass from our waters drop back down the Channel and gather in great shoals off the West Country coast where they are fished for by large British and French trawlers up to 150 feet long which work in pairs, that's two boats pulling one net. These nets can be almost a mile in circumference. Last year a Scottish team caught 32 tons in one trip. If they weighed in at, say, $3\frac{1}{2}$ lbs each that is over 20,000 bass in one hit. These fish are caught just before and during spawning and the damage done in the last few years can be seen in the results of

MAFF's latest survey, *The Offshore Bass Fishing Pilot Study*, (MO802) which shows that all the big fish have gone, leaving only the young fish that joined the main stock in the last two years.

One point that is often forgotten is 'Whose fish are they anyway?' Sea fish are the property of 'The Commons', they are ours, yours, mine and we entrust those we vote into office to manage and share those fish in a responsible and fair way. Quite simply we anglers want our share. After all, in their 'Charter for Anglers' the Labour Party promised they would introduce a coastal planning policy to recognise important areas for sports fishing, and introduce closed areas for spawning and preserving breeding stocks. Or was it just another election-winning ploy. Well now is the time for us anglers to find out. In the next few weeks, the Fisheries Minister, Elliot Morley MP, will be deciding whether to introduce a limit on what these boats are allowed to take each week. The commercials are fighting as always, claiming that they are being deprived yet again and that it is not fair that there are no other fish to catch. If their life is so tough why did they spend 10 million on their new, all-singing and all-dancing high-tech boats in the first place. If they had not ruined all other fish stocks they would have no need to wipe out the bass.

It was anglers who campaigned for protection for bass in the 1980s and anglers who have both supported the 36 cm size limit and respected the nursery areas, set aside for young bass. Now the offshore opportunists want to benefit from our investment. Don't let them: write to the man who has to make that decision and strengthen his hand, help him make the right decision. Write to your MP at the House of Commons – now, before it's too late.

BIG BAITS FOR BIG BASS

Big bass think nothing of swallowing prey fish equal to a fifth of their own bodyweight. A 1½ lbs mackerel for example is merely a quick swallow to a chunky 8 lb bass. Like all members of the perch family to which both the European freshwater perch and the giant Nile perch belong, bass swallow their prey head first and quickly. Engulfed within wide expandable jaws, prey fish such as sandeels, pouting, mackerel and crabs are gulped down post haste, into a cavernous stomach cavity, where powerful juices quickly digest the largest food items. So if a sizeable bass is your dream catch don't pussyfoot about. Sure there will be occasions when ragworms, lugworms and small crab baits will produce quality bass, but they are hardly selective offerings as everything from pouting to young bass are likely to grab hold.

If out on a charter boat working over deepwater wrecks, or rock pinnacles etc., feather up some jumbo-sized launce (greater sand-eels) or mackerel and put down a lively close to the feature lie on a size 5/0 wide gap hook. You'll soon know when a good bass is imminent, the bait fish will start to rattle the rod tip violently, followed by a good solid thump and pull over. At this stage don't strike like a maniac, simply lower the rod tip for the bait to be properly taken and then firmly 'wind' into your bass. This is especially important when using non-stretch braided reel lines, for it's so easy to pull the hook out by striking too fiercely. Braided reel lines are also excellent for working artificials such as small pirks and yans in deep water over rocky gullies and pinnacles after big bass because the 'non-stretch factor' allows maximum rod movement to be transferred to the artificial, many hits actually coming on the drop as the lure freefalls in that tantalising 'fluttering' wounded fish motion. So be ready for a hit literally at any time throughout the 'lift and fall' routine of pirking.

It's quality bass all round for (L-R) Weymouth skipper Chris Cains, The Rev. Hugh Middleton and me, while working a deep water Dorset wreck on the drift, using whole live mackerel.

Rugged coastline features of rocky pinnacles and promontories where bass work ridiculously close in shore can be most effectively worked with plugs. For deep water try Rapala's CD 14 in blue mackerel colouration. The CD means countdown, allowing you to choose the depth at which you envisage bass to be working by counting the plug down at around one foot per second, before commencing the retrieve. For shallow areas try Rapala's J13 jointed floating diver, possibly the most effective bass lure of all time, which is particularly effective in fire tiger and perch patterns. And if all else fails go for broke with Rapala's CD 18 in either olive green or blue mackerel. With this mackerel-sized plug you may not hit into many bass, but like as not they'll be big.

NORTH NORFOLK TOPE

It's been several years since I last fished for tope off the North Norfolk coast, so an invitation from local skipper Brian Riches, who throughout the spring and summer months operates 27 foot *Tilley* out of the creek at Thornham village near Hunstanton, was more than welcome. Brian specialises in tracking down Britain's most popular shark over a bar of rough ground running between six and 10 miles out due east of Thornham where depths vary between 15 and 30 feet. Past trips have resulted in specimens to well in excess of 60 lbs, but our first task was to feather for mackerel on the drift in order to gather a good supply of fresh bait. In the early spring Brian catches dabs to use for bait, upon which tope commonly feed along the shallow waters of the Wash and North Norfolk coastline. But now good shoals of mackerel were in evidence and there is no better fresh natural bait for just about every saltwater predator.

Once we had enough mackerel Brian put the anchor down over what was to be the first potential tope mark of the day, with a view to moving position, several times if need be. But the only time it came up was when we headed back into Thornham. The action was surprisingly that good. I say surprisingly because for two days previously only one tope run had materialised. Yet within minutes of rigging up three uptide rods apiece with baits placed across the tide on both sides of the boat the fun began. I was presenting on my three rods a flapper, a cone and a large fillet. And within a 30 minute spell all three were taken resulting in lovely screeching runs from the multiplier's ratchet.

The first was a baby of around 12 lbs but on a 25 lb test low-diameter, non-stretch braided reel line (to hold out in the strongly ebbing tide) it provided great fun. As I lowered it back into the North Sea to grow bigger, my second bait was grabbed and by a much larger specimen which ran and ran across the tide directly away from the boat for over 50 yards before I could slow it down. Then it went and bit through the 100 lb mono trace. But I didn't have time to dwell on my misfortune for the third bait was taken whilst I was tying on another 7/0 hook. This 40 lbs-plus beauty, a female in pup, stayed on and put up an incredible scrap which included several powerful runs before I could manoeuvre it alongside for Brian to lean over and lift it out by grabbing one of its large pectoral fins and dorsal.

Sport was so manic at times as packs of tope suddenly passed through, I cannot remember exactly how many tope between 20 and 30 lbs were boated from a dozen or so runs. Six or seven good fish is I think a fair estimation and I took home enough fresh mackerel to freeze down for pike fishing trips this coming winter. What a fabulous day's fishing. Thanks a million Brian.

North Norfolk tope are renown for not turning up when they should. But skipper Brian Riches who operates 27 foot Tilley *out of Thornham produced the goods for me.*

RITCHIE BOATS A 'BIG UN' AND SPIKE LANDS RECORD

To the best of my knowledge there are few offshore charter boat skippers on the south coast who cater especially for and actually encourage wheelchair sea anglers. One who does is Spike Spears, skipper of 38 foot *Bessie Vee*, operating out of Langstowe harbour at picturesque Hayling Island in Hampshire. And it was my good fortune just recently to venture out with Spike to a mark some 12 miles south of Selsey Bill in the company of my good friend, and wheelchair angling fanatic, Ritchie Powell from Burry Port, near Swansea.

Now to mention Ritchie's list of phenomenal successes outside the world of angling would fill a page in itself: in athletics in Ireland, Australia, Germany, Spain, Canada, etc., and in the London Marathon and in both the Commonwealth and Para Olympic Games In fact a favourite quote of his, 'Don't think about what you can't, only what you can do' – says it all. So I'll simply concentrate on our memorable day out on board *Bessie Vee* along with the camera crew from Anglia Television, in pursuit of a sea fishing section for my programme *Go Fishing*. Our target species was jumbo-sized smooth-hounds and tope which frequent a particular area of rough ground in just 30 feet of water. It was uptide sport at anchor at its very, very best. And in the course of just six hours' fishing, offering a mixture of hermit and softback crabs, plus fresh mackerel heads and cones, we virtually took the place apart, boating over 20 common and starry smooth-hounds averaging between 10 and 20 lbs plus a new British record of $29\frac{1}{2}$ lbs. This easily eclipsed the old record of 28 lbs but captor Spike rightly decided not to kill such a fine specimen in order for it to be weighed ashore (imperative for those wishing to claim a record) so it was returned to fight another day after being duly recorded for my television series. The first British record fish ever landed during the making of 102 programmes I've now made in the last 16 years for Anglia and Meridian Television. Boy, was I pleased.

Whilst the cameras were rolling on Spike's giant smooth-hound, the brakes on Ritchie's wheelchair were coming under severe strain as he battled away with what materialised into a fine 38 lbs male tope. What a fight, easily beating his previous personal best weight of any species. What did I catch? Well, I did manage to net Spike's record 'smoothie' even if the net handle did snap as I heaved it on board. All good stuff for the two cameras. And amid all the chaos I landed my own personal best smooth-hound of $15\frac{1}{2}$ lbs, plus what I thought was another record smoothie (so did Spike) but which materialised into a 40 lbs tope. What a day. I can't ever remember when big fish were coming over the gunnel so frequently or so fast. And all on sporting uptide rods, small multiplier reels and 30 lb braid.

A LATE TOPE SAVES THE DAY

The way weather patterns have been affecting offshore fishing this spring and summer there's no way I'd fancy earning my living as an East Coast skipper. Yet stalwarts like John Rawle who operates 33 foot *Kingfisher* out of Bradwell Marina in Essex, accepts those inevitable cancellations with surprising nonchalance. Having my first trip kicked into touch by a sudden low accompanied by torrential rain and a force 7, I was delighted when John rang and confirmed that the reserve trip to get amongst those smooth-hounds and tope of the Thames Estuary 'was on'. And with just one day budgeted for a segment of my long-running TV series *Go Fishing* (series 17 no less) the camera crew and I assembled early at the moorings for some leaving clips followed by a push against a strong flooding tide to reach an area of extremely rough ground in 80 feet of water, lasting over two hours.

By the time we had arrived over the desired mark and dropped anchor the tide was just starting to ebb nicely, picking up all the time and we quickly put out three uptide outfits each - two for tope, the 100 lb mono trace and 6/0 hooks baited with five inch sections of eel and the third with just a 50 lb trace and 3/0 hook baited with fresh hermit crab which, along with peeler crab, smooth-hounds absolutely adore.

These two members of the shark family have different feeding preferences entirely. Smooth-hounds have no canine teeth, merely crushing pads, hence their liking for crabs. Whereas tope are fast tooth-laden killers following the mackerel shoals though they will, of course, feed from the bottom on flatfish and eels etc., dead or alive. Both provide great scraps especially on light tackle and our 20 lb monofilament reel lines were soon being stretched in the strong ebbing tide as an assortment of common smooth-hounds, starry smooth-hounds and small tope, all between 4 and 12 lbs were hoisted over the side. But where were the large tope our camera needed? Only the day before John's boat had accounted for no fewer than three tope over 50 lbs. And, yes, as a TV presenter I have

My old mate Essex skipper John Rawle certainly saved our bacon with this huge male tope when the 'Go Fishing' TV crew and I chartered his boat Kingfisher out of Bradwell.

become used to all the 'You should have been here yesterday' cliches. Then quite out of the blue the multiplying reel on one of John's tope rods squealed like the proverbial stuck pig as what was obviously a sizeable tope shot off downtide. Fortunately the hook held throughout a magnificent battle lasting fully 20 minutes in the strong tide from what materialised into a huge male tope fully five feet long, weighing 44 lbs. Yours truly bundled it into the net at the first attempt and so far as our TV segments were concerned it was 'job sorted'.

WONDERFUL WEYMOUTH

Of all our South Coast ports I personally rate Weymouth as the most prolific: not only in the wealth of competent charter boat skippers who operate from the huge marina, but in the sheer diversity of saltwater locations and options all within short steaming time of the harbour. You can drift over rocky ground or alongside wrecks using live sand-eels or mackerel for bass and pollack; anchor over rough ground for a stack of different rays and flatfish, plus cod, tope, bull huss and conger; go for a truly mixed bag of smaller species on light tackle including corkwing, ballan and the highly coloured cuckoo wrasse, plus garfish, mackerel and schoolie-sized bass or pollack etc. Or even book a three or four day excursion during the summer months over to the Channel Islands for tope, turbot, brill and specimen bass with some hectic, deepwater wrecking for cod and pollack on the way across using jellyworm rigs, shads or heavy pirks according to the depth and tide.

There's great shore fishing around this part of Dorset too, with wrasse, pollack and bass from many of the rocks areas, plus excellent sport with the thick-lipped grey mullet in and around the marina and within Portland harbour itself. If you go further west then you have the full length of famous Chesil beach to explore where in addition to most of the previously mentioned species, there is a real chance during the present warm weather of catching a trigger fish which is actually a sub-tropical species that comes in with the gulf stream.

Just recently my wife Jo and I made the long journey down from Norfolk to enjoy a fabulous day's sport just a couple of miles offshore from Weymouth on board 36 foot *Tiger Lily*, skippered by good friend Chris Caines. Unfortunately, following several extremely hot days, the weather turned turtle on the very morning our boat left harbour, with the promise of rain and a freshening wind from the south-west. So our original plan of heading a fair way out to wait with big baits on the bottom in a strong tide rip, specifically to attract a big blonde ray or two, had to be shelved. It would have been just too uncomfortable for Jo who, though a fair sailor, soon started to feel cold in the freshening wind. So Chris anchored us over an incredibly steep bank which shelved from 150 feet down to over 200 feet with a fertile fish-packed trough at the bottom renowned for conger eels, dogfish, bull huss, plus of course the inevitable hordes of pouting which continually peck away at your bait.

Having already spent 20 minutes enjoying feathering for fresh mackerel off Portland Bill on the way out, we used a combination of large mackerel, mackerel flappers and cocktails of squid and mackerel fillets on our simple bottom rigs. The hook trace was 5 feet of 150 lb mono with a swivel at one end and a size 6/0 O'Shaunassey on the business end. Above this, on a 15 ft rubbing trace of 50 lb mono tied to our 30 lb braided reel lines ran a plastic boom and $1\frac{1}{2}$ lbs lead which just about held bottom as the ebb tide was starting to slow down. Chris suggested we step down to lighter weights of 1 lb and then

Prior to my wife Jo and I catching this lovely brace of bull huss while out with Weymouth skipper Chris Cains, I had never before featured the species in my 'Go Fishing' programmes.

finally to just 10 ozs as the current slowed right down to slack water, which worked an absolute treat and permitted maximum enjoyment from everything we hooked. Besides, continually retrieving and lowering heavy leads when the fish are hard on is not pleasant.

The first fish, a bull huss, approaching double figures, came to my rod having nobbled a mackerel flapper, which overall proved on the day to be by far the most productive bait. Then Chris caught a small conger, followed immediately afterwards by a larger bull huss from Jo who really had to use every ounce of her energy in pumping it up from 200 feet against a fair lick of tide.

Once the tide had slackened right off Chris had promised the action would really liven up and he was right. Jo got stuck into a lively conger of around 30 lbs by far her largest ever, while Chris and I shared a mixture of strap congers and the beautifully spotted bull huss, which is, of course, none other than the greater spotted dogfish and a true shark. The last fish and best conger of the day was caught by Chris before a squall of rain set in and we decided to pull anchor. Jo said she still felt numbness in her hauling arm two days later. So we must have had a great day.

CONGER MAGIC

Skipper Roger Bayzand hadn't long steered around the famous Needles, off the Isle of Wight and set *Sundance* on a course into the middle of the English Channel, when a school of dolphins suddenly appeared beside the boat. There were at least 30 of these curious, magnificent creatures looking all of 500 – 600 lbs apiece, cavorting around the boat, jumping in our wake and giving the party of eight local Lymington wreck fishermen and myself a rare treat indeed, all thoughts of hauling up conger being immediately put to one side.

Following half an hour of marvelling at the antics of our newfound friends it was sadly time to go, and everyone set about making up their tackle in readiness for one of Roger's favourite wartime conger wrecks lying out in mid-channel down on the bottom in 140 feet of water. Good friend 'stainless steel' Steve Bachelor had arranged this pre-Christmas trip and it was he who quickly hooked into a real lump of a conger within minutes of Roger setting the anchor immediately uptide of the wreck. Sadly, to Steve's disgust this particular eel managed to throw the hook, as indeed did several throughout the day. Despite great conditions combining warm, sunny weather, a gentle force 3 sea and a slow neap tide those eels proved particularly finicky. Bites from conger were rarely as aggressive as the horde of pouting and black bream continually pecking away at our mackerel and cuttlefish hookbaits mounted on size 8/0 hooks to thick 150 lb test mono traces. In fact half the party soon switched over to much lighter outfits presenting jigs of baited

Super Skipper and pal Roger Bayzand (right) uses a 'T' bar to unhook a nice conger for Steve 'stainless steel' Batchelor, (left), during our pre-Christmas trip out from Lymington.

feathers purposefully to enjoy the black bream fishing, Ady Hulme catching a real specimen for the species weighing 4lb s 6 ozs.

Amongst the bream came a real mixed bag of species including pouting, mackerel, dogfish, bull huss and pollack, but conger were what we wanted and eventually eels in the 20 – 30 lb bracket started picking up our large baits. Not monsters but really good action on our sporting outfits.

Regularly lowering down fresh baits to the bottom which inaugurates a continual scent trail and hauling up lots of fish, often attracts other predators to the wreck, sharks in particular, and our trip proved no exception. Both 'stainless steel' Steve and I had baits grabbed in mid-water on the drop by what we thought to be tope, but unfortunately were bitten through, the teeth chaffing our 40 lb test monofilament rubbing leaders above the hook trace. Best conger of the day was a fish of 40 lbs plus boated and returned (like all the eels taken) by Eddie Taylor who also accounted for another slightly smaller. What a fabulous day out for everyone. I must make the effort and long drive down to the South Coast from my Norfolk home more often. Big eels really do give you a great work-out.

SEARCHING OUT THOSE ELUSIVE AND ENIGMATIC SHAD

A special British migratory sea fish will soon be entering a handful of our major river systems for the sole purpose of spawning in fresh water. Only during the following month at locations such as Tewkesbury Weir on the River Severn and the River Wye where it joins forces with the River Monnow in South Wales, is the freshwater enthusiast likely to see, let alone catch, one of our rarest fish, the twaite shad. These silvery, herring-like plankton feeders enter our estuaries by the thousand during May and wherever they congregate there is a real chance of catching them using a super-light spinning outfit and tiny vibratory spinners in the 00 size range. They can also be great fun to catch on the fly rod using attractor patterns, especially silver-bodied fish fry imitations – zonkers being my favourite.

Shad share the characteristics of leaping repeatedly in a show of shimmering iridescence, not unlike a miniature tarpon. The British record is a little over 2 lbs, so there is no chance of a monster. But due to their acrobatics these lively fish, which average over the pound, more than compensate.

Personally I am always delighted at catching a new species I have not previously seen so when my old pal Dave Lewis of Newport first invited me across country to sample twaite shad fishing in his nearby River Wye a few years back I was like a kid in a toyshop. Fortunately we got the timing right and filled our boots throughout a hectic morning's session, catching several dozen shad from 1 lb up to almost 2 lbs, all of which were returned unharmed.

What you immediately notice about this enigmatic species is the notch cut into the centre of its upper jaw, into which fits its protruding lower jaw. It's a purpose-built strainer mechanism designed for plankton feeding at sea. It's cavernous, expanding mouth is, however, quite capable of swallowing sand-eels, sprats and immature herrings. Hence its willingness to grab artificial lures. Colouration along the back is a mix of pewter and pale grey, sometimes with a distinct blue tinge. And one of the shad's most recognisable features is a line of several dark round blotches along the shoulder which are often visible in the water. The twaite shad has deeply compressed flanks covered in silvery scales which easily become dislodged and a most defined keel along the belly. In fact, from the small

The silvery enamelling, protruding lower jaw and deeply forked tail of twaite shad, likens the species to tarpon and herring. They certainly jump like tarpon.

dorsal fin it tapers rapidly towards the sharply forked tail.

Confusion with another species is hardly likely – except that is with the now incredibly rare allis shad which, due to pollution and the construction of weirs and locks, no longer migrate into British freshwater to breed. Allis Shad grow to more that 4 lbs and are much deeper in the body. Occasionally one is caught at sea, usually by someone feathering for mackerel, although I have regularly used Allis shad for barracuda and shark baits when sea fishing in tropical waters. Shark fishing in the mouth of the Gambia River in West Africa immediately springs to mind, where allis shad are called bonga fish. They are commonly seen in local fish markets, and due to their oily flesh are one of the most effective baits for large predatory sea fish. I have a pair of bonga fish fillets to thank for the 300 lbs lemon shark which provided the cameras with some exciting footage during the making of a TV *Go Fishing* programme in The Gambia during the early 1990s.

It wasn't until I caught my first shad from the River Wye three years later and recognised that unique notch in its upper jaw that I realised Gambian bonga fish were none other than allis shad. Incidentally the allis shad is now considered a threatened species and is protected under the Wildlife and Countryside Act of 1981. It is an offense to capture one intentionally. But let's be honest, you've a better chance of hooking a basking shark under London Bridge.

223

MULLET MANIA

If you ever find yourself at a loss this summer and unsure about which technique or species to target next, then try your hand at catching the elusive thin-lipped grey mullet. It is an estuary and tidal river fish and I'm sure that even the majority of most coarse anglers will already own a suitable tackle combo. For instance, a basic 13 foot float rod with a centre-pin or fixed-spool reel, holding 4 lb test monofilament, is ideal for presenting a piece of fluffy white breadflake on a size 10 or 12 hook, in conjunction with regular helpings of mashed bread to keep the mullet working where you want them. It's then a simple matter of trotting the float along as though you are roach or chub fishing, except that pound for pound, mullet knock the spots off most coarse species. For a fish averaging between just $1\frac{1}{2}$ and 3 lbs their power and speed is quite phenomenal.

Alternatively you can enjoy a day's spinning as I did just recently using an ultra-light outfit comprising of an 8-9 foot rod and small fixed-spool reel filled with just 4 lb test monofilament. You'll need to doctor your spinners, mind, replacing the weighted brass barrel of, say, a Mepps No. 3 with a line of small beads on the wire stem. This is to ensure the lure works high up near the surface where the thin lips are most likely to grab hold. The treble hook can be replaced with a pennel rig of 2 single hooks on two inches of 8 lb mono, one a size 12 and the other a long shank size 8 or 6, to ensure the tail end of half a ragworm will flutter enticingly behind the attractor blade.

My good friend and guide for the day, 'stainless steel' Steve Batchelor from Lymington, had painstakingly doctored a dozen or so spinners to ensure we had a good supply for our day out in Christchurch harbour where the fertile waters of both the Hampshire Avon and the Dorset Stour converge. Now Christchurch harbour is like mullet city, with enormous concentrations of thin lips, plus the occasional bass to ensure those who try the spinning technique are kept on their toes; the secret being to retrieve as slow as you can in the strong flow.

Every now and again a sizeable sea trout or salmon crashes out but when the rod tip is yanked round, a lively thin lip is usually responsible and don't they go on a 4 lb reel line. My best weighed around $3\frac{1}{2}$ lbs and it's difficult to think of another species of identical size that would have fought so hard or for as long. Give mullet a try.

EVERYMAN'S FISH

Though pollack do not attain massive weight (the British record is $29^{1/4}$ lbs), in my book they are amongst the hardest fighting of all our popular saltwater species, and I only wish they were common off my local East Coast. But this is one sea fish I am only too pleased to travel in order to catch.

Being a member of the cod family pollack sport three dorsal and two anal fins, the first of which is noticeably long. The species is perhaps most recognisable, however, for its protruding bottom jaw which easily distinguishes it from its cousin, the coalfish, whose lips are almost level. In addition, the lateral line of the coal fish is straight compared to that of the pollack which curves above its pectoral fin. Pollack are beautifully enamelled in brownish coppery beige along the back fusing down the flanks into highly polished metallic brass. To say they shimmer when lifted clear of the sea would indeed be a gross understatement. And it is this colourful, yet powerful persona of the pollack that I love, for in eating qualities it comes a poor second to cod, though its flesh does improve from being filleted and stored in the freezer for a few weeks prior to cooking.

What I like most about this particular species, however, is that it is truly Everyman's fish and can be caught from many locations around the British Isles whether you are shore or wreck fishing. The west coast of Ireland offers fabulous shore fishing for pollack as do many of the rugged feature locations in the south-west of England and all around the coastline of Wales.

Armed with a heavy spinning outfit and an assortment of bar spoons and small pirks the wandering fisherman has a wealth of great pollack fishing ahead, for they are always aggressive and willing to feed. But you do need to live dangerously and count the lure down amongst the rocks before commencing the retrieve. For this reason I prefer the direct drive and fast retrieve of a small multiplying reel loaded to the brim with 12 – 14 lb test. A 20 foot shock leader of say 22 – 25 lb test will also help against abrasions from the rocks.

For 'pollack pirates' who venture well offshore by charter boat to plunder the deep water of sunken reefs and wartime wrecks, well, there is no finer more exciting light tackle adversary to be found in temperate saltwater. The favourite way for coming to grips with the huge pollack inhabiting wrecks is to drift fish over the wreck on a neap tide (spring tides pull the boat along too fast) using a 20 – 30 lb outfit presenting a jellyworm or red-gill-type rubber eel on a long trace and French or plastic boom rig to which a 6 – 10 oz lead is attached. You allow the lead to hit the wreck taking care the long trace doesn't become tangled around the lead and reel line and then slowly wind the lure upwards for 10 to 25 turns of the reel handle. If a pollack doesn't hit it after 30 turns you lower the lure down to the wreck and start the retrieve again. Though a slow retrieve is recommended by most charter boat skippers when 'gilling', it's always worth trying an erratic-fast retrieve. You may be pleasantly surprised – but hang on, hits are often deliciously savage and the way in which your uptide rod is wrenched over into an alarming bend bears little relation to the size of pollack that has grabbed hold. Even a 10 pounder can pull away ripping several yards of line from the spool each time it dives for the sanctuary of the wreck. It's worth mentioning here that in really deep marks, say between 130 to 200 feet of water using a low-stretch, low diameter braided reel line makes everything so much more positive and exciting, compared to monofilament. Due to its inherent 25 per cent stretch monofilament line becomes totally insensitive for working artificial rubber lures and especially heavy pirks down deep. So often the large treble

No wonder Norfolk angler Mike Mcgregor looks happy, this massive south-coast pollack weighed well into double figures and gave him a real workout from a wreck 200 feet down.

hooks on pirks do not find purchase on the initial impact of the strike and promptly fall out when the pollack is halfway up; whereas with 'no-stretch braid' they are pulled well in on the fish's first dive for freedom.

Incidentally, don't tie your pirk directly to the braided reel line. Use a mono shock absorber trace of 6-8 feet of a lower breaking strain than your reel line. Then if the pirk gets caught up in the wreck when you wrap the line around a cleat so the drifting boat does the breaking off (saves a nasty accident with your hands) and only the pirk is lost. Of course, big pollack also fall to fish baits ledgered close up to wrecks and intended for conger eels. I've taken some whopping great double-figure pollack on whole mackerel, mackerel flappers and on whole pouting. And I think the most endearing quality of this species is that it is nearly always ready to have a go wherever you fish. It is indeed Everyman's fish.

MINI BILLFISH ARE FUN

From around the beginning of June through until the end of the summer the acrobatic garfish will be foraging through the upper water layers close inshore around piers, breakwaters, rocky headlands and in harbours all around the British Isles. And it's probably the closest that many sea fishermen will come to a taste of big game fishing, certainly in our temperate seas. If only the garfish grew 10 feet long and as thick as a man's leg, I then doubt anyone would ever want to catch salmon. But just because this minuscule gladiator, with its long beak full of needle-sharp teeth, rarely exceeds 3 feet and a weight of 3 lbs, doesn't mean you can't enjoy its willingness to be caught on float tackle and acrobatic jumping ability.

Gars catapult their long metallic greeny-blue bodies high into the water and start tailwalking usually within seconds of taking your bait, providing unrivalled sport on light tackle. Incidentally, anyone who owns an 11-12 feet rod used for chub, carp or pike etc., is already well equipped for gars. Add a fixed-spool reel filled with around 8 lb test, a few cylindrical 'through the middle' sliding pike floats, plus bullet weights, small swivels and size 6 longshank eyed Aberdeen hooks, and that's it. You're ready to go. For bait you can use thin, quarter-inch strips of fresh mackerel, or once one is landed strips from the garfish itself. Like the mackerel garfish are delicious to eat, so don't be put off by the colour of its bones which turn a strange shade of green when cooked.

A simple float rig consists of the float set between 3 and 8 feet above the hook, stopped at the desired depth by a small bead and a sliding stop knot. This you can tie using several inches of reel line or the same of power gum. Use a 3 foot hook trace of slightly heavier mono (say 12 lb test) to alleviate abrasion from its teeth and thread the bullet used to cock the float on to the line immediately above the size 10 swivel with a bead in between. Don't worry about a cylindrical pike float seeing too big. When fishing up to 50 yards out you need something large to watch. Besides, so ferocious is the take from a garfish, the float fair zooms away with the result that

the gar virtually hooks itself when pulling the large buoyant float under. Alternatively, if the gar swims upwards with the bait, the float will simply lie flat, so bend the rod into it immediately.

The most productive areas for garfish are where the turbulence around rocky headlands makes shoals of small bait fish disorientated and easy pickings. So use the tide flow to your advantage by trotting the bait along in the currents with the reel's bale arm open. Try various depths until a taking band is found and be prepared to move about from one area to another as the flooding or ebbing tide provides the garfish with unlimited areas in which to locate small shoal fish.

Harbour garfish can often be seen close to the surface at the end of a pier or breakwater, and you can sometimes actually watch them grab your bait. To keep them working through a particular area, a smelly groundbait can be concocted from minced oily fish, blood and bran. An old spoon is recommended for ladling out a dollop every so often otherwise the stink on your hands might prove upsetting. These harbour garfish, particularly in flat calm clear water conditions, can prove exceedingly finicky at times. So be prepared to scale right down to freshwater waggler or trotting floats, a lighter hook link and even smaller hooks when you can see them gobbling up the loose-feed particles but not your hookbait. When fresh fish strip is in short supply, or simply as a change, try using a slither of raw steak on the hook. Replace regularly when the blood washes out and it loses its attraction.

Finally don't forget to rinse both rod and especially your reel in clean fresh water afterwards to remove all traces of salt.

GENTLEMEN PREFER BLONDES

I experienced a really smashing day's sea fishing offshore from Weymouth in Dorset just recently aboard Colin Penny's 37 foot charter boat *Flamer* when, although the actual intention of the trip was to bag some big blonde rays, I cannot ever remember catching so many species, despite our fairly substantial tackle. To put us in with a chance of these big rays, which can top 30 lbs, (the British record is in fact $37^{3/4}$ lbs), Colin felt our best bet was to fish at anchor in depths between 70 and 100 feet on top of a rocky and shingle slope, so our baits could be fished down the slope during the flood tide and whilst it eased down.

Our tackle consisted of 50 lb class outfits with the gel spun polyethylene braided reel line, which due to its exceedingly narrow diameter, requires far less lead to hold bottom in the fierce tide run than monofilament. Even then during the full force of the flood, 2 lb of lead was needed to anchor the baits down. At the business end were simple downtide running ledgers with 5 feet of 80 lb mono hook lengths holding two hook Pennel rigs. As the top hook runs free on the line it can be positioned to accommodate any length bait simply by winding the line twice around the shank. This two-hook arrangement not only ensures the bait is held out straight for maximum attraction, it also stops it from wodging down over the bottom hook and impairing penetration when a ray sucks it up.

Colin illustrated his simple most attractive method for preparing 6 – 8 inch squid bait, by first removing the head, then making four two inch cuts up the body with a sharp knife creating a skirt that wavers and flutters in the tide. The head is then nicked on to the lower hook once the squid's body has been mounted. For extra scent and visual attraction we sometimes also added a thin silvery strip of fresh mackerel to the lower hook.

We started slowly at our first mark south of the Lulworth banks at the end of the ebb

When filming for television I honestly don't care who catches the target species, and Weymouth skipper Colin Penny certainly obliged with this 20 lb plus blonde ray.

tide by taking doggies and large pouting plus the occasional spotted ray, but once the flood started to build and the boat swung round to hold steady, for a good hour the rods were nodding regularly to more pouting, red gurnard, small-eyed rays, thornback rays and even small tope. It was fabulous non-stop action but Colin wanted that blonde and so we moved position to east of the Adamant bank.

Once the anchor was in, over a slightly deeper and certainly steeper slope, I just couldn't evade catching doggies except for a cod around 10 lbs which came right out of the blue, whilst Colin chuckled away at my misfortune, boating small-eyed rays and thornbacks. Then he really rubbed the salt in by finally latching on to what we had set out for, a big blonde ray. The way it was holding bottom in the strong tide flow Colin said it couldn't have been anything else and he was right. Despite the 50 lb class outfit that ray took ages to come up, every so often tearing line from the spool against the clutch as it dropped downtide using the incredible power and water resistance of its wide wings. But eventually it tired and when totally exhausted on the surface I managed to bungle it into the salmon-sized landing net and heaved it over the gunnel. A superbly marked fish from the deeps, resplendent in an overall beige-honey colouration overlaid with lighter patches and completely covered in small spots, and it pulled the scales down to over 20 lbs.

A DAY OVER THE 'SHAMBLES'

I must admit that in over 50 years a fisherman I have never set out specifically to catch plaice. Yes, I'd taken the odd fish of up to a pound or so whilst catching dabs from the beach, but until friend Stewart Smalley invited me to join his party of Suffolk plaice enthusiasts, who each April make a pilgrimage to fish the famous 'shambles' bank off Weymouth, I cannot remember even seeing a specimen plaice boated. Truth is, big plaice, and we are talking 3-6 lbs beauties here, resplendent in huge orangey spots with a pure white fringe around glistening brown bodies the size of a turkey serving plate, rarely get caught by accident. In fact, as I was to experience on board Chris Caines boat, *Tiger Lily*, the drifting technique used to lure these jumbo flatties is as highly skilled as it is fascinating.

For a start, booking the right set of tides for plaice fishing is imperative, and over the 'shambles' situated seven miles out from Weymouth in depths varying from 30 to over 80 feet, experienced skippers like jovial Chris Caines expect short 'catching' windows at the end of the ebb and again at the end of the flood tide. It's all about being able to drift with your lead bumping the clean, sandy banks extremely slowly. To slow the boat's drift right down Chris puts out a fairly short anchor chain and a 50 lb weight which gently bumps bottom.

On the business end of a light, sensitive-tipped 15-20 lb class boat rod coupled to a small multiplier loaded with 20-30 lbs braid, is a 6 foot flowing trace of 20 lb monofilament. Above the swivel on to a running link goes a 6-10 oz flat watch type lead to bump smoothly over the sand. And on to the 2/0 fine wire, Aberdeen hook are crammed as many large king ragworm as is physically possible. This results in an 8-10 inch wodge of bait, most of it on the line above the hook, and resting above this are between 20 and 30 coloured beads, some of which contain a tiny rattle. It's all about attracting plaice to the bait and to this end some anglers prefer a 3 inch 'flasher' spoon incorporated into the rig 20 inches above the worms.

Once the skipper has set his craft on a good drift, everyone lowers their rigs and gives an extra 10 foot of free line upon reaching the bottom, to encourage a gentle bow in the braided line between rod tip and lead. You then wait expectantly for the gentle tap, tap, tap of a plaice mouthing your worms and instantly free spool line so it gets the bait well down before putting the reel back into gear and winding into one of the best meals swimming in the English Channel. My first weighed $3\frac{1}{2}$ lbs and fought surprisingly strongly on the light tackle, as did all of the 17 specimens landed by our party of six the largest being a whopper of $4\frac{1}{2}$ lbs taken by David Hicks of Woodbridge, who also craftily caught the lion's share, by adding chunks of peeler crab to his ragworms.

GET OUT THERE WRECKING

The vast majority of coarse and game fishermen, even sea anglers who only ever cast from the beach and pier, are all taken aback by the sheer power and exhilarating fights from species like cod and pollack when hooked deep down in clear water over wartime wrecks. And once you have had a taster you want more. Nowadays to fish the most productive wrecks skippers are having to motor further and further offshore each year. Those, for instance, who operate charter boat trips from ports along our South Coast between Kent and Dorset are invariably fishing closer to France than England. But then so long as

For extra attraction and additional hooking power I like to add a colourful rubber eel to the top of my 'pirk' when deep water wreck fishing for big cod. Nuff said.

everybody gets their string well and truly pulled travelling time is not a problem to most sea stalwarts. Those who part with their breakfasts rather easily, however, would perhaps give you an argument. Sea sickness sufferers, therefore, would be well advised not to try wrecking.

To be fairly sure of success you need not only to book with a competent skipper who specialises in drifting over wrecks, but make that booking well in advance so as to be fishing on the very best set of neap tides which ensure the boat drifts slowly over the wreck. And with the most productive skippers that means up to a year ahead – such is the demand.

Sure, it is expensive due to the amount of diesel used. Sure, you may experience an uncomfortable trip back if the weather turns for the worse, and your limbs will feel as though you've been arm wrestling with Arnold Schwarzanegger if the wreck happens to be really stacked up. But there's no more gut-busting, adrenalin-pumping action than fighting a big cod or pollack up from 200 feet down when it doesn't fancy coming up. Such fish never want their eyes to see the light of day and use every muscle in their bodies to stay down close to the wreck and even wind your line into the steelwork should you allow excess slack.

Until non-stretch low-diameter braided reel lines hit the market a few years ago the inherent elasticity in monofilament of around 25 per cent meant that a likely fish could reach the sanctuary of the wreck without ever ripping a yard of line from the reel. Monofilament also deadened the action of working artificial lures in deep water, particularly heavy pirks. But with braid it is a different ball game and because there is next to no stretch you feel each and every twist and turn of a powerful fish. You can almost feel it blinking. Everything upwards of double figures will pull the rod over in several arm-wrenching dives and to alleviate a break-off during the early stages of a fight, experienced wreck fishermen do not have the clutch screwed down too tight, as with mono, preferring to thumb the spool when required for more controlled braking.

Of course, none of this would be possible without the very latest in DGPS installed in the wheelhouse which allows the skipper to put his boat right over the wreck, as if by magic, after steaming towards the horizon for two or three hours, drift after drift after drift. The Differential Global Positioning System utilises land-based stations to intercept the GPS signals from satellites and transmit that upgraded data to the boat's receiver. So we are talking about an exact science here to within yards. Mind you, days when the wreck's inhabitants aren't in a co-operative mood still occur. Thankfully nothing can ever change that.

Should you fancy some wrecking on the drift invest in an uptide-type boat rod of around 9–9½ feet long with a softish, forgiving tip but plenty of power in the butt section. Then you can enjoy the best of both worlds by obtaining maximum sport from modest-sized fish with enough backbone in reserve for leaning into the biggies.

Almost any reliable medium-format multiplier with a smooth dependable clutch will suffice and should be filled with 30 – 40 lb braid, to which a 9-10 foot monofilament trace of around 25 lb test should be added via a swivel. This not only helps cushion the non-forgiving non-stretch qualities of braid during the fight, but ensures that when your pirk or jellyworm trace becomes snagged in the wreck, as it surely will, that's all you lose. It becomes the perfect weak link. But don't try to break off by holding the line. Simply wrap the braid a few times around a cleat and let the drifting boat do what is a potentially dangerous task for you.

To minimise tackle and hooked fish losses whilst drifting over the wreck, endeavour to work a vertical line which can be effectively lifted or lowered over the rusting ironwork as it appears on the sonar screen. Some skippers constantly yell out their boat's position (and your lines) in relation to the wreck. If you can actually keep an eye on the sonar screen inside the wheelhouse whilst fishing then so much the better. Otherwise listen to the skipper's advice and do not let out an excess of line. When it starts to hang out in the tide quickly retrieve and lower your lure back down again. And hang on.

WHAT A MARVELLOUS BRACE

Good friend Brian Joslin and I have much in common. We are the same age and approaching 60 far quicker than we'd both like (sorry Brian), having been commercially involved one way or another in the pursuit of angling for much of our working lives. Myself in the tackle trade and then as a writer and television presenter, and Brian both as a trout fishery and reservoir manager and as a charter boat skipper working out of Rye harbour in East Sussex.

It was in fact during the filming of my early *Go Fishing* television programmes back in the early 1990s. that Brian and I first teamed up, producing for the cameras double-figure trout from Hanningfield Reservoir in Essex, and conger eels over 70 lbs from deepwater wrecks in the English Channel. His experience of South Coast offshore fishing is literally second to none, so when I was invited on board his 38 foot boat *Christyann* just recently to share a day's wreck fishing 20 miles out with a group of seven jovial Essex lads from Ongar, my optimism level was running high.

We were fishing on a falling spring tide with a potential window of action that included all of the ebb plus the first of the flood. And in just over an hour's steaming from our 6.00 a.m. departure, Brian cut the engines followed by those immortal words, 'Down you go boys.' On the finder good shoals of fish were marking between 10 and 30 feet off bottom immediately uptide of the wreck which lay in 140 feet of water.

Upon Brian's advice everyone was presenting small redgills on 12 foot monofilament traces above just 6 oz of lead on a boom, and slowly retrieving for 20 or 30 turns of the reel handle once the lead hit bottom, before lowering the rubber lures down again into the 'target' area. It's a great light tackle technique which on the day can account for several different species.

During the first few drifts both cod and pollack into double figures were taken by the Essex lads, but I couldn't encourage a hit on a 7 inch orange lure. A switch over to a smaller black 'gill', however, produced an extremely

Yes, I'm totally ecstatic having boated this 26 lb cod and 17 lb coalfish while aboard south coast skipper Brian Joslin's boat Christyann *pirking a deep water wreck out from Rye in Sussex. What a brace.*

powerful fish on the first retrieve One that crash dived so deeply I feared it would snag in the wreck. But thanks to non-stretch braided reel line I managed to get its head up and Brian was at hand to finally net what I initially assumed was a big pollack, but which materialised into a fabulous 17 lb coal fish. Our only coal fish of the day. My biggest ever and the heaviest landed from Brian's boat in several years. Yes, it was one of those days. The fish boxes began to fill, the sun never stopped shining and despite a decidedly lumpy sea everyone caught all day. Freshwater angler Jeff Mason, on his first sea trip, ever boated a magnificent 22 lb cod and as slack water approached I changed over to a 10 oz KC pirk with a red vinyl eel attached to the swivel for extra attraction. This produced an even larger cod which fought all the way up and pulled Brian's spring balance down to $26\frac{1}{2}$ lbs. My largest ever. Two personal bests in a day, great company, a freezer full of cod fillets - what more can a man want from his sport?

A BIGGIE FOR JINX

If, like me, you love arm-wrenching battles from summer cod inhabiting deepwater wrecks, then you'll already know there is no better time for bumper action with both specimens and fish in quantity than now in June. A recent trip proved exactly this when I accepted an invitation to join good friend John (Jinx) Davey and his party of six workmates from Waveney District Council on board skipper Colin Clarke's 38 foot

Aided by skipper Colin Clarke (left) Jinx Davey proudly shows his $24\frac{1}{2}$ lb North Sea cod to the camera. It's always nice to share in a friends success.

Mistress II out of Southwold in Suffolk, our destinations being several of the 150 First and Second World War wrecks lying in between 120 and 160 foot of water, all within steaming distance of Southwold up to 40 miles out.

Only one of the six wrecks we drifted over failed to hold fish and the first produced double-figure cod for everyone using large chromium-plated pirks. Being non-stretch and a much finer diameter than monofilament of the same test, a braided reel line allows the pirk to be worked more attractively in the extreme depths these wrecks are situated. But you must be prepared to lose a fair amount of gear in the ironwork when cod pack tightly around it, in order to induce hits. And this was certainly one of those days. Using a 6 foot shock absorber trace of lighter test monofilament between pirk and the braided reel line results in it breaking first but the wreck still gets your pirk despite the braided reel line and top swivel remaining intact.

When enough double-figure cod are coming over the side, however, no-one minds losing tackle and it was a case of feverishly getting geared up again between drifts for those who had broken off, while skipper Colin repositioned *Mistress II* uptide of the wreck again. As is often the case when wrecking for cod the friendly banter on board got around to who was going to get stuck into a 20 pounder and claim the £5 a head stake money. For a while I was in there with a chance when my rod hooped over into an alarming bend as a real clonker ripped line from the reel in a frantic dive. I couldn't stop it and, yes, – it made the wreck. Shortly afterwards we moved to the last wreck of the day which, being so small, took every ounce of Skipper Colin's experience to set up a suitable drift over it. His prophetic words of 'It's a big fish or nothing here, boys', had hardly left his mouth when Jinx yelled, 'I'm in,' and he was too, within seconds of the pirk bumping the wreck and being jerked upwards, and the ark of his rod said it all. Until afterwards I wasn't aware Jinx had not caught a 20 pounder but he made up for monsters lost in the past by playing to the boat and what a lovely sight it made spiralling up through such clear water, a simply massive fish over 3 feet in length. In spawn it would have topped 30 lbs but the grin on my best friend's face said he was more than happy with his 24$^{1}/_{4}$ lbs specimen.

A COD WORK-OUT FOR LEE

It's not often these days that I manage to talk my 30-year-old son, Lee, into a fishing trip. That is unless it's to the Florida Keys or some of the more exciting parts of equatorial Africa. He's never really been bitten by the angling bug as his sport is body building but I thought he just might enjoy accompanying me down to Lymington in Hampshire for a day's deepwater wreck fishing on Roger Bayzand's spanking new 32 foot purpose-built catamaran *Sundance*. After all, prizing hard-battling cod to 20 lbs plus and double-figure pollack away from a rusting hulk and over 200 feet up to the surface is work-out enough for anyone, believe me.

After leaving the moorings at Lymington we were soon shooting across the Solent and passing the famous Needles off the Isle of Wight. I was amazed at the stability of Roger's new boat which has an unbelievable beam of 16 foot, allowing anglers to fish all around, including along each side of the wheelhouse. Fitted with a pair of 215 hp Sabre Perkins diesel engines, *Sundance* can do up to 24 knots but cruises nicely at 17 knots. The hull has a high bow for an exceptionally dry ride and a high forward bridge deck end to prevent slamming. I can see more and more British skippers turning their attentions towards this

My son Lee really enjoyed our wrecking trip out with Roger Bayzand. It was arm-wrenching sport all day long with cod to over 20 lbs and big, double figure pollack. He must come again.

new breed of catamaran fishing boats. They are without question the ultimate fishing platform.

During a run of less than two hours our 9 foot uptide rods were made up and stories of past trips were swapped. Then Roger slowed the boat down as the chosen wreck came up on the finder and motored 100 yards uptide before switching the engines off for our first drift of the day. Our multipliers were full to the brim of 40 lb braid to which 20 feet of 30 lb mono was added as a rubbing leader, being far more abrasion resistant against rusting metal than low-diameter braid. On the business end of a plastic boom and 10 ozs lead we fished 15 feet, 30 lb mono traces with Roger's new twin-tail lures. These orange and red synthetic cod catchers are sleeved on to a $1\frac{1}{2}$ ozs leaded jig sporting a strong size 5/0 hook, and once lowered down on to or beside the wreck are erratically wound upwards 20 – 30 feet. The twin tails gyrate and throb away and being leaded keep working away low down where the cod are situated close to the bottom. Within seconds all three rods were hooped over with fish on, and Lee's first work-out of the day began. He was smiling throughout and so must have enjoyed the scrap. And who wouldn't have? His first cod ever weighed close on 20 lbs.

There were so many fish on the wreck I enjoyed working several different lures including another lead head called a Toothy Critter head case, which has interchangeable different-coloured rubber shad-like bodies. All caught cod. Every now and again someone would latch on to a big pollack, always recognisable by their fast, juddering fight all the way to the top, and by the end of the day everyone had had their string well and truly pulled.

IT'S UPTIDE FISHING FOR COD AND CHIPS

Due to the sheer distances involved from my Norfolk home I would not generally drive across country all the way to Wales for a day's cod fishing, but as local expert Dave Lewis promised the Bristol Channel off Penarth in South Wales would be really 'stacked up' at the end of November, Neil Mackellow and I eagerly joined him for some uptide fishing action on board *Kobe*, a 27 foot charter boat skippered by 'Groucho', arguably Penarth's most experienced offshore man.

Now because I had also booked a film crew for the day in order to capture some video footage for *Sea Angler* magazine, we badly needed both sunshine and fish in plenty. And luckily we were treated to both, with numbers of quality whiting and some super cod up to 14 lbs, all on light uptide rods coupled to just 15 lb test mono. Rather a fluke really, isn't it, picking just the one day out of the hat in the middle of storms, snow blizzards, grey skies and rough seas amid a generally inclement weather pattern for November? But in this game you do need a little luck, or is it the dried toad skins that my wife Jo insists she keeps shuffling around on the evening before I have a TV fishing shoot? I still don't know whether she's kidding or not, honestly! Either way, thanks to Kobe's owner, Mike Miles of nearby Cardiff Angling Supplies, we were treated to some wonderful bait in the way of frozen squid, fresh king ragworm, some razor fish and the largest black lugworms I have ever seen, over a foot long and as thick as your thumb. And, of course, we were all using the devastatingly effective uptide boat fishing technique (pioneered on the East Coast incidentally by skippers John Rawle and Bob Cox) which is now the accepted and indeed the only way of keeping a grip lead on the bottom in front of feeding cod in the

Through the efforts of fellow angling journalist and old pal Dave Lewis, we managed once again to shoot enough footage out of Penarth in South Wales, to put a cod fishing video together for Sea Angler *magazine.*

237

unbelievably fast tide flow of the Bristol Channel, where until the fish hits the surface you literally cannot see it. The water is that thick.

I felt rather sorry for some of the anglers leaving harbour on other boats who were totally ill equipped with heavy wrecking rods and over-large multiplying reels holding 30 and 40 lbs test lines which then, of course, necessitate at least 2 lb of lead to stand any chance of anchoring their bait to the bottom in 50 – 60 feet of water where the fish are. Needless to say, few returned to the marina with any cod to show for their efforts and I suspect that for the greater part of the day until the tide started to ease, their heavy leads were actually 'floating' well off bottom in the 6 – 9 knot tide rip.

Boosted by floodwaters of several rivers, like the Wye and, of course, the mighty Severn, fishing just a mile offshore from Penarth into the Bristol Channel provides a truly daunting experience to newcomers. So whilst trying not to preach to the converted let alone teaching them to suck eggs, let's explore why uptide boat fishing works and why comparatively light 5-8 oz breakaway grip wire leads hold out even in fierce currents. After casting well uptide (as close to the anchor rope as you can get the lead when it's really pulling) you allow the lead to touch bottom and dig in and keep the reel in free spool, while a huge bow of line forms in the tide between lead and rod tip. Only when an accentuated bow has developed, which greatly reduces water pressure, (hence the need for using just 15 lb low-diameter line), do you put the reel into gear and rest the rod. Bites then register in two ways. Should a large fish like a cod swallow the bait and move downtide, thus hooking itself and tripping the lead simultaneously, the rod tip springs back. You then quickly wind down until the fish is felt and continue winding until the rod arches over. So do not strike. The fish is, of course, already hooked well.

What often happens, however, especially with small fish such as whiting, codling and even the very odd large cod, is that they just sit there having gorged the bait, the only indication being the occasional tap or nod on the rod tip. One good reason why the bait should never be left out too long. If you suspect a fish is already there simply wind up the bow, which is held downtide until the lead trips, and retrieve. Basically, so long as you appreciate that in no way can your line ever be taut in a straight line between bait and rod tip when boat fishing and that there must always be a bow to minimise water pressure, you will enjoy and undoubtedly benefit from adopting the uptide method for overcoming fast tide runs.

WRECKING 'N' ROLLING

I allowed the 10 oz lead to bump the wreck momentarily before slamming the multiplier into gear and starting a fairly fast retrieve to flutter the jellyworm enticingly upwards through the clear blue water, but something down there had other ideas and the rod suddenly lurched over the gunnel into an alarming bend while the clutch screamed out in pain. No! Wilson wasn't back swanning it up in the tropics again connected to an exotic sports fish, simply enjoying the delights of wreck fishing off our south coast. Some 20 miles from Lymington, to be exact, in the company of Andy Benham and Mel Russ from EMAP's *Sea Angler* magazine, on board *Sundance II* skippered by my old mate Roger Bayzand.

Our mission was to catch enough cod plus the inevitable, hard-battling pollack (which are also attracted by deepwater wrecks) to make a specialist cod video for *Sea Angler* magazine. And we were all having a real beanfeast, providing fish after fish for the

E.M.A.P. editorial duo, (L-R) Mel Russ and Andy Benham, may well be laughing holding these plump cod, but like mine, their arms were aching badly following several hours of 'hauling' over one of the most productive wrecks I've ever fished.

cameraman, Paul Bennett, of Anglia Television. Now how Roger Bayzand does it I just don't know, because I have yet to board his boat without having an exciting day and this was certainly no exception. His knowledge of South Coast wrecks is quite phenomenal, because Mel Russ and I were literally into a big double-figure fish apiece on the very first drift, and double hook-ups happened again and again from then on.

Lying on the sea bed over 200 feet down (73 metres to be precise) the wreck was clearly shown by the sonar/fish finder to be absolutely stacked with fish. But at such depths it is all too easy to bump fish off the hook due to the inherent amount of stretch in monofilament which is around 25 per cent. So we chose 30 lb braided reel line which is made from gel spun polyethylene, connected to a 15 foot 30 lb monofilament trace (as a shock absorber) with a 12 inch rigid plastic boom above the junction swivel in order to stop the lead from tangling as the rig is lowered, with a plastic jellyworm on the business end threaded into a 5/0 hook. It is such a simple set-up but deadly.

Fortunately Roger had all the sundries including a massive selection of jellyworms on board *Sundance II* because the artificials I had brought along were either too big or of the wrong kind. And the live action is what turns cod and pollack on. After pumping up several bronze-backed pollack of between 11 and 13 lbs we started to get amongst arm-wrenching cod, which if anything averaged slightly larger. Andy Benham lost a real 'mother' due to his hook straightening and although we each missed out on a 20 by just a couple of pounds or so I have never enjoyed catching so many fish of such an exceptionally high average size. And you don't need to fight many 15-lbs-plus cod up from 200 feet down before both your back and groin start complaining. But then wrecking is a totally big boy's masochistic pastime. And while I wouldn't fancy the ensuing pain each and every single trip out, every now and again I revel in it.

The interesting aspect of our day, however, was that we didn't experience any of the usual plucks and abortive grabs which cod usually make when you're winding up imitation plastic or rubber sand-eels. With these incredibly lifelike latex-cum-jellyworms, which originated from the USA and were first used for tempting large-mouth bass on jigging rigs, both cod and pollack literally 'hang' themselves. You simply wind the 'jelly' erratically up over the wreck until the rod tip arches over and keep winding (without actually striking) until the reel's clutch screams. What truly wonderful fun and arguably the most exciting technique in saltwater offshore fishing around the British Isles.